Practical Maya Programming with Python

Unleash the power of Python in Maya and unlock your creativity

Robert Galanakis

BIRMINGHAM - MUMBAI

Practical Maya Programming with Python

First published: July 2014

Production reference: 1180714

Published by Packt Publishing Ltd.
Livery Place
35 Livery Street
Birmingham B3 2PB, UK.

ISBN 978-1-84969-472-8

www.packtpub.com

Cover image by Andrei Cosmin Cristea (Andrei@undoz.com)

Credits

Author
Robert Galanakis

Reviewers
Harry Boltz

Brian Escribano

Michael Tsai

Commissioning Editor
Akram Hussain

Acquisition Editor
Subho Gupta

Content Development Editor
Dayan Hyames

Technical Editors
Krishnaveni Haridas

Manal Pednekar

Copy Editors
Aditya Nair

Stuti Srivastava

Project Coordinator
Leena Purkait

Proofreaders
Stephen Copestake

Maria Gould

Paul Hindle

Indexers
Mariammal Chettiyar

Tejal Soni

Priya Subramani

Graphics
Sheetal Aute

Yuvraj Mannari

Abhinash Sahu

Production Coordinator
Pooja Chiplunkar

Cover Work
Pooja Chiplunkar

About the Author

Robert Galanakis is a technical artist cum programmer who has worked in various areas of game development. He is the Technical Director of EVE Online at CCP Games, Iceland, where he focuses on Python, Lean, and Agile training and evangelism. In 2008, Rob founded tech-artists.org, which is the largest and the most active community focused on tech art on the Internet. He has spoken at Game Developers Conference several times and has also written many articles about tools, pipelines, and culture. His blog can be found at www.robg3d.com. He lives in Reykjavík, Iceland, with his wife Casady and their son Marcus.

About the Reviewers

Brian Escribano has over 11 years of experience working in the fields of education, TV, and games. He builds world-class character rigs and animation pipelines for companies such as Nickelodeon, Mirada, and Spark Unlimited. With his deep scripting knowledge in Python and MEL, Brian brings a wealth of expertise and experience to any team he works with.

Michael Tsai attended the Academy of Art University at San Francisco to study Visual Effects. After college, he worked on *Fantastic Four 2 – Rise of the Silver Surfer*, *Red Cliff 2 – The Battle of Red Cliff*, and the stereoscopic version of G-Force. In 2012, Michael received his Master of Entertainment Technology degree (MET) from the Entertainment Technology Center of Carnegie Mellon University. *Elysium* was another feature film he worked on before he joined Schell Games in Pittsburgh as a full-time game artist.

www.PacktPub.com

Support files, eBooks, discount offers and more

You might want to visit www.PacktPub.com for support files and downloads related to your book.

Did you know that Packt offers eBook versions of every book published, with PDF and ePub files available? You can upgrade to the eBook version at www.PacktPub.com and as a print book customer, you are entitled to a discount on the eBook copy. Get in touch with us at service@packtpub.com for more details.

At www.PacktPub.com, you can also read a collection of free technical articles, sign up for a range of free newsletters and receive exclusive discounts and offers on Packt books and eBooks.

http://PacktLib.PacktPub.com

Do you need instant solutions to your IT questions? PacktLib is Packt's online digital book library. Here, you can access, read and search across Packt's entire library of books.

Why Subscribe?

- Fully searchable across every book published by Packt
- Copy and paste, print and bookmark content
- On demand and accessible via web browser

Free Access for Packt account holders

If you have an account with Packt at www.PacktPub.com, you can use this to access PacktLib today and view nine entirely free books. Simply use your login credentials for immediate access.

Table of Contents

Preface   **1**

Chapter 1: Introspecting Maya, Python, and PyMEL   **9**

  Creating your library   **9**

    Using the interpreter   10

    Finding a place for our library   10

    Choosing a development root   11

    Creating a function in your IDE   12

    Reloading code changes   13

  Exploring Maya and PyMEL   **13**

    Creating an introspection function   15

    Understanding Python and MEL types   16

    Using the method resolution order   18

    PyNodes all the way down   19

    Understanding PyMEL data and math types   21

    Leveraging the REPL   23

  Building the pmhelp function   **24**

    Creating a query string for a PyMEL object   25

    Creating more tests   27

    Adding support for modules   29

    Adding support for types   30

    Adding support for methods   30

    Adding support for functions   33

    Adding support for non-PyMEL objects   34

    Designing with EAFP versus LBYL   37

    Code is never complete   38

    Opening help in a web browser   38

  Summary   **40**

Chapter 2: Writing Composable Code   41

Defining composability   41
Identifying anti-patterns of composability   42
Avoiding the use of Boolean flags   44
Evolving legacy code into composable code   45
Rewriting code for composability   46
Getting the first item in a sequence   46
Writing head and tail functions   48

Learning to use list comprehensions   48
Implementing is_exact_type   50
Saying goodbye to map and filter   51

Writing a skeleton converter library   51
Writing the docstring and pseudocode   52
Understanding docstrings and reStructured Text   53
Writing the first implementation   53
Breaking the first implementation   54
Understanding interface contracts   55
Extracting the safe_setparent utility function   56
Learning how to refactor   57
Simplifying the node to joint conversion   58
Learning how to use closures   60
Dealing with node connections   61
Dealing with namespaces   61
Wrapping up the skeleton converter   62

Writing a character creator   63
Stubbing out the character creator   64
Implementing convert_hierarchies_main   65
Implementing convert_hierarchies   66
Decomposing into composable functions   66
Implementing convert_hierarchy   68
Supporting inevitable modifications   69

Improving the performance of PyMEL   72
Defining performance   73
Refactoring for performance   73
Rewriting inner loops to use maya.cmds   75

Summary   75

Chapter 3: Dealing with Errors   77

Understanding exceptions   77
Introducing exception types   78
Explaining try/catch/finally flow control   79

Explaining traceback objects   81
Explaining the exc_info tuple   82
Living with unhandled exceptions   **83**
Handling exceptions at the application level   83
Golden rules of error handling   **84**
Focus on the critical path   85
Keep the end user in mind   85
Only catch errors you can handle   86
Avoid partial mutations   87
Practical error handling in Maya   **88**
Dealing with expensive and mutable state   88
Leveraging undo blocks   90
Dealing with Maya's poor exception design   91
Leveraging the Maya application   92
Dealing with the Maya application   92
Leveraging Python, which is better than MEL   92
Building a high-level error handler   **92**
Understanding sys.excepthook   93
Using sys.excepthook in Maya   94
Creating an error handler   95
Improving the error handler   96
Inspecting Python code objects   97
Adding filtering based on filename   98
Assembling the contents of an error e-mail   100
Sending the error e-mail   103
Installing the error handler   **104**
Obeying the What If Two Programs Did This rule   105
Improving the error handler   **106**
Adding a user interface   106
Using a background thread to send the e-mail   107
Moving beyond e-mail   107
Capturing locals   107
Attaching log files   108
Summary   **109**

**Chapter 4: Leveraging Context Managers and
Decorators in Maya**   **111**
Inverting the subroutine   **111**
Introducing decorators   **113**
Explaining decorators   113
Wrapping an exporter with a decorator   117

Introducing context managers   **118**
Writing the undo_chunk context manager   121
Writing the undo_on_error context manager   122
Contrasting decorators and context managers   123
Context managers for changing scene state   **124**
Building the set_file_prompt context manager   125
Building the at_time context manager   126
Building the with_unit context manager   126
Building the set_renderlayer_active context manager   127
Building the set_namespace_active context manager   127
Improving on future versions of Maya   129
Creating the denormalized_skin context manager   **129**
Safely swapping vertex influences   129
Addressing performance concerns   131
Creating a decorator to record metrics   **133**
Getting a unique key   134
Recording duration   134
Reporting duration   135
Handling errors   136
Advanced decorator topics   **138**
Defining decorators with arguments   138
Decorating PyMEL attributes and methods   139
Stacking decorators   139
Using Python's decorator library   140
Doing decorators the right way   140
Summary   **141**
Chapter 5: Building Graphical User Interfaces for Maya   **143**
Introducing Qt, PyQt, and PySide   **143**
Introducing Qt widgets   144
Introducing Qt layouts   145
Understanding Qt main windows and sorting   145
Introducing Qt signals   146
Establishing rules for crafting a GUI   **146**
Prefer pure PySide GUIs where possible   146
Use command-style UI building where necessary   146
Avoid the use of .ui files   147
Installing PySide   **147**
Supporting PySide and PyQt   **148**
Creating the hierarchy converter GUI   **149**
Creating the window   149

Running a Python file as a script	150
Introducing the QApplication class	151
Understanding the event loop	151
Running your GUI	152
Designing and building your GUI	153
Defining control, container, and window widgets	153
Adding the rest of the widgets	155
Hooking up the application to be effected by the GUI	156
Hooking up the GUI to be effected by the application	158
Simulating application events	160
Considering alternative implementations	161
Integrating the tool GUI with Maya	**162**
Opening the tool GUI from Maya	162
Getting the main Maya window as a QMainWindow	163
Making a Qt window the child of Maya's window	164
Using Python's reload function with GUIs	165
Emitting a signal from Maya	166
Connecting Maya to a signal	167
Verifying the hierarchy converter works	169
Working with menus	**169**
Creating a top-level menu	169
Getting the Qt object from a Maya path	170
Changing the font of a widget	171
Marking menus as new	172
Creating a test case	173
Adding a persistence registry	174
Verifying the new menu marker works	176
Using alternative methods to style widgets	176
Working with Maya shelves	**177**
Summary	**178**
Chapter 6: Automating Maya from the Outside	**179**
Controlling Maya through request-reply	**180**
Using a Python client and Maya server	180
Controlling Python through exec and eval	180
Handling problems with IPC	181
Installing ZeroMQ	181
Demonstrating request-reply with ZeroMQ	182
Explaining connection strings, ports, bind, and connect	183
Designing the automation system	**184**
Pairing one client and one server	184

Bootstrapping the server from the client   185
The client-server handshake   185
Defining the server loop   188
Serializing requests and responses   188
Choosing what the server does   189
Handling exceptions between client and server   189
Understanding the Maya startup routine   **191**
Using batch mode versus GUI mode   192
Choosing a startup configuration mechanism   192
Using command line options   192
Using environment variables   193
Building the request-reply automation system   **193**
Creating a Python package   194
Launching Maya from Python   194
Automatically killing the server   196
Creating a basic Maya server   197
Running code at Maya startup   198
Understanding eval and exec   199
Adding support for eval and exec   201
Adding support for exception handling   202
Adding support for timeouts   206
Adding support for the client-server handshake   208
Practical uses and improvements   **211**
Batch processing using Maya   211
Running a server in a Maya GUI session   213
Running automated tests in Maya   214
Adding support for logging   214
Supporting multiple languages and applications   215
Supporting control from a remote computer   215
Designing an object-oriented system   216
Evaluating other RPC frameworks   216
Summary   **216**
Chapter 7: Taming the Maya API   **217**
Explaining types   **218**
Dicts all the way down   218
Using custom types to simplify code   220
Introducing inheritance by drawing shapes   221
Introducing Maya's API and architecture   **225**
Understanding the OpenMaya bindings   226
Navigating the Maya API Reference   227

Understanding MObjects and function sets	229
Learning the Maya Python API by example	**230**
Converting a name to an MObject node	230
Getting the name of an MObject	231
Getting the hash of a node	231
Building a mesh	232
Setting mesh normals	238
Using MScriptUtil to call a method	241
Using OpenMaya for callbacks	243
Comparing Maya Python API and PyMEL	246
Creating a Maya Python plugin	**247**
The life of a Python plugin	248
Creating the sound player library	249
Creating the plugin file	250
Reloading plugins	252
Adding a command flag	252
Comparing the OpenMaya and scripting solutions	255
Using PyMEL in a plugin that loads during startup	**256**
Summary	**257**
Chapter 8: Unleashing the Maya API through Python	**259**
Understanding Dependency Graph plugins	**260**
Building a simple node plugin	260
Understanding plugin type IDs	262
Defining inputs, outputs, and the initializer	263
Creating the compute method	266
Taming the non-Pythonic Maya API	268
Demystifying Python metaprogramming	**268**
Rethinking type creation	269
Exploring the type function	270
The importance of being declarative	271
Designing the node factory	**273**
Designing plugin nodes	273
Designing the attribute specification	274
Designing the node type specification	275
Building the node factory	**276**
Specifying attributes	276
Creating attributes	277
Specifying a node	279
Using partial application to create attributes	281
Creating a node	282

Slaying the compute method   285
Extending the node factory   **289**
Supporting string and color attributes   289
Supporting enum attributes   290
Supporting transform nodes   292
Overriding MPxNode methods   293
Summary   **294**
Chapter 9: Becoming a Part of the Python Community   **295**
Understanding Open Source Software   **296**
Differentiating OSS from script download sites   296
Defining what a third-party module is   297
Creating a site directory for third-party modules   **298**
Explaining the site directory   298
Creating a new site directory for Maya   299
Establishing the site directory at startup   299
Working with Python distributions in Maya   **300**
Using the Python Package Index   300
Adding a source distribution to Maya   300
Adding an egg or wheel to Maya   301
Using binary distributions on Windows   302
Using pip to install third-party modules   303
Contributing to the open source community   **303**
Designing Maya Python code for open source   304
Starting an open source project   306
Distributing your project   307
Engaging with the wider community   **308**
Summary   **309**
Appendix: Python Best Practices   **311**
The args and kwargs parameters   **311**
String formatting   **313**
String concatenation   **315**
Raw strings and string literals   **316**
Path building and manipulation   **317**
Unicode strings   **318**
Using the doctest module   **319**
Adopting Test-Driven Development   **320**
Using the GitHub repository for this book   **321**
Index   **323**

Preface

When Autodesk added support for Python into Maya 8.5, few people understood the implications. It was a decision that has fundamentally changed the way 3D art gets done. Now, years later, we stand on the edge of realizing its promise.

The promise of Python in Maya goes beyond just a familiar language with a great syntax. Any language could have been chosen to bind to Maya; and most would have been more familiar, and with a better syntax than MEL, and easier to use than C++. So, why Python?

The promise goes beyond a powerful language with lots of built-in features. Python is said to have *batteries included*, but so do other languages, and Autodesk certainly has lots of batteries in Maya that now also exist in Python. So, again, why Python?

The promise goes beyond having a single language for scripting, API use, and plugins. It goes beyond the endless third-party libraries maintained by a large community. It goes beyond having powerful development tools.

The promise of Python in Maya is all of these things and more. You can learn how to use the language by leveraging a wide variety of resources that have nothing to do with Maya. You can easily translate what you know of MEL and the C++ API and use it in Python, but with an improved development velocity and maintainability of code. You can use your favorite standard Python editor and tools. You can learn about the language from a technical and design perspective and apply that to improve your programming in Maya. You can be part of a large, vibrant, diverse community of developers on the forefront of multiple areas of technology.

Join me as we explore topics that will allow you to unleash the power of Maya through Python. Together, we'll learn how Python works both under the hood and over it, how Maya integrates with Python, and how the elegant PyMEL builds on that integration. We will drill down into what makes Python code beautiful and idiomatic, and how we can use these concepts and Python's language features to make our Maya Python code expressive and elegant. We will leverage third-party solutions for networking and user interfaces, to compliment and extend what is included with Maya and Python. We will decouple Python code from Maya dependencies, making our work go smoother and faster

This book is not a reference. It is not a cookbook, and it is not a comprehensive guide to Maya's Python API. It is a book that will teach you how to write better Python code for use inside of Maya. It will unearth interesting ways of using Maya and Python to create amazing things that wouldn't be possible otherwise. While there is plenty of code in this book that I encourage you to copy and adapt, this book is not about providing recipes. It is a book to teach skills and enable.

This is a book which, I hope, helps realize the promise of Python in Maya.

What this book covers

Chapter 1, *Introspecting Maya, Python, and PyMEL*, explores how Maya and Python work individually and together to create a powerful programming and scripting environment. It covers some of the key technical underpinnings for the rest of the book.

Chapter 2, *Writing Composable Code*, introduces the practice of writing code that can be reused in many places. Composable code is a fundamental concept for the rest of the skills taught in this book.

Chapter 3, *Dealing with Errors*, teaches you all about exceptions and errors in Maya and Python. We explore several strategies for handling them effectively.

Chapter 4, *Leveraging Context Managers and Decorators in Maya*, covers context managers and decorators, which are two powerful features of Python, and how they can be used to simplify your code.

Chapter 5, *Building Graphical User Interfaces for Maya*, demonstrates the PySide and PyQt frameworks, how to abstract your user interface code from underlying logic, and a strategy of building GUIs to maximize maintainability and productivity.

Chapter 6, *Automating Maya from the Outside*, shows how Maya can be controlled from another process, explains how request-reply systems work, and builds a fully featured automation system on these principles.

Chapter 7, Taming the Maya API, introduces the Maya Python API and how types and classes work in Python and Maya. It contains a number of examples to demonstrate the API, as well as a Maya command plugin.

Chapter 8, Unleashing the Maya API through Python, covers the creation of a library to easily create Maya plugin nodes, demonstrating how to map the Maya API onto Pythonic idioms using metaprogramming.

Chapter 9, Becoming a Part of the Python Community, goes over the concepts behind open source software, demonstrates how to find and use third-party modules, explains how to create your own open source project, and tours the Python and Maya programming communities.

Appendix, Python Best Practices, explains in detail various Python language features and miscellaneous, but very relevant, topics.

What you need for this book

You will need a copy of Autodesk Maya 2013 for this book. Newer versions are fine, and older versions that use Python 2.6 (2011, 2012) should be acceptable as well. Any operating system capable of running Maya (Windows, OS X, Linux) should work, though you will need to translate things such as file paths to what is appropriate on your system.

I would also suggest having an install of Python 2.6 or 2.7 outside Maya for exploring and running some of the samples that can be run from the interactive interpreter prompt. You can download Python 2.6 or 2.7 from `http://www.python. org/download`, or it may be installed on your Mac or Linux OS already!

Finally, I strongly suggest installing both a powerful text editor and an **Integrated Development Environment (IDE)**. Python is a real programming language, and you should use the powerful tools available. If you are an experienced Python user already happy with `vim`, I don't expect to convert you. But if you are a converted MEL scripter playing around in Notepad, it is time to embrace your good fortune!

For a text editor, **Sublime Text** (`http://www.sublimetext.com`) is popular, cross-platform, and free to use on an unlimited trial. **Notepad++** (`http://notepad-plus-plus.org`) is excellent if you are on Windows and prefer free and open source. There are dozens of other good text editors, and if the two editors mentioned here do not tickle your fancy, you should keep trying until you find one that does.

Finally, the choice of IDE is usually a contentious topic. For Python, however, I can confidently say **PyCharm** (http://www.jetbrains.com/pycharm/) by JetBrains is the premiere IDE, and my personal favorite. It has a free and quite powerful Community Edition as well. Other popular options are **Wing IDE** (http://www.wingware.com) and **Eclipse** with **PyDev** (http://pydev.org). Experiment with a few different programs, but whatever you do, move past IDLE, the IDE bundled with Python!

Who this book is for

- Do you currently use Python with Maya and ask yourself: "Can I do better?"
- Are you a MEL scripter who has started using Python and want to know what all the fuss is about?
- Are you a Python programmer who is starting with Maya and believes there must be a better way?
- Have you been using Python in Maya for a while but work hard to continuously improve?

Some basic experience with Python and Maya is expected. This book does not cover those most primitive topics that are inevitably learned through introductory Maya and Python use.

Even more than experience, this book requires a willingness to learn. Some of the more advanced or unfamiliar topics may feel a bit like learning how to ride a bicycle, but keep peddling and you'll get the hang of things in no time.

Conventions

In this book, you will find a number of styles of text that distinguish between different kinds of information. Here are some examples of these styles, and an explanation of their meaning.

Code words in text are shown as follows: "We can include other modules through the use of the import statement."

A block of code is set as follows:

```
def spam():
    return 'spam!'
```

When we wish to draw your attention to a particular part of a code block, the relevant lines or items are set in bold:

```
def more_spam():
    spams = ' '.join([spam()] * 5)
    return spams
```

Any command line input or output is written as follows:

```
> mayapy --version
Python 2.6.4
```

Code meant to be entered by the Python interactive interpreter uses its familiar conventions. Input lines are prefixed with ">>>". Continuations for multiline statements are prefixed with "...". Output from the interpreter has no prefix:

```
>>> 'This is input'.replace('in', 'out')
'This is output'
>>> if True:
...     print 'Hello!'
Hello
```

New terms and **important words** are shown in bold. Words that you see on the screen, in menus or dialog boxes for example, appear in the text like this: "Clicking on the **Next** button moves you to the next screen".

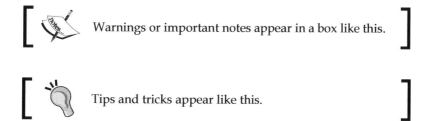

Warnings or important notes appear in a box like this.

Tips and tricks appear like this.

Reader feedback

Feedback from our readers is always welcome. Let us know what you think about this book—what you liked or may have disliked. Reader feedback is important for us to develop titles that you really get the most out of.

To send us general feedback, simply send an e-mail to feedback@packtpub.com, and mention the book title via the subject of your message.

If there is a topic that you have expertise in and you are interested in either writing or contributing to a book, see our author guide on www.packtpub.com/authors.

Customer support

Now that you are the proud owner of a Packt book, we have a number of things to help you to get the most from your purchase.

Downloading the example code

You can download the example code files for all Packt books you have purchased from your account at http://www.packtpub.com. If you purchased this book elsewhere, you can visit http://www.packtpub.com/support and register to have the files e-mailed directly to you.

The code for this book is also available on GitHub, at https://github.com/rgalanakis/practicalmayapython. See the *Appendix, Python Best Practices,* for more information about the GitHub repository.

Errata

Although we have taken every care to ensure the accuracy of our content, mistakes do happen. If you find a mistake in one of our books—maybe a mistake in the text or the code—we would be grateful if you would report this to us. By doing so, you can save other readers from frustration and help us improve subsequent versions of this book. If you find any errata, please report them by visiting http://www.packtpub.com/submit-errata, selecting your book, clicking on the **errata submission form** link, and entering the details of your errata. Once your errata are verified, your submission will be accepted and the errata will be uploaded on our website, or added to any list of existing errata, under the Errata section of that title. Any existing errata can be viewed by selecting your title from http://www.packtpub.com/support.

Piracy

Piracy of copyright material on the Internet is an ongoing problem across all media. At Packt, we take the protection of our copyright and licenses very seriously. If you come across any illegal copies of our works, in any form, on the Internet, please provide us with the location address or website name immediately so that we can pursue a remedy.

Please contact us at copyright@packtpub.com with a link to the suspected pirated material.

We appreciate your help in protecting our authors, and our ability to bring you valuable content.

Questions

You can contact us at questions@packtpub.com if you are having a problem with any aspect of the book, and we will do our best to address it.

You can also contact the author, Robert Galanakis, at rob.galanakis@gmail.com.

1
Introspecting Maya, Python, and PyMEL

Maya and Python are both excellent and elegant tools that can together achieve amazing results. And while it may be tempting to dive in and start wielding this power, it is prudent to understand some basic things first. Knowledge of the fundamentals will provide the platform from which we will grow great skills and conquer our obstacles throughout the rest of this book.

In this chapter, we will look at Python as a language, Maya as a program, and PyMEL as a framework. We will begin by briefly going over how to use the standard Python interpreter, the Maya Python interpreter, the Script Editor in Maya, and your **Integrated Development Environment** (**IDE**) or text editor in which you will do the majority of your development. Our goal for the chapter is to build a small library that can easily link us to documentation about Python and PyMEL objects. Building this library will illuminate how Maya, Python and PyMEL are designed, and demonstrate why PyMEL is superior to `maya.cmds`. We will use the powerful technique of **type introspection** to teach us more about Maya's node-based design than any Hypergraph or static documentation can. Along the way we will explore some core concepts that will reoccur throughout later chapters.

Creating your library

There are generally three different modes you will be developing in while programming Python in Maya: using the mayapy interpreter to evaluate short bits of code and explore ideas, using your Integrated Development Environment to work on the bulk of the code, and using Maya's Script Editor to help iterate and test your work. In this section, we'll start learning how to use all three tools to create a very simple library.

Using the interpreter

The first thing we must do is find your mayapy interpreter. It should be next to your Maya executable, named `mayapy` or `mayapy.exe`. It is a Python interpreter that can run Python code as if it were being run in a normal Maya session. When you launch it, it will start up the interpreter in **interactive mode**, which means you enter commands and it gives you results, interactively. The `>>>` and `...` characters in code blocks indicate something you should enter at the interactive prompt; the code listing in the book and your prompt should look basically the same. In later listings, long output lines will be elided with `...` to save on space.

 Most of the interactive samples can be run as code through `doctest`. See *Appendix, Python Best Practices*, for more information.

Start a `mayapy` process by double clicking or calling it from the command line, and enter the following code:

```
>>> print 'Hello, Maya!'
Hello, Maya!
>>> def hello():
...     return 'Hello, Maya!'
...
>>> hello()
'Hello, Maya!'
```

The first statement prints a string, which shows up under the prompting line. The second statement is a multiline function definition. The `...` indicates the line is part of the preceding line. The blank line following the `...` indicates the end of the function. For brevity, we will leave out empty `...` lines in other code listings. After we define our `hello` function, we invoke it. It returns the string `"Hello, Maya!"`, which is printed out beneath the invocation.

Finding a place for our library

Now, we need to find a place to put our library file. In order for Python to load the file as a module, it needs to be on some path where Python can find it. We can see all available paths by looking at the path list on the `sys` module.

```
>>> import sys
>>> for p in sys.path:
...     print p
C:\Program Files\Autodesk\Maya2013\bin\python26.zip
C:\Program Files\Autodesk\Maya2013\Python\DLLs
C:\Program Files\Autodesk\Maya2013\Python\lib
```

```
C:\Program Files\Autodesk\Maya2013\Python\lib\plat-win
C:\Program Files\Autodesk\Maya2013\Python\lib\lib-tk
C:\Program Files\Autodesk\Maya2013\bin
C:\Program Files\Autodesk\Maya2013\Python
C:\Program Files\Autodesk\Maya2013\Python\lib\site-packages
```

A number of paths will print out; I've replicated what's on my Windows system, but yours will almost definitely be different. Unfortunately, the default paths don't give us a place to put custom code. They are application installation directories, which we should not modify. Instead, we should be doing our coding outside of all the application installation directories. In fact, it's a good practice to avoid editing anything in the application installation directories entirely.

Choosing a development root

Let's decide where we will do our coding. We'll call this location the development root for the rest of the book. To be concise, I'll choose C:\mayapybook\pylib to house all of our Python code, but it can be anywhere. You'll need to choose something appropriate if you are on OS X or Linux; we will use ~/mayapybook/ pylib as our path on these systems, but I'll refer only to the Windows path except where more clarity is needed. Create the development root folder, and inside of it create an empty file named minspect.py.

Now, we need to get C:\mayapybook\pylib onto Python's sys.path so it can be imported. The easiest way to do this is to use the PYTHONPATH environment variable. From a Windows command line you can run the following to add the path, and ensure it worked:

```
> set PYTHONPATH=%PYTHONPATH%;C:\mayapybook\pylib
> mayapy.exe
>>> import sys
>>> 'C:\\mayapybook\\pylib' in sys.path
True
>>> import minspect
>>> minspect
<module 'minspect' from '...\minspect.py'>
```

The following is the equivalent commands on OS X or Linux:

```
$ export PYTHONPATH=$PYTHONPATH:~/mayapybook/pylib
$ mayapy
>>> import sys
>>> '~/mayapybook/pylib' in sys.path
True
>>> import minspect
>>> minspect
<module 'minspect' from '.../minspect.py'>
```

There are actually a number of ways to get your development root onto Maya's path. The option presented here (using environment variables before starting Maya or mayapy) is just one of the more straightforward choices, and it works for mayapy as well as normal Maya. Calling `sys.path.append('C:\\mayapybook\\pylib')` inside your `userSetup.py` file, for example, would work for Maya but not mayapy (you would need to use `maya.standalone.initialize` to register *user paths*, as we will do later).

Using `set` or `export` to set environment variables only works for the current process and any new children. If you want it to work for unrelated processes, you may need to modify your global or user environment. Each OS is different, so you should refer to your operating system's documentation or a Google search. Some possibilities are `setx` from the Windows command line, editing `/etc/environment` in Linux, or editing `/etc/launchd.conf` on OS X. If you are in a studio environment and don't want to make changes to people's machines, you should consider an alternative such as using a script to launch Maya which will set up the `PYTHONPATH`, instead of launching the `maya` executable directly.

Creating a function in your IDE

Now it is time to use our IDE to do some programming. We'll start by turning the path printing code we wrote at the interactive prompt into a function in our file. Open `C:\mayapybook\pylib\minspect.py` in your IDE and type the following code:

```
import sys
def syspath():
    print 'sys.path:'
    for p in sys.path:
        print '  ' + p
```

Save the file, and bring up your mayapy interpreter. If you've closed down the one from the last session, make sure `C:\mayapybook\pylib` (or whatever you are using as your development root) is present on your `sys.path` or the following code will not work! See the preceding section for making sure your development root is on your `sys.path`.

```
>>> import minspect
>>> reload(minspect)
<module 'minspect' from '...\minspect.py'>
>>> minspect.syspath()
C:\Program Files\Autodesk\Maya2013\bin\python26.zip
C:\Program Files\Autodesk\Maya2013\Python\DLLs
C:\Program Files\Autodesk\Maya2013\Python\lib
```

```
C:\Program Files\Autodesk\Maya2013\Python\lib\plat-win
C:\Program Files\Autodesk\Maya2013\Python\lib\lib-tk
C:\Program Files\Autodesk\Maya2013\bin
C:\Program Files\Autodesk\Maya2013\Python
C:\Program Files\Autodesk\Maya2013\Python\lib\site-packages
```

First, we import the `minspect` module. It may already be imported if this was an old mayapy session. That is fine, as importing an already-imported module is fast in Python and causes no side effects. We then use the `reload` function, which we will explore in the next section, to make sure the most up-to-date code is loaded. Finally, we call the `syspath` function, and its output is printed. Your actual paths will likely vary.

Reloading code changes

It is very common as you develop that you'll make changes to some code and want to immediately try out the changed code without restarting Maya or mayapy. You can do that with Python's built-in `reload` function. The `reload` function takes a module object and reloads it from disk so that the new code will be used.

When we jump between our IDE and the interactive interpreter (or the Maya application) as we did earlier, we will usually reload the code to see the effect of our changes. I will usually write out the `import` and `reload` lines, but occasionally will only mention them in text preceding the code.

Keep in mind that reload is not a magic bullet. When you are dealing with simple data and functions as we are here, it is usually fine. But as you start building class hierarchies, decorators, and other things that have dependencies or state, the situation can quickly get out of control. Always test your code in a fresh version of Maya before declaring it done to be sure it does not have some lingering defect hidden by reloading.

Though once you are a master Pythonista you can ignore these warnings and figure out how to reload just about anything!

Exploring Maya and PyMEL

Now we will start digging into Maya and PyMEL. Let's begin by initializing Maya in the mayapy interpreter so we can use more than just standard Python functionality. We do this by calling `maya.standalone.initialize`, as shown in the following code:

```
>>> import maya.standalone
>>> maya.standalone.initialize()
>>> import pymel.core as pmc
>>> xform, shape = pmc.polySphere()
```

The import of `pymel.core` will implicitly call `maya.standalone.initialize` automatically, but I do it explicitly here so it's clear what's going on. In the future, you can generally skip the call to `maya.standalone.initialize` and just import `pymel.core`.

There is a lot we can discover about these PyMEL objects, which represent Maya nodes, using basic Python. For example, to see the **type** of either of our objects, we can use the built-in `type` function (we will dig much deeper into types later in this chapter).

```
>>> type(xform)
<class 'pymel.core.nodetypes.Transform'>
>>> type(shape)
<class 'pymel.core.nodetypes.PolySphere'>
```

To see the names of all the attributes on our shape, we can use the built-in `dir` function:

```
>>> dir(xform)
['LimitType', 'MAttrClass', ..., 'zeroTransformPivots']
```

We can use the built-in `getattr` function with an object and a name of one of its attributes to get the value of the attribute.

```
>>> getattr(xform, 'getShape')
<bound method Transform.getShape of nt.Transform(u'pSphere1')>
>>> getattr(xform, 'translate')
Attribute(u'pSphere1.translate')
```

Note that we are using the `getattr` built-in Python function, not to be confused with the `maya.cmds.getAttr` function or its equivalent PyMEL version. We will not use the `getAttr` function at all in this book. While using `getAttr` may be more familiar if you are coming from the world of MEL and `maya.cmds`, using `getattr` is familiar if you are coming from the much saner world of Python. We should take full advantage of Python and do things the Python, not MEL, way.

We can combine all of these techniques and use the `inspect` module from Python's standard library (commonly referred to as the `stdlib`) to filter for interesting information about our object.

```
>>> import inspect
>>> methods = []
>>> for a in dir(xform):
...     attr = getattr(xform, a)
...     if inspect.ismethod(attr):
```

```
...            methods.append(attr)
>>> attrs = xform.listAttr()
>>> methods
[<bound method Transform.__add__ of nt.Transform(u'pSphere1')>, ...]
>>> attrs
[Attribute(u'pSphere1.message'), ...]
```

In the preceding code, we use the `dir` function to get every Python attribute from our PyMEL transform instance, and then filter them into a list of methods. We then use the `listAttr` method to get a list of Maya attributes on the transform. Based on this data, we can begin to see how the node is structured. Maya attributes are represented by instances of `Attribute`, and methods are usually helpers.

 Using `for` loops and `if` statements that append to a list is not a good practice. We'll replace them with a much nicer syntax called **list comprehensions** in *Chapter 2, Writing Composable Code*.

Creating an introspection function

We'll create a new function in `minspect.py` that will print out interesting information about the object we pass it. Open `C:\mayapybook\pylib\minspect.py` in your IDE or text editor. First, we will add an import to the top of the file (`import sys` should already be there). As a matter of style, imports should always go at the top of the file, one per line, divided into groups. Refer to Python's style guide, called **PEP8**, at `http://www.python.org/dev/peps/pep-0008/#imports`. We will refer back to **PEP8** several times throughout this book.

```
import pymel.core as pmc
import sys
```

Now let's use our earlier techniques and our understanding of Maya to print some information about an object. We can use the `name` method on `PyNode` to provide a simple string representation for a node.

```
def info(obj):
    """Prints information about the object."""

    lines = ['Info for %s' % obj.name(),
             'Attributes:']
    # Get the name of all attributes
    for a in obj.listAttr():
        lines.append('  ' + a.name())
    result = '\n'.join(lines)
    print result
```

You'll notice that instead of repeatedly printing, we put our data into a list and print it only once at the end. We do this for three reasons.

First, appending substrings to a list of strings is faster than incrementally concatenating (adding) them into a large string. Never concatenate many strings together in Python. For example, consider the following expression.

```
'Hello, ' + username + ', it is ' + now + ' right now.'
```

Evaluating this expression creates several unnecessary intermediate strings that are immediately thrown away. Ideally we should minimize transient objects.

Second, joining a list of strings is a well-known pattern. It is said to be more Pythonic than string concatenations.

There is no formal definition for what Pythonic means, but here is an attempt: *something is said to be Pythonic when enough people have said it is Pythonic, or it is very similar to something that is Pythonic*. You should learn to use Pythonic idioms wherever possible, and I will point them out when we run across them.

Finally and most importantly, building a list and printing at the end is more maintainable and easier to test because we are separating decisions (creating the result string) from dependencies (the output stream we print to). If this were production code we'd remove the `print` (dependency) entirely so we can easily test the decisions in `info`. We facilitate that future change by putting `print` into the last line so our dependency is in one place instead of on every line.

Note the use of the `%` operator in the `info` function. We are using **string formatting**. If you are not familiar with string formatting in Python, refer to *Appendix, Python Best Practices*, for more information about it.

We can continue adding to this function to express more information about a node. Try adding support for printing relatives by using `obj.listRelatives()` if you are comfortable.

Understanding Python and MEL types

Python's `type` function, which we used earlier, returns the type of an object. Every object in Python, including the `type` object, has a type, and PyMEL is no different.

```
>>> type([])
<type 'list'>
```

```
>>> type(type([]))
<type 'type'>
>>> type(xform)
<class 'pymel.core.nodetypes.Transform'>
```

You may also be familiar with MEL's *type strings*. Because MEL does not possess a rich type system like Python, *typing* (if it can be called that) is done with strings, as we can see in the following example. The usages of MEL type strings are highlighted.

```
>>> pmc.joint()
nt.Joint(u'joint1')
>>> pmc.polySphere()
[nt.Transform(u'pSphere2'), nt.PolySphere(u'polySphere2')]
>>> pmc.ls(type='joint')
[nt.Joint(u'joint1')]
>>> pmc.ls(type='transform')
[...nt.Joint(u'joint1'), nt.Transform(u'pSphere1'), ...]
>>> pmc.ls(type='shape')
[...nt.Mesh(u'pSphereShape1'), ...]
```

This MEL type, as we'll call it, is very useful while scripting, but not very descriptive. For example, we need to know in advance that a joint is a specific type of transform, and thus returned from invoking `pmc.ls(type='transform')`. This relationship is not clearly expressed.

In contrast, these taxonomic relationships are much better expressed through Python's type system. If we go to the PyMEL documentation for its `Joint` class, we can see the following diagram of its type hierarchy:

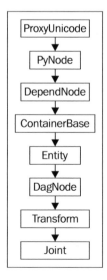

This type hierarchy mimics Maya's underlying object oriented architecture, and we can use it to understand things about nodes we may not be totally familiar with. For example, we can know that a `Joint` has `translate/rotate/scale` attributes because it is a subclass of `Transform`. A subclass inherits the behavior, such as the attributes and methods, of its base class. A subclass is commonly called a **child class**, and a base class is commonly called a **parent class** or **superclass**.

Notice in the example below how the `__bases__` attribute indicates that `Transform` is the base class of the `Joint` class.

```
>>> j = pmc.joint()
>>> j.type()
u'joint'
>>> type(j)
<class 'pymel.core.nodetypes.Joint'>
>>> type(j).__bases__
(<class 'pymel.core.nodetypes.Transform'>,)
>>> j.translate, j.rotate
(Attribute(u'joint2.translate'), Attribute(u'joint2.rotate'))
```

We will look into PyMEL's type hierarchies for the next few sections as a means of understanding how PyMEL nodes work. Don't get intimidated if these concepts are new. We won't be creating any of our own types in this section, and if you are familiar with Maya's nodes, the type hierarchies we are going to examine should be rather intuitive. Later in the book, once we are more familiar with Python and PyMEL, several exercises will require creating our own types.

Using the method resolution order

Even more useful than the `__bases__` attribute is the `__mro__` attribute. **Method Resolution Order (MRO)** is the order Python visits different types so it can figure out what to actually call. You generally don't need to understand the MRO mechanisms (they can be complex), but looking at the MRO will help you understand all the type information about an object. Let's look at the MRO for the `Joint` type:

```
>>> type(j).__mro__
(<class 'pymel.core.nodetypes.Joint'>,
<class 'pymel.core.nodetypes.Transform'>,
<class 'pymel.core.nodetypes.DagNode'>,
<class 'pymel.core.nodetypes.Entity'>,
<class 'pymel.core.nodetypes.ContainerBase'>,
<class 'pymel.core.nodetypes.DependNode'>,
<class 'pymel.core.general.PyNode'>,
<class 'pymel.util.utilitytypes.ProxyUnicode'>,
<type 'object'>)
```

This makes sense: a joint node is a special type of transform node, which is a type of DAG node, which is a type of dependency node, and so on, mirroring the inheritance diagram we previously saw. The fact that reality meets expectation here is a great testament to Maya and PyMEL.

When a call to j.name() is invoked, Python will walk along the MRO looking for the first appropriate method to call. In the case of PyMEL, looking at the MRO often tells us a lot about how an object behaves. This is not always the case, however. Python allows much more dynamic resolution mechanisms. We will not use these mechanisms, such as __getattr__ or __getattribute__, much in this book, but you should be aware that the MRO may not always tell the whole story.

Let's add the collection of type and MRO information into the minspect.py file's info function:

```
def info(obj):
    """Prints information about the object."""

    lines = ['Info for %s' % obj.name(),
             'Attributes:']
    # Get the name of all attributes
    for a in obj.listAttr():
        lines.append('  ' + a.name())
    lines.append('MEL type: %s' % obj.type())
    lines.append('MRO:')
    lines.extend(['  ' + t.__name__ for t in type(obj).__mro__])
    result = '\n'.join(lines)
    print result
```

PyNodes all the way down

In Python, there's a saying, "Its objects all the way down." This means that everything in Python, including numbers, strings, modules, functions, types, and so on, are all just objects. In MEL and maya.cmds I like to say, "Its strings all the way down." Because the type system in MEL and maya.cmds is so rudimentary, many things must be handled through strings. And in PyMEL, I like to say, "It's PyNodes all the way down."

The saying is adapted from "Its turtles all the way down." It is left as an exercise to the reader to uncover the origin of this quote. It may also be said in Python that, "Its dicts all the way down." Python is a language of many clever sayings.

Let's look at our PyMEL transform node to better understand how it is "PyNodes all the way down."

```
>>> type(xform).__mro__
(<class 'pymel.core.nodetypes.Transform'>,
<class 'pymel.core.nodetypes.DagNode'>,
<class 'pymel.core.nodetypes.Entity'>,
<class 'pymel.core.nodetypes.ContainerBase'>,
<class 'pymel.core.nodetypes.DependNode'>,
<class 'pymel.core.general.PyNode'>,
<class 'pymel.util.utilitytypes.ProxyUnicode'>,
<type 'object'>)
>>> type(xform.translate).__mro__
(<class 'pymel.core.general.Attribute'>,
<class 'pymel.core.general.PyNode'>,
<class 'pymel.util.utilitytypes.ProxyUnicode'>,
<type 'object'>)
```

There are a number of very interesting things going on in this short listing.

First, our two types—along with all PyMEL types, in fact—inherit from both `PyNode` and `ProxyUnicode` (as well as `object`, which all Python types inherit from). The `PyNode` type represents any Maya node (DAG/dependency nodes, attributes, Maya windows, and so on). Vitally, `Attributes` are also `PyNodes`. If we look at the PyMEL help for `PyNode`, we can see the distinguishing features of `PyNodes` are that they have a name/identity, connections, and history.

Second, anything that inherits from `DependNode` has attributes. So predictably, `Attributes` are not a `DependNode`, but our `Transform` is.

Third, `Transform` is also a `DagNode`. We can use our knowledge of Maya (or graph theory, if you're into that) to infer that this means the object can have a parent, children, instances, and so on. This is a great example where our knowledge of Maya maps directly onto PyMEL, and we aren't required to learn a new paradigm to understand how the PyMEL framework works.

 We build custom Maya nodes in *Chapter 7, Taming the Maya API*.

Finally, if we look at the __mro__ for a `Joint`, we will see the following information:

```
>>> type(pmc.joint()).__mro__
(<class 'pymel.core.nodetypes.Joint'>,
<class 'pymel.core.nodetypes.Transform'>,
...,
<type 'object'>)
```

We can immediately understand much of how a PyMEL Joint works if we already understand Transform. In fact, everything about Transform is also true for every Joint. The deduction that every Joint behaves like a Transform is known as the **Liskov substitution principle**. It states, roughly, that *if S is a subclass of T, then a program can use an instance of S instead of T without a change in behavior.* It is a fundamental principle of good object-oriented design and manifests itself in well-designed frameworks such as PyMEL.

The fact that types inherit the behavior of their parents is important to keep in mind as you go through the rest of this book and program with PyMEL. Don't worry if you don't fully understand how inheritance works or how to best leverage it. It will become clearer as we proceed on our journey.

> The ProxyUnicode class should be treated as an implementation detail. The only important user-facing detail is that it allows PyNodes to have string methods on them (.replace, .strip, and so on). As of writing this book, I've never used the string methods on a PyNode. Maybe there are valid uses but I can't imagine them. There are always better, more explicit ways of dealing with the node. If you need to deal with its name, call a name-returning method (name(), longName(), and the like) and manipulate that. Use the rename method to rename the node.

Understanding PyMEL data and math types

PyMEL's intuitive use of type hierarchies does not end with Maya node types. It also provides a very useful wrapper around Maya's mathematical data types, including vectors, quaternions, and matrices. These types are located in the pymel.core.datatypes namespace.

Let's take a closer look at xform's transform information.

```
>>> xform.translate
Attribute(u'pSphere1.translate')
>>> t = xform.translate.get()
>>> print t
[0.0, 0.0, 0.0]
```

The translation value of the sphere transform, which is highlighted, appears to be a list. It isn't. The translation value is an instance of `pymel.core.datatypes.Vector`. Sometimes we need to more aggressively introspect objects. I think this is one of the few areas where PyMEL made a mistake. Calling `str(t)` returns a string that looks like it came from a list, instead of looking like it came from a `Vector`. Make sure you have the correct type. I've spent hours hunting down bugs where I was using a `Vector` instead of a `list`, or vice versa.

```
>>> vect = xform.translate.get()
>>> lst = [0.0, 0.0, 0.0]
>>> str(vect)
'[0.0, 0.0, 0.0]'
>>> str(lst)
'[0.0, 0.0, 0.0]'
>>> print t, lst # The print implicitly calls str(t)
[0.0, 0.0, 0.0] [0.0, 0.0, 0.0]
>>> repr(t) # repr returns a more detailed string for an object
'dt.Vector([0.0, 0.0, 0.0])'
>>> repr(lst)
'[0.0, 0.0, 0.0]'
```

Using `repr` as highlighted in the preceding code shows us that vect is not a list. It is one of PyMEL's special data types. This has a number of benefits, despite its bad string representation.

First of all, `Vector` and other data types are list-like objects. The __iter__ method means we can iterate over it, just like a list.

```
>>> t = xform.translate.get()
>>> for c in t:
...      print c
0.0
0.0
0.0
```

The __getitem__ method means we can look up an index.

```
>>> t[0], t[1], t[2]
(0.0, 0.0, 0.0)
```

But it also behaves more like we would expect it to mathematically. When we add two vectors, we get the summed vector, instead of a six item list.

```
>>> [1, 2, 3] + [4, 5, 6] # Regular Python lists
[1, 2, 3, 4, 5, 6]
>>> repr(t + [1, 2, 3])
'dt.Vector([1.0, 2.0, 3.0])'
```

And finally, `Vector` has several useful methods on it, including name-based accessors and helper methods.

```
>>> t.x += 5 # Familiar name-based access
>>> t.y += 2
>>> t.x
5.0
>>> t.length() # And helpers!
5.385...
```

This sort of design, where a custom type implements several different interfaces or protocols, is powerful. For example, if you wanted to move a transform by some vector, you can just write the following code:

```
>>> def move_along_x(xform, vec):
...     t = xform.translate.get()
...     t[0] += vec[0]
...     xform.translate.set(t)
>>> j = pmc.joint()
>>> move_along_x(j, [1, 0, 0])
>>> j.translate.get()
dt.Vector([1.0, 0.0, 0.0])
>>> move_along_x(j, j.translate.get())
>>> j.translate.get()
dt.Vector([2.0, 0.0, 0.0])
```

Notice that at no point did we need to check whether `vec` was an instance of list or of `Vector`. We just require it to implement `__getitem__` so we can access an index. Think about how much more natural this pattern makes using `Vector`, `Quaternion`, `Matrix`, and the other data types in `pymel.core.datatypes`.

When you need to represent some mathematical data or measurement, take a look at the `pymel.core.datatypes` namespace. The classes and functions there are quite important and useful!

Leveraging the REPL

The `info` function we've been building isn't just a useful learning exercise. It can be helpful in everyday programming. A major advantage of dynamic, interpreted languages such as Python has been their **REPL: Read-Evaluate-Print Loop** (REPL). We've actually been using a REPL all throughout this chapter.

Let's write some simple code in the interpreter to demonstrate the REPL:

```
>>> pmc.joint
<function joint at 0x0...>
>>>
```

Now let's see how this fits into the REPL flow:

1. The interpreter prompts for input, indicated by the `>>>` characters.
2. We type `pmc.joint` and hit *Enter*.
3. The input string `pmc.joint` is parsed into a data structure. This is the **read**.
4. The interpreter **evaluates** the data structure, finding PyMEL's `joint` function.
5. The interpreter **prints** the result to the output stream.
6. The interpreter prompts for more input (the loop).

The alternative to the REPL is the Edit-Compile-Run Loop of compiled languages. This is a much longer process, often lasting minutes instead of seconds and requiring a full restart of the application. In recent years, several compiled languages have created interpreters or REPL environments, but this is unavailable to C++ in Maya right now.

It stands to reason that anything we can do to improve our REPL experience will help us learn and explore our language and environment more effectively. Whereas `minspect.info` allows us to see runtime information about some object, next we'll write a function to bridge the gap from runtime information to static documentation.

Building the pmhelp function

Python has a built-in `help` function that, when paired with the REPL described previously, is very useful for rapid exploration.

```
>>> help
Type help() for interactive help, or help(object) for help about
object.
```

However, `help` can be difficult to use with PyMEL (along with many other libraries). The documentation may be missing from the actual object, or may be defined somewhere else. Commonly, the documentation is too verbose to read comfortably in a terminal window. And in the case of a GUI Maya session, it is just more convenient to have documentation in your browser than in the Script Editor.

To better use the online documentation, we'll write an `minspect.pmhelp` function that will link us to PyMEL's excellent online documentation.

As useful as something like pmhelp can be, this exercise will be even more useful for understanding how PyMEL and Maya work. So even if you don't think you have a use for pmhelp or if you get stuck with some of the more technical snippets in this chapter, keep going and at least read through how we build the function.

Calling help(pmc.polySphere) is sort of like calling print pmc.polySphere.__doc__. The help function actually uses the interesting pydoc module, which can do much more, but printing a **docstring** is the most common use case. A docstring is the triple-quoted string that describes a function/method/class, as we had for our minspect.info function. The triple-quoted string gets placed into the function or method's __doc__ attribute.

Invoking the pmhelp function will bring us to the PyMEL web help page for an object or name, searching for it if we do not get a direct match. We'll be able to use this function from within the mayapy interpreter, the Script Editor in Maya, and even a shelf button. We will use the introspection techniques we've learned to get enough information to search properly.

Let's start by typing up our functions into **pseudocode**. Pseudocode is prose that we will eventually turn into actual code. It declares exactly what our function needs to do.

```
# Function converts a python object to a PyMEL help query url.
  # If the object is a string,
    # return a query string for a help search.
  # If the object is a PyMEL object,
    # return the appropriate url tail.
    # PyMEL functions, modules, types, instances,
    # and methods are all valid.
  # Non-PyMEL objects return None.

# Function takes a python object and returns a full help url.
  # Calls the first function.
  # If first function returns None,
  #   just use builtin 'help' function.
  # Otherwise, open a web browser to the help page.
```

Creating a query string for a PyMEL object

First, open a web browser to the PyMEL help so we can understand the URL schema. For our examples, well use the Maya 2013 English PyMEL help at http://download.autodesk.com/global/docs/maya2013/en_us/PyMel/index.html.

Then, open C:\mayapybook\pylib\minspect.py and write the following code at the bottom of the file (the comments with numbers are for the explanation following the code sample and do not need to be copied):

```
def _py_to_helpstr(obj): #(1)
    return None
def test_py_to_helpstr(): #(2)
    def dotest(obj, ideal): #(3)
        result = _py_to_helpstr(obj)
        assert result == ideal, '%s != %s' % (result, ideal) #(4)
    dotest('maya rocks', 'search.html?q=maya+rocks') #(5)
```

Let's pick apart the preceding code.

1. The leading underscore means this is a protected function. It indicates that we shouldn't call it from outside the module. It is for implementation only.

2. This function will contain all of our tests for the different possible objects we can pass in. We can write what we expect, and then assert that our function returns the correct result.

3. Defining a function within a function is normal in Python. Since we don't need dotest outside of our test function, just define it inside.

4. The assert statement means that if the expression following the assert is False, raise an AssertionError with the message after the comma. So in this case, we're saying if the result is not equal to ideal, raise an error that tells the user the gotten and ideal values.

5. We call our inner function. All of the rest of our tests for this function will look very similar.

And in the mayapy interpreter, you can test the code by evaluating the following:

```
>>> import minspect #(1)
>>> reload(minspect)
<module 'minspect' from '...\minspect.py'>
>>> minspect.test_py_to_helpstr() #(2)
Traceback (most recent call last): #(3)
AssertionError: ...
```

Let's walk over how we are running our tests:

1. Import and reload minspect.

2. We invoke our test function, which evaluates our assertion.

3. Since we didn't actually implement anything, our assertion fails and an AssertionError is raised.

The next step is to implement code to pass the test:

```
def _py_to_helpstr(obj):
    if isinstance(obj, basestring):
        return 'search.html?q=%s' % (obj.replace(' ', '+'))
    return None
```

Now we can run our test by calling `test_py_to_helpstr` again and looking for an error:

```
>>> reload(minspect).test_py_to_helpstr()
```

No errors. Congratulations! You have just done **Test Driven Development (TDD)**, which puts you into an elite group of programmers. And we're only in the first chapter!

 Test Driven Development is a technique of developing code where you write your tests first. It is a really an excellent way to program, though not always possible in Maya. See *Appendix, Python Best Practices*, for more information about TDD.

Creating more tests

Let's go ahead and write more test cases. We will add tests for the `pymel.core.nodetypes` module, the `pymel.core.nodetypes.Joint` type and instance, the `Joint.getTranslation` method, and the `pymel.core.animation.joint` function.

```
def test_py_to_helpstr():
    def dotest(obj, ideal):
        result = _py_to_helpstr(obj)
        assert result == ideal, '%s != %s' % (result, ideal)
    dotest('maya rocks', 'search.html?q=maya+rocks')
    dotest(pmc.nodetypes,
            'generated/pymel.core.nodetypes.html'
            '#module-pymel.core.nodetypes')
    dotest(pmc.nodetypes.Joint,
            'generated/classes/pymel.core.nodetypes/'
            'pymel.core.nodetypes.Joint.html'
            '#pymel.core.nodetypes.Joint')
    dotest(pmc.nodetypes.Joint(),
            'generated/classes/pymel.core.nodetypes/'
            'pymel.core.nodetypes.Joint.html'
            '#pymel.core.nodetypes.Joint')
    dotest(pmc.nodetypes.Joint().getTranslation,
```

```
                    'generated/classes/pymel.core.nodetypes/'
                    'pymel.core.nodetypes.Joint.html'
                    '#pymel.core.nodetypes.Joint.getTranslation')
        dotest(pmc.joint,
                    'generated/functions/pymel.core.animation/'
                    'pymel.core.animation.joint.html'
                    '#pymel.core.animation.joint')
```

I got the ideal values simply by going to the PyMEL online help and copying the appropriate part of the URL. Building code is simpler when your expectations are crystal clear!

The actual implementation of _py_to_helplstr can be considered simple or complex depending on your experience with Python. It uses lots of double-underscore attributes and demands some understanding of Python's types and inner workings. Memorizing every detail of every line is less important than understanding the basic idea of the code.

We'll use various *double underscore* attributes such as __class__ and __name__. They are called either **dunder methods** or **magic methods**, though there's nothing magical about them. Single leading underscore attributes, as we've seen, indicate *implementation* or *protected* attributes that callers outside of a module or class should not use. Double leading underscore indicate *private* attributes, though you can think of them the same as single leading underscore attributes (they cannot be called in a straightforward manner, however). Magic methods are generally not called directly but are for protocols such as the __getitem__ method we saw earlier allowing an object to be indexed like a list or dictionary.

We'll add support for the different types of objects in the order they are listed in the test function until every test passes. We'll start with modules.

In the _py_to_helpstr function, we make heavy use of the isinstance function. This sort of design may seem intuitive, but it is typically a bad practice to check if something is an instance of the class. It is generally better to check if something has functionality or behavior rather than checking what type it is. In this case, though, we do actually want to check if something is an instance. The type of the object is the behavior we are checking for.

Adding support for modules

pymel.core.nodetypes is a module, as are pymel and pymel.core. The implementation of _py_to_helpstr for modules is straightforward. We use the __name__ attribute to identify the module (we will see other uses for __name__ throughout this book).

```
>>> import pymel.core.nodetypes
>>> pymel.core.nodetypes.__name__
'pymel.core.nodetypes'
```

To test if something is a module, we can check if the type is the **module type** by importing the types module and checking if an object is an instance of types.ModuleType.

```
>>> import types
>>> isinstance(pymel.core.nodetypes, types.ModuleType)
True
```

We will continue to use the types module throughout the rest of this chapter. The code should be mostly self-explanatory so I will only remark on the members we use when their usage is not obvious.

We also need to understand how documentation for modules is laid out in PyMEL's help. URLs to module documentation take the following form:

```
<base_url>/generated/<module name>.html#module-<module_name>
```

To support modules, the _py_to_helpstr function should look like the following (don't forget to add import types at the top of minspect.py):

```
def _py_to_helpstr(obj):
    if isinstance(obj, basestring):
        return 'search.html?q=%s' % (obj.replace(' ', '+'))
    if isinstance(obj, types.ModuleType):
        return ('generated/%(module)s.html#module-%(module)s' %
                dict(module=obj.__name__))
    return None
```

If we reload our module and run the test_py_to_helpstr test function, you will see that the test now passes for pmc.nodetypes and fails for pmc.nodetypes.Joint.

Adding support for types

To add support for types such as `pymel.core.nodetypes.Joint`, we will use the same technique as we did for modules. We will use the `__module__` and `__name__` attributes of the `Joint` type:

```
>>> pmc.nodetypes.Joint
<class 'pymel.core.nodetypes.Joint'>
>>> pmc.nodetypes.Joint.__name__
'Joint'
>>> pmc.nodetypes.Joint.__module__
'pymel.core.nodetypes'
```

The PyMEL help format for types is almost the same as the one for modules:

```
generated/classes/<module>/<module>.<type>.html#<module>.<type>
```

We'll treat a type as the default (last) case. If we pass in something that is not a type, we can just get the object's type and use that. Let's add support for types into our function:

```
def _py_to_helpstr(obj):
    if isinstance(obj, basestring):
        return 'search.html?q=%s' % (obj.replace(' ', '+'))
    if isinstance(obj, types.ModuleType):
        return ('generated/%(module)s.html#module-%(module)s' %
                dict(module=obj.__name__))
    if not isinstance(obj, type):
        obj = type(obj)
    return ('generated/classes/%(module)s/'
            '%(module)s.%(typename)s.html'
            '#%(module)s.%(typename)s' % dict(
                module=obj.__module__,
                typename=obj.__name__))
```

If you reload and invoke the test function, the test should fail for the `Joint.getTranslation` method.

Adding support for methods

When we use something like `mylist.append(1)`, we can say we are "invoking the `append` method with an argument of `1` on the `list` instance named `'mylist'`." Methods are things we call on an instance of an object. Things we call on a module are called functions, and we'll cover them after methods.

It's important to define what a method is with precise vocabulary. While speaking with other people, it's not so important if you mix up "function" with "method", but when you're writing code, you must be very clear what you are doing.

The following code creates a `Joint` and inspects the type of the instance's `getTranslation` method. We can see the method's type is `instancemethod`, and it is an instance of `types.MethodType`:

```
>>> joint = pmc.nodetypes.Joint()
>>> type(joint.getTranslation)
<type 'instancemethod'>
>>> isinstance(joint.getTranslation, types.MethodType)
True
```

There are actually several other types of methods in Python. Fortunately, they are largely unimportant for our purposes here. We'll run through them quickly, in case you want to follow up on your own.

```
>>> class MyClass(object):
...     def mymethod(self):
...         pass
...     @classmethod # (1)
...     def myclassmethod(cls):
...         pass
...     @staticmethod # (2)
...     def mystaticmethod():
...         pass
>>> MyClass().mymethod # (3)
<bound method MyClass.mymethod of <__main__.MyClass object athh...
>>> MyClass.mymethod # (4)
<unbound method MyClass.mymethod>
```

Given this class definition, we can observe the following method types:

- **Class methods**: These use the `@classmethod` decorator and are called with the type of the instance (`cls`) instead of the instance itself. We cover decorators in *Chapter 4, Leveraging Context Manager and Decorators in Maya*.

- **Static methods**: These use the `@staticmethod` decorator and are called with no `cls` or `self` argument. I always advise against the use of static methods. Just use module functions instead. And in fact, static methods aren't really methods when you inspect their type; they are functions as described in the next section.

- **Bound methods**: `MyClass().mymethod` refers to a bound method. A method is said to be bound when it is associated with an instance. For example, we can say `bound = MyClass().mymethod`. When we later invoke `bound()`, it will always refer to the same instance of `MyClass`.

- **Unbound method**: `MyClass.mymethod` refers to an unbound method. Note we're accessing `mymethod` from the class itself, not an instance. You must call unbound methods with an instance. Calling `MyClass().mymethod()` and `MyClass.mymethod(MyClass())` is roughly equivalent. You rarely use unbound methods directly.

Methods also have three special attributes that link them back to the type and instance they are bound to. The `im_self` attribute refers to the instance bound to the method. The `im_class` attribute refers to the type the method is declared on. The `im_func` refers to the underlying function.

```
>>> MyClass().mymethod.im_self
<__main__.MyClass object at 0x0...>
>>> MyClass().mymethod.im_class
<class '__main__.MyClass'>
>>> MyClass().mymethod.im_func
<function mymethod at 0x0...>
```

The important one for us is the `im_class` attribute so we can get the class for this method.

Let's go ahead and add support for methods. The pattern should be very familiar now. The help string format is just the same for types, but with an additional "`.`" and the name of the method. The new code is highlighted in the following listing:

```
def _py_to_helpstr(obj):
    if isinstance(obj, basestring):
        return 'search.html?q=%s' % (obj.replace(' ', '+'))
    if isinstance(obj, types.ModuleType):
        return ('generated/%(module)s.html#module-%(module)s' %
                dict(module=obj.__name__))
    if isinstance(obj, types.MethodType):
        return ('generated/classes/%(module)s/'
                '%(module)s.%(typename)s.html'
                '#%(module)s.%(typename)s.%(methname)s' % dict(
                    module=obj.__module__,
                    typename=obj.im_class.__name__,
                    methname=obj.__name__))
    if not isinstance(obj, type):
        obj = type(obj)
```

```
return ('generated/classes/%(module)s/'
        '%(module)s.%(typename)s.html'
        '#%(module)s.%(typename)s' % dict(
            module=obj.__module__,
            typename=obj.__name__))
```

Adding support for functions

A function is just like a method, but it isn't part of a class.

```
>>> def spam():
...     def eggs():
...         pass
...     pass
```

The preceding code contains two functions: spam and eggs. Basically, any def that isn't part of a class definition (the first argument is not self or cls in regular methods and class methods described previously) is considered a function. In addition to these earlier simple functions, lambdas and staticmethods are also functions, as we see in the following code:

```
>>> get10 = lambda: 10
>>> type(get10)
<type 'function'>
>>> class MyClass(object):
...     @staticmethod
...     def mystaticmethod(): pass
>>> type(MyClass.mystaticmethod)
<type 'function'>
>>> type(MyClass().mystaticmethod)
<type 'function'>
```

Both get10 and MyClass.mystaticmethod are considered functions by Python and will be handled by the logic in this section.

The PyMEL help URL for functions is straightforward and in fact very similar to types. Implementing functions has no surprises. The code added for handling functions is highlighted in the following listing:

```
def _py_to_helpstr(obj):
    if isinstance(obj, basestring):
        return 'search.html?q=%s' % (obj.replace(' ', '+'))
    if isinstance(obj, types.ModuleType):
        return ('generated/%(module)s.html#module-%(module)s' %
                dict(module=obj.__name__))
```

```
    if isinstance(obj, types.MethodType):
        return ('generated/classes/%(module)s/'
                '%(module)s.%(typename)s.html'
                '#%(module)s.%(typename)s.%(methname)s' % dict(
                    module=obj.__module__,
                    typename=obj.im_class.__name__,
                    methname=obj.__name__))
    if isinstance(obj, types.FunctionType):
        return ('generated/functions/%(module)s/'
                '%(module)s.%(funcname)s.html'
                '#%(module)s.%(funcname)s' % dict(
                    module=obj.__module__,
                    funcname=obj.__name__))
    if not isinstance(obj, type):
        obj = type(obj)
    return ('generated/classes/%(module)s/'
            '%(module)s.%(typename)s.html'
            '#%(module)s.%(typename)s' % dict(
                module=obj.__module__,
                typename=obj.__name__))
```

If you reload `minspect` and run the `test_py_to_helpstr` test function, no error should be raised by the `assert`. If there is, ensure your test and implementation code is correct.

Adding support for non-PyMEL objects

Right now we only have tests and support for PyMEL objects. We can add support for non-PyMEL objects by returning None if our argument does not have a module under the `pymel` namespace. The check can be a straightforward function using several of the things we've learned about the special attributes of objects. Add the following function somewhere in `minspect.py`:

```
def _is_pymel(obj):
    try: # (1)
        module = obj.__module__ # (2)
    except AttributeError: # (3)
        try:
            module = obj.__name__ # (4)
        except AttributeError:
            return None # (5)
    return module.startswith('pymel') # (6)
```

This logic is based on what we already know about Python objects. All user-defined types and instances have a __module__ attribute, and all modules have a __name__ attribute. Let's walk through the preceding code.

1. We use try/except in this function, rather than checking if attributes exist. This is discussed in the following section, *Designing with EAFP versus LBYL*. If you are not familiar with Python's error handling mechanisms including try/except, we discuss it more in *Chapter 4, Leveraging Context Managers and Decorators in Maya*.

2. If obj has a __module__ attribute (for example, if it is a type or function), we will use that as the namespace.

3. If it does not, an AttributeError will be raised, which we catch.

4. Try to get the __name__ attribute, assuming obj is a module. There's a possibility obj has a __name__ and no __module__ but is not a module. We will ignore this possibility (see the *section Code is never complete* later in this chapter).

5. If obj does not have a __name__, give up, and return None.

6. If we do find what we think is a module name, return True if it begins with the string "pymel" and False if not.

We don't need to test this function directly. We can just add another test to our existing test function. The new tests are in highlighted in the following code.

```
def test_py_to_helpstr():
    def dotest(obj, ideal):
        result = _py_to_helpstr(obj)
        assert result == ideal, '%s != %s' % (result, ideal)
    dotest('maya rocks', 'search.html?q=maya+rocks')
    dotest(pmc.nodetypes,
            'generated/pymel.core.nodetypes.html'
            '#module-pymel.core.nodetypes')
    dotest(pmc.nodetypes.Joint,
            'generated/classes/pymel.core.nodetypes/'
            'pymel.core.nodetypes.Joint.html'
            '#pymel.core.nodetypes.Joint')
    dotest(pmc.nodetypes.Joint(),
            'generated/classes/pymel.core.nodetypes/'
            'pymel.core.nodetypes.Joint.html'
            '#pymel.core.nodetypes.Joint')
    dotest(pmc.nodetypes.Joint().getTranslation,
            'generated/classes/pymel.core.nodetypes/'
            'pymel.core.nodetypes.Joint.html'
            '#pymel.core.nodetypes.Joint.getTranslation')
```

```
        dotest(pmc.joint,
            'generated/functions/pymel.core.animation/'
            'pymel.core.animation.joint.html'
            '#pymel.core.animation.joint')
    dotest(object(), None)
    dotest(10, None)
    dotest([], None)
    dotest(sys, None)
```

Reload `minspect` and run the test function. The first new test should fail. Let's go in and edit our code in `minspect.py` to add support for non-PyMEL objects. The changes are highlighted.

```
    def _py_to_helpstr(obj):
        if isinstance(obj, basestring):
            return 'search.html?q=%s' % (obj.replace(' ', '+'))
        if not _is_pymel(obj):
            return None
        if isinstance(obj, types.ModuleType):
            return ('generated/%(module)s.html#module-%(module)s' %
                    dict(module=obj.__name__))
        if isinstance(obj, types.MethodType):
            return ('generated/classes/%(module)s/'
                    '%(module)s.%(typename)s.html'
                    '#%(module)s.%(typename)s.%(methname)s' % dict(
                        module=obj.__module__,
                        typename=obj.im_class.__name__,
                        methname=obj.__name__))
        if isinstance(obj, types.FunctionType):
            return ('generated/functions/%(module)s/'
                    '%(module)s.%(funcname)s.html'
                    '#%(module)s.%(funcname)s' % dict(
                        module=obj.__module__,
                        funcname=obj.__name__))
        if not isinstance(obj, type):
            obj = type(obj)
        return ('generated/classes/%(module)s/'
                '%(module)s.%(typename)s.html'
                '#%(module)s.%(typename)s' % dict(
                    module=obj.__module__,
                    typename=obj.__name__))
```

It's important that the `_is_pymel` check comes early so we don't try to generate PyMEL URLs for non-PyMEL objects. We now have a relatively complete function we can be proud of. Reload and run your tests to ensure everything now passes.

Designing with EAFP versus LBYL

In _is_pymel, we used a try/except statement rather than check if an object has an attribute. This pattern is called **Easier to Ask for Forgiveness than Permission (EAFP)**. In contrast, checking things ahead of time is called **Look Before You Leap (LBYL)**. The former is considered much more *Pythonic* and generally results in shorter and more robust code. Consider the differences between the following three ways of writing the second try/except inside the _is_pymel function.

```
# Version 1
>>> module = None
>>> if isinstance(obj, types.ModuleType):
...     module = obj.__name__

# Version 2
>>> module = None
>>> if hasattr(obj, '__name__'):
...     module = obj.__name__

# Version 3
>>> module = getattr(obj, '__name__', None)

# Version 4
>>> try:
...     module = obj.__name__
... except AttributeError:
...     module = None
```

Version 1 is thoroughly LBYL and should generally be avoided. We are interested in the __name__ attribute, not whether obj is a module or not, so we should look for or access the attribute instead of checking the type. Versions 2 and 3 are using LBYL by checking for the __name__ attribute but would be an improvement over version 1 since they are not checking the type. These two versions are about the same, with version 3 being more concise. Version 4 is fully EAFP. Use the style of code that results in the most readable result, but err on the side of EAFP.

There is much more to the debate, and we'll be seeing more instances of EAFP versus LBYL throughout this book.

Code is never complete

Note that the code in this chapter may not be complete. As Donald Knuth said:

> *Beware of bugs in the above code; I have only proved it correct, not tried it.*

There are likely problems with this chapter's code and undoubtedly bugs in the rest of this book. While math may be provably correct, production code that depends on large frameworks (like PyMEL), which themselves rely on complex, stateful systems (like Maya) will never be provably correct. No practical amount of testing can ensure there are no bugs for edge cases.

But there are many types of bugs. In _py_to_helpstr, a user can pass in a string that may be illegal for a URL. If this were externally released code, we'd want to handle that case, but for personal or in-house code (the vast majority of what you'll write) it is perfectly fine to have "bugs" like this. When the need arises to filter problematic characters, you can add the support.

In the same way, when we find a PyMEL object that isn't compatible with _is_pymel, or some object that causes an unhandled error, we can edit the code to solve that problem.

The alternative is to try and write bug-free code all the time while predicting all the ways your code can be called. Good luck!

Understanding that we can't write perfect code is one reason why having automated tests is so important. When we find a use case we need to support, we can just go back to our test function, add the test, make sure our test fails, implement the change, make sure our test passes, and then **refactor** our implementation to make sure our code looks as good as it can. We cover refactoring in *Chapter 2, Writing Composable Code*.

Opening help in a web browser

Now that all of our tests pass, we can put together our actual pmhelp function. We need to assemble our generated URL tail with a site, and open it in the web browser. This is actually very simple code because Python comes with so many *batteries included*. The following code should go into minspect.py:

```
import webbrowser # (1)
HELP_ROOT_URL = ('http://download.autodesk.com/global/docs/'
                 'maya2013/en_us/PyMel/')# (2)


def pmhelp(obj): # (3)
    """Gives help for a pymel or python object.
```

```
    If obj is not a PyMEL object, use Python's built-in
    'help' function.
    If obj is a string, open a web browser to a search in the
    PyMEL help for the string.
    Otherwise, open a web browser to the page for the object.
    """
    tail = _py_to_helpstr(obj)
    if tail is None:
        help(obj) # (4)
    else:
        webbrowser.open(HELP_ROOT_URL + tail) # (5)
```

Let's walk through the preceding code.

1. The `webbrowser` module is part of the Python standard library and allows Python to open browser pages. It's awesome!

2. Define the documentation URL root. Point it to the correct source for your version of Maya and PyMEL.

3. Define the `pmhelp` function, and give it a docstring because we are responsible programmers.

4. If `_py_to_helpstr` returns `None`, just use the built-in `help` function.

5. If `_py_to_helpstr` returns a string, open the URL.

You can now reload your module once more and try it out, for real.

```
# Will open a browser and search for "joint".
>>> minspect.pmhelp('joint')
# Will open a browser to the pymel.core.nodetypes module page.
>>> minspect.pmhelp(pmc.nodetypes)
# Will print out help for integers.
>>> minspect.pmhelp(1)
Help on int object:
class int(object)
 |  int(x[, base]) -> integer
...
```

Note that doing `minspect.pmhelp(minspect.pmhelp)` is totally valid and will show your docstring. This sort of robustness is the hallmark of well-designed code.

We can also hook up `pmhelp` to be available through Maya's interface: select an object, hit the `pmhelp` shelf button, and a browser page will open to its help page. Just put the following Python "code in a string" into a shelf button (all one line, broken into two here for print):

```
"import pymel.core as pmc; import minspect;
minspect.pmhelp(pmc.selected()[0])"
```

If you're not sure how to do this, don't worry. We will look more at using Python code in shelf buttons in *Chapter 5, Building Graphical User Interfaces for Maya*. Also be aware this code will error if nothing is selected, but you'll see how to better handle high-level calls from shelf buttons in *Chapter 2, Writing Composable Code*.

You may also notice we didn't write any automated tests for `pmhelp` like we did for `_py_to_helpstr`. Normally I would, especially if this function grows at all. But for now, it's so simple and would take more advanced techniques so we should be pretty confident to leave it alone.

Summary

In this chapter, we learned how Maya and Python work together to create PyMEL. First we learned how to use the mayapy interpreter, and how to create and use Python libraries and modules. Then we explored PyMEL via introspection: how it mirrors Maya concepts such as DAG nodes and attributes, how every Maya object is represented as a first-class PyMEL node, and PyMEL's special math data types. Finally, we built a function that can bring us to the PyMEL online help when we want more information about a PyMEL node. Along the way, we learned about concepts central to Python, such as types, the standard library, magic methods, a definition of the term Pythonic, and easier to ask for forgiveness than permission versus look before you leap.

In the next chapter, we will learn more about writing practical Maya Python with PyMEL by investigating the important concept of *composability*.

2
Writing Composable Code

In this chapter, we'll explore the concept of **composable code**. We start by defining the term. We then examine composable and non-composable examples to better understand what composability is, and improve code by refactoring. We will learn about important techniques to maximize composability, such as predicates, list comprehensions, contracts, closures, and docstrings. We put these techniques to work by building a library to convert a hierarchy of transforms into joints. After that, we compose this library into a configurable higher-level tool for creating characters. Finally, we will look at some issues and solutions surrounding PyMEL, composability, and performance.

Defining composability

The idea of composability is to write code as small and well-defined **units** that can be combined with other units in flexible and predictable ways. Composable code is **decoupled** and **cohesive**. That is, the code has few dependencies and is responsible for a single responsibility. Writing composable code is the key to creating maintainable systems and libraries you'll use for years.

A *unit* is a function, class, or method. It is generally the smallest piece of independently useful code, and should be smaller than a module or group of classes (system). There is no black and white definition, so prefer smaller and simpler to larger and more complex.

Maya's utility nodes, such as the `MultiplyDivide` node, are examples of composable units. They are very clear in their inputs, outputs, and descriptions of what they do. The input to a `MultiplyDivide` node can be a number from any source, such as a Maya transform, another utility node, or a constant. The `MultiplyDivide` node does not care, as long as the input is a number. The node just does what it is asked to do — multiply or divide two numbers — and returns the result. It has no undefined behavior, since it will error for any unexpected inputs, and does not rely on system state at all. It relies only on its inputs.

A utility node such as `MultiplyDivide`, then, can be said to have *clear contracts*. The idea of contracts is a key to writing composable code and is something we'll explore in greater detail later in this chapter. But first, let's look at an example of non-composable code.

Identifying anti-patterns of composability

In contrast to Maya's utility nodes, the design of MEL and `maya.cmds` is profoundly non-composable. Let's start by creating a couple of nodes, and viewing them with the `ls` function as follows:

```
>>> import maya.cmds as cmds
>>> j1 = cmds.joint()
>>> j2 = cmds.joint()
>>> cmds.ls(type='transform')
[...u'joint1', u'joint2'...]
>>> cmds.ls(exactType='joint')
[u'joint1', u'joint2']
```

The `type='transform'` argument returns the joints because joints are a type of transform, as we learned in the last chapter. If our scene had other transforms, they would be part of the results. In contrast, the `exactType='joint'` argument returns only the joints in the scene, and not other transforms.

We would expect that most *listing* functions in Maya would support the `type` and `exactType` flags, as `ls` does. And if not, at least we'd expect these flags to work consistently. I have bad news. Behold the `listConnections` function:

```
>>> cmds.listConnections(j1, type='transform')
[u'joint2']
>>> cmds.listConnections(j1, exactType='transform')
Traceback (most recent call last):
TypeError: Invalid arguments for flag 'exactType'...
```

Using a string for the `exactType` argument in `listConnections` results in a `TypeError`. The argument must be a Boolean value, as shown in the following example:

```
>>> cmds.listConnections(j1, type='joint', exactType=True)
[u'joint2']
```

We see this unintuitive pattern repeated in multiple places. In this next example, we can see that the `listRelatives` function doesn't even support the `exactType` flag!

```
>>> cmds.listRelatives(j1, type='joint')
[u'joint2']
>>> cmds.listRelatives(j1, exactType='transform')
Traceback (most recent call last):
TypeError: Invalid flag 'exactType'
```

What do these strange design choices have to do with composability?

Composable functions generally do a single thing. The problematic functions called out previously are combining two behaviors into one function. There is the **selection** behavior (list relatives, connections, or all objects in the scene) and the **filtering** behavior (of the selection, choose only objects of a certain type). We can imagine that as this filtering behavior grows more complex, it becomes impossible to keep all selection functions providing filtering in sync.

 It should be clear but it bears pointing out: the term *selection* here does not refer to selecting an object in Maya. It refers to the computer science term of choosing something.

What would it look like if we broke the filtering out into a distinct function? The following code uses functions that we will build later in this chapter.

```
>>> import minspect
>>> [o for o in pmc.listConnections(j1)
...    if minspect.is_exact_type(o, 'joint')]
[nt.Joint(u'joint2')]
```

The `listConnections` function still handles the selection, but now the `is_exact_type` function handles the filtering. We combine the two using a list comprehension, which we'll learn about in the *List Comprehensions* section later in this chapter. As more filtering functionality needs to be provided, nothing except `is_exact_type` needs to change. Likewise, as `listConnections` needs to change, it would never conflict with the type filtering behavior.

Avoiding the use of Boolean flags

As a rule of thumb, avoid multiple Boolean flags as function parameters. Multiple Boolean flags indicate problematic code, or what is often called a *code smell*. While a single flag is usually acceptable, multiple flags become exponentially more difficult to maintain. Once you get past two flags, you should almost always split your function into two or more smaller functions, or rethink how it works.

 A *code smell* is something in the design or implementation of a program that indicates deeper problems. Generally, multiple Boolean flags in a function's signature is a code smell that indicates an overly complex function body.

Additionally, you should never have arguments that are mutually exclusive or interfere with each other, flags or not. The use_stdout argument in the following example has no effect when the stream argument is not None.

```
>>> import os
>>> import sys
>>> def say(s, use_stdout=True, stream=None):
...     if stream is None:
...         if use_stdout:
...             stream = sys.stdout
...         else:
...             stream = sys.stderr
...     stream.write(s + os.linesep)
```

The preceding say function may seem contrived but it is not. You could have a function similar to this lurking in your codebase! I would expect that the evolution of the say function went like this:

```
>>> # Someone needs a simple debug printer to stdout
>>> say('hi')
>>> # Someone needed to print to stderr, so adds a flag.
>>> say('hi', use_stdout=True)
>>> # Someone needed an arbitrary stream, so adds support.
>>> say('hi', use_stdout=True, stream=None)
```

You should err on the side of not using Boolean flags. It is better to be verbose and pass in what's needed than it is to perform calculations in controlled by flags. You can always wrap a general and verbose function with a function that has a signature better suited to the context in which it is used.

As we've already seen, the teams at Autodesk (and Alias | Wavefront before them) could not keep all of their flags in sync. This isn't because they aren't smart enough or don't work hard enough. It is simply the way software evolves. For comparison, the Unix ls command supports almost 60 options!

Flags lead to users having a hard time remembering how something works. It makes a single function difficult to maintain and extend. It also adds an insurmountable burden to systems, such as Maya's listing functions, that should have consistency.

Due to MEL's limitations as a language, flags were probably a good decision at the time. But we are using the much more powerful language of Python and should take advantage of it by writing composable code and avoiding the use of Boolean flags.

Evolving legacy code into composable code

Have you ever seen code like the following?

```
>>> def get_all_root_joints():
...     roots = []
...     for jnt in pmc.ls(type='joint'):
...         if jnt.getParent() is None:
...             roots.append(jnt)
...     return roots
>>> get_all_root_joints()
[nt.Joint(u'joint1')]
```

The get_all_root_joints function returns a list of all joints in the scene that have no parent. There are a number of issues with the preceding function, but in general we can say *it lacks composability*.

Perhaps this function is already somewhere in your codebase. Now you have a new use case for this root-finding behavior: a user merges a Maya scene into one with existing skeletons, and you want to get only the skeleton roots from the new scene. Unfortunately, you cannot use the same logic inside get_all_root_joints unless you copy and paste it (which you shouldn't do, and won't have to do after reading this chapter). The get_all_root_joints function has a limited design that makes re-using it for new purposes impossible.

In what ways is it limited? Just like the listRelatives and previously discussed examples, we've combined selection and filtering in the same function. For example, the ls command has both selection (select all objects) and filtering (keep only joints), and the next line also filters (keep only objects without a parent). We also have several lines of boilerplate for creating the list, appending to the list, and returning it.

Wouldn't it be great if we could write our code in such a way so that it's more easily re-usable?

Rewriting code for composability

Rewriting existing code for composability usually involves splitting up a larger function into smaller pieces, each responsible for a single task. In the case of `get_all_root_joints`, we will just create a function to filter root joints.

```
>>> def is_root_joint(obj):
...     return obj.type() == 'joint' and obj.getParent() is None
>>> all_roots = [o for o in pmc.ls() if is_root_joint(o)]
>>> new_roots = [o for o in pmc.importFile(some_file_path)
...              if is_root_joint(o)]
```

We've pulled all of our filtering logic into a simple *predicate*, the `is_root_joint` function. A *predicate* is a fancy name for a function that returns `True` or `False`. We combine that predicate with a selection (`ls` or `importFile`) and suddenly the root-finding logic is usable everywhere.

Let's take this splitting of selection and filtering further.

Getting the first item in a sequence

It's very common to find code to select the first item in a sequence, unless the sequence is empty, in which case we select `None`. To do this, we create the sequence, assign our result variable a default value of `None`, check if the sequence contains items, and if so, assign the result variable to be the first item in the sequence.

The following code illustrates this process:

```
>>> all_roots = [o for o in pmc.ls() if is_root_joint(o)]
>>> first_root = None
>>> if all_roots:
...     first_root = all_roots[0]
>>> first_root
nt.Joint(u'joint1')
```

There are several problems with this implementation. First, accessing `all_roots[0]` only works if `all_roots` is indexable with an integer. Examples of compatible types are lists and tuples. However, there are many sequences in Python that are not indexable. We won't go over them now (they include `sets` and generators), so you'll just have to take my word for it. This pattern will not work for those types, so the common workaround is to cast the object into a list before indexing. Yuck!

The second problem (and more important for our current purposes) is that the preceding code involves a lot of **boilerplate**. Boilerplate is code that must be included with little modification. We use four lines for a single expression: *return a value that is the first item in a sequence or a default if the sequence is empty.* Instead of being happy with boilerplate, we should write a function to remove it, as we do in the following code:

```
>>> def first_or_default(sequence, default=None):
...     for item in sequence:
...         return item  # Return the first item
...     return default  # Return default if no items
```

Now our code to select the first root joint looks like this:

```
>>> first_root = first_or_default(
...     o for o in pmc.ls() if is_root_joint(o))
>>> first_root
nt.Joint(u'joint1')
```

Can we do one better? What if we combine the `is_root_joint` predicate with our `first_or_default` logic? Let's add a `predicate` parameter to the `first_or_default` function.

```
>>> def first_or_default(sequence, predicate=None, default=None):
...     for item in sequence:
...         if predicate is None or predicate(item):
...             return item
...     return default
```

Now our code looks as follows:

```
>>> first_root = first_or_default(pmc.ls(), is_root_joint)
>>> first_root
nt.Joint(u'joint1')
```

Pretty neat! We've taken what normally shows up as several lines of boilerplate imperative code, and broken it down into two totally reusable functions.

One of the benefits of developing this way is that our code is not tied to Maya. There is nothing specific to Maya in the `first_or_default` function. This means that your code is totally reusable, testable, and much more easy to develop. In fact, I always develop functions like this completely outside Maya.

```
>>> first_or_default([1, 2, 3])
1
>>> first_or_default([], default='hi!')
'hi!'
```

We're well on our way to writing composable code!

Writing head and tail functions

Another example of argument-driven behavior that is better served as distinct functions is the `head` and `tail` parameters in the `ls` function. The `head` argument specifies how many items to return from the start of the list, and the `tail` argument specifies the opposite. We can see the two in action in the following example:

```
>>> pmc.ls(type='joint', head=2)
[nt.Joint(u'joint1'), nt.Joint(u'joint2')]
>>> pmc.ls(type='joint', tail=2)
[nt.Joint(u'joint2'), nt.Joint(u'joint3')]
```

Instead of using arguments to control this behavior, it can be rewritten as `head` and `tail` functions, as shown in the following example;

```
>>> def head(sequence, count):
...     result = []
...     for item in sequence:
...         if len(result) == count:
...             break
...         result.append(item)
...     return result
>>> head(pmc.ls(type='joint'), 2)
[nt.Joint(u'joint1'), nt.Joint(u'joint2')]

>>> def tail(sequence, count):
...     result = list(sequence)
...     return result[-count:]
>>> tail(pmc.ls(type='joint'), 2)
[nt.Joint(u'joint2'), nt.Joint(u'joint3')]
```

The new `head` and `tail` functions can be re-used for any collection, do not depend on Maya, and do not have the special behavior of the `ls` arguments.

Learning to use list comprehensions

Let's look at list comprehensions in depth now that we've used simpler versions several times. It's a powerful-yet-simple syntax that has been in Python since version 2.0. List comprehensions are described very succinctly and with very clear examples in PEP 202 at `http://www.python.org/dev/peps/pep-0202/`.

A **Python Enhancement Proposal (PEP)** is a design document for a Python feature (or similar). Often it can be very long and technical. PEP 202 is a very straightforward PEP that is well worth reading, consisting of three paragraphs and one example block. Some other notable PEPs will be mentioned in this book and in the appendices.

Oh, and PEP 1 describes PEPs and the PEP process, of course.

A list comprehension has the following form:

```
[<map> for <variable> in <selection> | if <predicate>]
```

The `map` is the item that ends up in the list. It can be the same as `variable` if no transformation is to take place. It's commonly a function that transforms `variable`. The `variable` is the item in `selection` being iterated over. The `selection` is the sequence being iterated. The `predicate` is optional expression, but is a function that takes `variable` and returns `True` if the item should be included in the result or `False` if not. For example, the following list comprehension generates a list of uppercase letters from an input string:

```
>>> s = 'hi!'
>>> [c.upper() for c in s if c.isalpha()]
['H', 'I']
```

In the preceding example:

- `s` is the `selection`.
- `c` is the `variable`.
- `c.alpha()` is the `predicate`.
- `c.upper()` is the `map`.

Let's look at some more simple examples.

```
>>> [i + 1 for i in [1, 2, 3]]
[2, 3, 4]
>>> [i for i in [1, 2, 3] if i > 2]
[3]
>>> [(i, chr(i)) for i in [65, 66, 67]]
[(65, 'A'), (66, 'B'), (67, 'C')]
```

You can also nest list comprehensions, but we'll avoid that for this book. PEP 202 includes many examples of nested list comprehensions, and they can be very useful. However, only attempt them once you are comfortable with regular list comprehensions.

List comprehensions are vital when writing composable code, and we'll use them repeatedly throughout the rest of the book. If you're still uncomfortable, fire up a Python interpreter and get comfortable!

Implementing is_exact_type

With our experience building composable code and using list comprehensions, let's take a stab at creating an `is_exact_type` function that will replace the need for the `exactType` parameter in Maya's listing functions.

First, we need to choose a place to put the function. The `minspect.py` file we created in *Chapter 1, Introspecting Maya, Python, and PyMEL,* is a reasonable location for it. Let's put the new `is_exact_type` function there.

```
def is_exact_type(node, typename):
    """node.type() == typename"""
    return node.type() == typename
```

The `is_exact_type` function is very simple, checking whether two type strings are equal.

We can add more predicates just as easily. The following `is_type` function returns `True` if the type of `node` has a MEL type of `typename` or a subclass.

```
def is_type(node, typename):
    """Return True if node.type() is typename or
    any subclass of typename."""
    return typename in node.nodeType(inherited=True)
```

Let's look at some examples that use our new predicates. Notice how `is_exact_type` matches only the camera node, but `is_type` finds the joint, sphere transform, and camera nodes.

```
>>> objs = pmc.joint(), pmc.polySphere(), pmc.camera()
>>> [o for o in pmc.ls() if minspect.is_exact_type(o, 'camera')]
[...nt.Camera(u'cameraShape1')]
>>> [o for o in pmc.ls() if minspect.is_type(o, 'transform')]
[...nt.Joint(u'joint1'), nt.Transform(u'pSphere1'),
nt.Transform(u'camera1')]
```

When a list comprehension uses a simple predicate, we may not even want to create a function for it. We can define our predicate expression right in the comprehension. The following code selects all joints with a positive *x* translation:

```
>>> j1, j2 = pmc.joint(), pmc.joint()
>>> j2.translateX.set(10)
>>> [j for j in pmc.ls(type='joint') if j.translateX.get() > 0]
[nt.Joint(u'joint2')]
```

Though this code may be less familiar for a MEL guru, it is much more easily understandable for anyone used to Python. And more importantly, it is far easier to maintain, and especially compose.

Saying goodbye to map and filter

Instead of list comprehensions, it used to be popular to use the built-in `map` and `filter` functions. For example, the two preceding examples could be written as follows:

```
>>> map(lambda i: i + 1, [1, 2, 3])
[2, 3, 4]
>>> filter(lambda i: i > 2, [1, 2, 3])
[3]
```

In some cases, the `map` and `filter` form can actually be more concise than the list comprehension form, as demonstrated by finding all root joints.

```
>>> filter(is_root_joint, pmc.ls())
[nt.Joint(u'joint1')]
>>> [o for o in pmc.ls() if is_root_joint(o)]
[nt.Joint(u'joint1')]
```

In full disclosure, I sometimes use `map` and `filter` when it's more concise. But as a rule, use list comprehensions. We'll use list comprehensions exclusively instead of `map` and `filter` in this book, to reduce confusion and enforce style.

If you're interested in why this book and the Python community at large encourages list comprehensions of `map` and `filter`, a simple Internet search should turn up lots of good reading. List comprehensions are now *Pythonic* and `map` and `filter` are not.

Refer to *Chapter 1, Introspecting Maya, Python, and PyMEL,* for a discussion of what Pythonic means.

Writing a skeleton converter library

Let's put composability to work for us. We'll implement a true rite of passage for programming in Maya—a routine to automatically convert a hierarchy of nodes into a hierarchy of joints (a skeleton). This task allows us to focus on building small, composable pieces of code, and string them together so that the character creator tool we build later in the chapter can be very simple. These composable pieces won't just serve our character creator. They'll serve us all throughout the book and our coding lives.

Writing the docstring and pseudocode

Before we start coding, we need a place to put the code. Create the `skeletonutils.py` file inside the development root you chose in *Chapter 1, Introspecting Maya, Python, and PyMEL*. This book's examples use `C:\mayapybook\pylib`.

After creating `skeletonutils.py`, open it in your IDE. Add the following code. The code defines a function, a docstring that explains precisely what it will do, and pseudocode describing the implementation. Docstrings are explained in more detail in the next section:

```python
def convert_to_skeleton(rootnode, prefix='skel_', _parent=None):
    """Converts a hierarchy of nodes into joints that have the
    same transform, with their name prefixed with 'prefix'.
    Return the newly created root node.
    The new hierarchy will share the same parent as rootnode.

    :param rootnode: The root PyNode.
      Everything under it will be converted.
    :param prefix: String to prefix newly created nodes with.
    """
    # Create a joint from the given node with the new name.
    # Copy the transform and rotation.
    # Set the parent to rootnode's parent if _parent is None,
    # Otherwise set it to _parent.
    # Convert all the children recursively, using the newly
    # created joint as the parent.
```

We explicitly state that `rootnode` should be a `PyNode` object. It helps to be clear what you're expecting, and just take in what you need rather than try to convert it inside the function. That is, do not take in a string and convert it into a `PyNode`. The less the function does, the easier it is to understand and maintain. It will also run faster.

The pseudocode says the function works recursively. If you don't know what recursion is, don't worry. We'll explain it when we get to that part of the code.

And finally, the leading underscore of the `_parent` parameter indicates it is a `protected` parameter. Callers outside the module should not pass it in. Recall that we used a leading underscore in the name of `minspect._py_to_helpstr` in *Chapter 1, Introspecting Maya, Python, and PyMEL*, to indicate the function is protected.

Understanding docstrings and reStructured Text

In the preceding code, we used a *docstring* to explain what our function does. We've used docstrings already, for example in the `minspect.pmhelp` function in *Chapter 1, Introspecting Maya, Python, and PyMEL*. The more advanced usage in the preceding code, however, warrants more explanation.

Docstrings are any literal string directly following a definition (module, function, class, or method). By convention, triple-double-quotes are used (`"""`), which allows easy multiline strings. PEP 257 (`http://www.python.org/dev/peps/pep-0257/`) defines Docstring Conventions and is well worth a read.

The `:param rootnode:` lines in the previous docstring are **reStructured Text** markup (abbreviated **rst** or **reST**). This allows special formatting of your docstrings in a way that is also readable as plain text. reStructured Text is standard for Python so I'd suggest getting into the habit of using it. Many IDEs support special rendering for it and the popular Sphinx project (`http://sphinx-doc.org/`) can turn your Python docstrings into HTML and other forms of documentation.

In addition to `param`, there are other directives, such as `type`, which can give hints to your IDE about what members exist on a parameter, providing a richer experience. You can see more information about how Sphinx renders reStructured Text at `http://sphinx-doc.org/markup/desc.html`. In particular, I suggest getting comfortable with the `param`, `type`, `rtype`, `return`, and `raises` directives. You should also be familiar with the text styling markup, such as `*italics*`, `**bold**`, and `''code''`.

Start simple, and even if you don't go any further in reStructured Text, you should get used to documenting your code with docstrings.

Writing the first implementation

Now that we've written what our code is supposed to do, let's go ahead and write a rough implementation:

```
import pymel.core as pmc

def convert_to_skeleton(rootnode, prefix='skel_', _parent=None):
    """Converts a hierarchy of nodes into joints that have the
    same transform, with their name prefixed with 'prefix'.
    Return the newly created root node.
    The new hierarchy will share the same parent as rootnode.
```

```
:param rootnode: The root PyNode.
  Everything under it will be converted.
:param prefix: String to prefix newly created nodes with.
"""
# Create a joint from the given node with the new name.
j = pmc.joint(name=prefix + rootnode.name())
# Copy the transform and rotation.
j.translate.set(rootnode.translate.get())
j.rotate.set(rootnode.rotate.get())
# Set the parent to rootnode's parent if _parent is None,
# Otherwise set it to _parent.
if _parent is None:
    _parent = rootnode.getParent()
j.setParent(_parent)
# Convert all the children recursively, using the newly
# created joint as the parent.
for c in rootnode.children():
    convert_to_skeleton(c, prefix, j)
return j
```

All our code does is what the pseudocode says. The recursion that we mentioned previously happens where we call convert_to_skeleton inside convert_to_skeleton. If a function calls itself, the function is said to be recursive. Recursion is a powerful technique that should not be overused, but it is indispensable when walking a tree or a hierarchy.

Breaking the first implementation

It's not difficult to see all the places this code can break, where it is ambiguous, and the axes of likely change:

- What happens if rootnode is not a valid PyNode? This is acceptable. The only way this can happen is if code calls it with a non-PyNode, and we clearly state in the docstring that rootnode must be a PyNode, so we should not guard against this error. We look at these sorts of decisions more in *Chapter 3, Dealing with Errors*.

- What happens if rootnode is inside of a Maya namespace? Will the new hierarchy be part of that namespace?

- If the value of rootnode.getParent() is the same as j.getParent(), some versions of Maya will raise an error.

- What should happen to the inputs and outputs of the node being converted, such as any shape or materials? Should they be duplicated or connected to the new joint?

- Right now we preserve the name/parent/translation/rotation of the source transform, but what if we want to preserve additional information, such as scale or custom attributes? How would we customize the joint with different parameters, such as color or size?

Nearly any code you write is liable to have many unanswered questions about its behavior and will need to change at some point. This is especially true of very high-level code, and anything having to deal with Maya nodes is high-level. The complexity is introduced by the scope of the node's interface. The interface of a Maya node is so complex, and the surface area of what it can affect is so great, that it is impossible to fully enumerate an operation's contract.

Understanding interface contracts

We use the term **contract** in the sense popularized by Bertrand Meyer's *Design by Contract*. The idea, in a simplified form, says that every function has:

- **A set of preconditions**: Preconditions are the things that must be true for the function to do its work. For example, the `convert_to_skeleton` function requires an existing PyMEL `Transform` instance.

- **A set of postconditions**: Postconditions are the things that are guaranteed to be true after the function returns. For example, the `convert_to_skeleton` function returns a new PyMEL `Joint` instance.

Keeping this simple idea of contracts in mind can greatly help your design. However, when we are programming with Maya, we have to accept many limitations.

An operation such as setting an item in a dictionary (`my_dict[key] = value`) has a very clear contract. The precondition would be that `key` is hashable (implements a valid `__hash__` method). The postcondition would be that the value exists for the key, so `my_dict[key] == value` would return `True` immediately after the value is set.

But, let's say we have a Maya locator node. What should happen when we copy it? Should any children also be copied? Should the new node be under the existing node's parent? Should it be under the existing node's namespace or the active one? In these cases we need very precise semantics, which Maya makes available under the **Edit | Duplicate Special** tool. Similar options usually exist in Maya's script commands.

We will have to be forever vigilant against where Maya sets us up for failure by not allowing strong contracts. As we go through turning our initial naive implementation into something more robust, we'll build composable pieces with very precise semantics. If each piece of code does just what it says, and does only what it can comfortably guarantee, our codebase will be simpler overall.

Extracting the safe_setparent utility function

Given what we know about contracts and where the existing code can break, the first thing we can do is pull out some small functionality into **utility functions**. Utility functions are general purpose helpers that people tend to consolidate into a Python library.

 Utility functions are necessary, but too many can be dangerous. Unless they are of obvious and immediate general use, utility functions should be put next to where they are used. Utility libraries tend to grow with functions that end up being used only in one place, and effectively managing a utility library requires thorough documentation and high reliability, usually achieved through automated testing. So, try to defer the creation of utility functions and libraries until you have more than one actual use for it.

The easiest thing to fix is the potential `j.setParent(_parent)` error we documented previously. We only want to set the parent if the new value is different from the existing value. Let's change our code into the following, adding the `safe_setparent` function:

```python
def safe_setparent(node, parent):
    """'node.setParent(parent)' if 'parent' is
    not the same as 'node''s existing parent.
    """
    if node.getParent() != parent:
        node.setParent(parent)


def convert_to_skeleton(rootnode, prefix='skel_', _parent=None):
    j = pmc.joint(name=prefix + rootnode.name())
    if _parent is None:
        _parent = rootnode.getParent()
    safe_setparent(j, _parent)
    j.translate.set(rootnode.translate.get())
    j.rotate.set(rootnode.rotate.get())
    for c in rootnode.children():
        convert_to_skeleton(c, prefix, j)
    return j
```

We took the *only set the parent if it will succeed* approach (LBYL) rather than *try to set the parent and just pass if it fails* (EAFP) approach here. Recall the discussion about EAFP versus LBYL in *Chapter 1, Introspecting Maya, Python, and PyMEL*. LBYL was chosen in this case because `setParent` raises a very unhelpful `RuntimeError`, which can be raised for any number of reasons (for example, creating a circular parent/ child relationship). Rather than potentially swallowing an unexpected error, or doing something ugly like parsing the error message, we use LBYL. And while LBYL is not always considered *Pythonic*, this sort of pragmatism is.

So we've added the `safe_setparent` utility function, which handles the *I wish it worked this way in the first place* behavior we are trying to hide. Using utility functions in this way is smart.

 If you find yourself having to patch default behaviors often, you should consider following the advice in *Chapter 9, Becoming a Part of the Python Community*, and submit this as an improvement to the PyMEL source. In fact, that's already been done, so Maya 2011 and newer should not display this behavior.

While it's always best when problems can be fixed at the source, sometimes in order to create composable code, you need to take matters into your own hands.

Learning how to refactor

What we just did with `safe_setparent` is called **refactoring**. Martin Fowler gives the following definition of refactoring.

> *Refactoring is a disciplined technique for restructuring an existing body of code, altering its internal structure without changing its external behavior. Its heart is a series of small behavior preserving transformations.*

We identified a bug (if the current parent is the value to `setParent`, an exception is raised), identified a fix to the bug (check if the problematic condition exists), and implemented that fix by changing the function's internal structure. Fixing bugs is not an intrinsic part of refactoring, though it's often a motivation.

Making these small deliberate changes to our code facilitates building reliable modules that we can grow and maintain. Refactoring includes removing duplication, enhancing clarity, and making the code easier to work with. The importance of the practice cannot be understated.

To truly do safe refactoring, we'd need a full suite of automated tests to run, to make sure the refactoring does not break existing functionality. We'll build these tests where we can (such as in the `minspect._py_to_helpstr` example in *Chapter 1, Introspecting Maya, Python, and PyMEL*), but much of the book is void of them. Unit tests can be found in the code accompanying this book, along with instructions on how to run the tests. Refer to *Appendix, Python Best Practices*, for more information about acquiring and running the tests for the code in this book.

Simplifying the node to joint conversion

The next area of our implementation that needs work is the copying of attributes from the old object to the new joint. This is an area that will likely change as new features are added. For example, if this library were part of an auto-rigger, the dummy locators that define a pre-rigged character may have important custom attributes that need to be transferred to the joints.

Let's perform the highlighted refactoring, creating the `_convert_to_joint` function from code originally in the `convert_to_skeleton` function. The extracted code is highlighted in the following listing.

```python
def _convert_to_joint(node, parent, prefix):
    j = pmc.joint(name=prefix + node.name())
    safe_setparent(j, parent)
    j.translate.set(node.translate.get())
    j.rotate.set(node.rotate.get())
    return j


def convert_to_skeleton(rootnode, prefix='skel_', _parent=None):
    if _parent is None:
        _parent = rootnode.getParent()
    j = _convert_to_joint(rootnode, _parent, prefix)
    for c in rootnode.children():
        convert_to_skeleton(c, prefix, j)
    return j
```

Now when additional attributes need to be copied, locked, or reconnected, we have a good place to put them. For example, let's suppose we want to color our joints depending on their position on the *x* axis. We have a clear home for the changes, which are highlighted in the following listing.

```python
GREEN = 14
BLUE = 6
YELLOW = 17
```

```
def _convert_to_joint(node, parent, prefix):
    j = pmc.joint(name=prefix + node.name())
    safe_setparent(j, parent)
    j.translate.set(node.translate.get())
    j.rotate.set(node.rotate.get())
    x = j.translateX.get()
    if x < 0.001:
        col = GREEN
    elif x > 0.001:
        col = BLUE
    else:
        col = YELLOW
    j.overrideColor.set(col)
    return j
```

You can, of course, put this choosing and setting of the wire color into a function. It would help keep things organized. So let's refactor this implementation just a small bit, creating a `calc_wirecolor` function nested inside of the `_convert_to_joint` function.

```
def _convert_to_joint(node, parent, prefix):
    j = pmc.joint(name=prefix + node.name())
    safe_setparent(node, parent)
    j.translate.set(node.translate.get())
    j.rotate.set(node.rotate.get())
    def calc_wirecolor():
        x = j.translateX.get()
        if x < 0.001:
            return GREEN
        elif x > 0.001:
            return BLUE
        else:
            return YELLOW
    j.overrideColor.set(calc_wirecolor())
    return j
```

Now when we add more code, we can just put it into tiny nested functions similar to `calc_wirecolor`, instead of polluting the module globals with single-use functions. This has the added and important benefit of keeping the code as close as possible to where it's actually used. Of course, if you need a nested function in multiple scopes, you should pull it into a more accessible place.

Learning how to use closures

In the preceding example, we use the variable j inside the calc_wirecolor function, even though it is not a parameter. This calc_wirecolor function is called a **closure**, also called a **nested function** or **inner function**. We create a closure when a function *closes over* an outside variable (or more loosely, whenever we define a function inside a function or method). The formal definition of a closure sounds very technical, but we only need to understand this: because j is in the scope of calc_wirecolor (sort of like a global variable is accessible from within a function), it can be used inside the function. Using closures is an incredibly powerful technique. We'll use and explore it more throughout this book.

If you're stumped by closures, this is an area where thinking too hard is a drawback. In the following code, which does not use a closure, the spamneggs function can obviously refer to the spam function.

```
>>> def spam(adjective):
...        return adjective + ' spam'
>>> def spamneggs(adjective):
...        return spam(adjective) + ' + eggs'
>>> spamneggs('Boring')
'Boring spam + eggs'
```

We can also just move spam into spamneggs, as we've done with the calc_wirecolor and _convert_to_joint functions. Nested functions in Python work great!

```
>>> def spamneggs(adjective):
...        def spam(adjective):
...            return adjective + ' spam'
...        return spam(adjective) + ' + eggs'
>>> spamneggs('Decent')
'Decent spam + eggs'
```

Finally, we can just get rid of the duplication of the adjective parameter in spam and just have it use the adjective argument passed into spamneggs:

```
>>> def spamneggs(adjective):
...        def spam():
...            return adjective + ' spam'
...        return spam() + ' + eggs'
>>> spamneggs('Wonderful')
'Wonderful spam + eggs'
```

Closures are a truly important feature in Python, along with every other language that supports them. You should become familiar with them over time. If you're not comfortable yet, just plan on getting there. There are definitely some gotchas (don't create closures inside of Python loops!) but closures can really simplify your programs.

Dealing with node connections

Dealing with node connections is a common source of bugs when manipulating nodes. Often we write code that treats a node as a standalone entity, something we can reason about in the abstract. Nodes are, however, part of a potentially complex network of other nodes, of history, and of internal state.

It's very important that when we change the state of a node, especially if we are copying or deleting it, we consider its connections. In this case, we are just creating a new node and copying the value of certain attributes from the source, so we need not worry about connections.

Dealing with namespaces

In contrast to handling connections, which are an **essential complexity** in Maya, Maya namespaces are a hideous and constant nuisance; a true **accidental complexity**.

 Accidental and essential complexities are terms in Fred Brooks' famous essay, *No Silver Bullet*. Accidental complexity is caused by our approach to a problem (an example would be MEL), while essential complexity is inherent in the problem being solved and is unavoidable (an example would be managing a hierarchy of objects).

For our skeleton converter, in what namespace do we want the newly created joints to be placed? Our three options are as follows:

- The root namespace. This doesn't seem very correct so we won't bother considering it.
- The namespace of the source object.
- The current namespace.

Though the second option is a valid design choice, we'll avoid it and choose the third option for two reasons. First, the second option is more code. Putting something in the current namespace happens automatically, so we don't need to write any extra code. Second, any non-default behavior is a decision that our code needs to make and manage; by not making a decision in our function, we let the caller make a decision, or let the caller let its caller make a decision, and so on. This is much more in the spirit of this chapter. Think about our discussion of contracts and composability earlier. Prefer to write the simplest code possible.

Wrapping up the skeleton converter

It turns out that our skeleton converter is relatively simple, just a few dozen lines of code. There's nothing complex here, nothing that would trick another programmer (or yourself) several years in the future. And though we'll use our skeleton converter for our character creator in the next section, nothing stops a programmer from using it for their own purposes.

The following listing is the contents of `skeletonutils.py` so far.

```
GREEN = 14
BLUE = 6
YELLOW = 17


def _convert_to_joint(node, parent, prefix):
    j = pmc.joint(name=prefix + node.name())
    safe_setparent(node, parent)
    j.translate.set(node.translate.get())
    j.rotate.set(node.rotate.get())
    def calc_wirecolor():
        x = j.translateX.get()
        if x < 0.001:
            return GREEN
        elif x > 0.001:
            return BLUE
        else:
            return YELLOW
    j.overrideColor.set(calc_wirecolor())
    return j


def convert_to_skeleton(rootnode, prefix='skel_', _parent=None):
    """Converts a hierarchy of nodes into joints that have the
    same transform, with their name prefixed with 'prefix'.
    Return the newly created root node.
```

```
:param rootnode: The root PyNode.
   Everything under it will be converted.
:param prefix: String to prefix newly created nodes with.
"""
if _parent is None:
    _parent = rootnode.getParent()
j = _convert_to_joint(rootnode, _parent, prefix)
for c in rootnode.children():
    convert_to_skeleton(c, prefix, j)
return j
```

The key takeaway from the skeleton creator code is this:

Write the absolute simplest code you can for as much of your code as you can. The fastest code is the code which does not run. The code easiest to maintain is the code that was never written. Defer decisions to callers unless they are an important part of a contract.

As we'll see in the next example and beyond, there will still be complexity and we still need to write code. Decisions still need to be made. But we should make them in the best place possible.

Writing a character creator

So far, we've written the code to convert a hierarchy of transforms into joints. Now we must write something that we can hook up to a menu and a workflow. An overly simplified solution is to convert the current selection by assigning the following expression into a shelf button:

```
map(skeletonutils.convert_to_skeleton, pmc.selection())
```

But that's a pretty bad high-level function. What about error handling, user feedback, and the high-level decisions that we put off while writing the converter?

What we really want is something like the following:

```
charcreator.convert_hierarchies_main()
```

This can be hooked up to a menu button, which provides a better experience for the user and a place to make those decisions that we kept out of the `skeletonutils` module.

Stubbing out the character creator

Create a `charcreator.py` file next to the `skeletonutils.py` file in your development root, and open it up in your favorite IDE. Go ahead and type the following code, which will stub out the functions we will build in this section.

```python
import pymel.core as pmc
import skeletonutils

def convert_hierarchies_main():
    """'convert_hierarchies(pmc.selection())'.
    Prints and provides user feedback so only call from UI.
    """

def convert_hierarchies(rootnodes):
    """Calls 'convert_hierarchy' for each root node in 'rootnodes'
    (so passing in '[parent, child]' would convert the 'parent'
    hierarchy assuming 'child' lives under it).
    """

def convert_hierarchy(node):
    """Converts the hierarchy under and included 'rootnode'
    into joints in the same namespace as 'rootnode'.
    Deletes 'rootnode' and its hierarchy.
    Connections to nodes are not preserved on the newly
    created joints.
    """
```

In the preceding code we've done some basic imports and defined three higher-level functions that we know we'll need. They are documented in terms of each other, and each one is quite clear in what it does. This also gives us a good idea of the utility functions we'll need to write. For example, we will need a way to select only unique root nodes from the input to `convert_hierarchies`, and a way to walk along a skeleton.

Let's begin by implementing `convert_hierarchies_main`, which works on the current selection, then `convert_hierarchies`, which converts a collection of hierarchies, and then finally, `convert_hierarchy`, which converts a single hierarchy.

Implementing convert_hierarchies_main

The entry point of any program has traditionally been called its **main**. For example, the Python idiom of having `if __name__ == '__main__':` at the bottom of a file asks, "is this file the script being run from the command line". Other languages may have a `main` method in a binary to indicate the program's entry point when executed. We use the same convention here to specify that "this function provides some feedback (such as printing), so use this from the user interface, such as the shelf or a menu, but not from other libraries." This is just a convention I've established because I rigorously keep user interface code out of libraries. User interface not only includes graphical elements such as dialogs, but also calls to `raw_input` and print statements. You can come up with your own convention, but keep UI code distinct from non-UI code.

Anyway, the implementation of `convert_hierarchies_main` has no surprises:

```
def convert_hierarchies_main():
    """'convert_hierarchies(pmc.selection())'.
    Prints and provides user feedback so only call from UI.
    """
    nodes = pmc.selected(type='transform') #(1)
    if not nodes:
        pmc.warning('No transforms selected.') #(2)
        return
    new_roots = convert_hierarchies(nodes) #(3)
    print 'Created:', ','.join([r.name() for r in new_roots]) #(4)
```

This code should be self-explanatory but here's a quick breakdown:

1.   Get all transforms that are currently selected.

2.   If no transforms are selected, warn and return.

3.   Convert selected transforms.

4.   Print out the newly created roots to inform the user what was converted. Recall that the pattern of `<delimiter>.join(<string list>)` was discussed in *Chapter 1, Introspecting Maya, Python, and PyMEL*.

So with that function out of the way, let's get further into the actual meat of our program.

Implementing convert_hierarchies

The `convert_hierarchies` function does two things: it pulls only the unique root nodes from the inputs, and invokes `convert_hierarchy` on each of them. We'll start by implementing the functionality to find the unique roots.

Decomposing into composable functions

One way to pull only the unique roots from the inputs is to go through each input, and if any of its **ancestors** are in a collection of unique roots, it is not a unique root and can be skipped. Ancestors of a node include all the nodes between the node itself and the tree's root. For node **N** in the following diagram, nodes **P1** and **P2** are its ancestors.

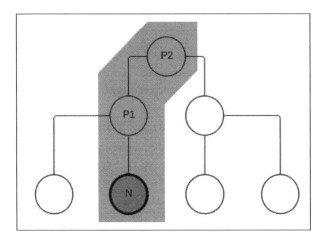

Getting a node's ancestors should sound tangential to creating a character and generally useful. These are clear indicators that it should live as a utility function. Open up `skeletonutils.py` and add the following function at the bottom:

```
def ancestors(node):
    """Return a list of ancestors, starting with the direct parent
    and ending with the top-level (root) parent."""
    result = []
    parent = node.getParent()
    while parent is not None:
        result.append(parent)
        parent = parent.getParent()
    return result
```

We know we've hit the root of the tree when `node.getParent()` returns `None`. We can see the ancestors function in action by walking through the following small joint hierarchy:

```
>>> j1 = pmc.joint(name='J1')
>>> j2 = pmc.joint(name='J2')
>>> j3 = pmc.joint(name='J3')
>>> import skeletonutils
>>> skeletonutils.ancestors(j1)
[]
>>> skeletonutils.ancestors(j3)
[nt.Joint(u'J2'), nt.Joint(u'J1')]
```

Remember that nothing about this function is tied to character creation or joint conversion at all. This makes it much easier to understand and to test, and also makes the character creator code simpler.

 We can clean the `ancestors` function up further by changing it to use the `yield` keyword. We'll look at `yield` in *Chapter 4, Leveraging Context Managers and Decorators in Maya.*

If we think about the code to find the unique roots, we'll find that there's nothing specific to character creation here either. Let's add the following code to the bottom of `skeletonutils.py` to find the unique roots of a collection of nodes:

```
def uniqueroots(nodes): #(1)
    """Returns a list of the nodes in 'nodes' that are not
    children of any node in 'nodes'."""
    result = []
    def handle_node(n): #(2)
        """If any of the ancestors of n are in realroots,
        just return, otherwise, append n to realroots.
        """
        for ancestor in ancestors(n):
            if ancestor in nodes: #(4)
                return
        result.append(n) #(5)
    for node in nodes: #(3)
        handle_node(node)
    return result
```

Let's walk through this code block by block:

1. There may be a better way to write this docstring, since this is a tricky algorithm to express. You'll also notice that the docstring expresses the idea, but the implementation is very different. We can very well implement the function the way the docstring is written, but it would be significantly slower and more complex. The docstring should express the what and not the how, but sometimes the two overlap (check out `help(dict.get)`).

2. We create a *closure* inside the `uniqueroots` function to handle each node. The closure "closes over" the result variable from the outer scope. We looked at closures in more detail earlier in this chapter, and will continue to use them throughout the book. Their importance cannot be overstated.

3. We call the closure with each node.

4. If the ancestor of any input node is another input node, the node we are looking at can be ignored; it will already be handled by its ancestor.

5. From inside the closure, we append to the `result` list.

Like `ancestors`, the `uniqueroots` function should be understandable and testable in the abstract.

```
>>> reload(skeletonutils)
>>> skeletonutils.uniqueroots([j1, j2])
[nt.Joint(u'J1')]
>>> skeletonutils.uniqueroots([j2])
[nt.Joint(u'J2')]
```

Since we are done with all of our utility functions, we can go back to `charcreator.py` and implement our `convert_hierarchies` function as follows. Notice how simple it is.

```
def convert_hierarchies(rootnodes):
    roots = skeletonutils.uniqueroots(rootnodes)
    result = [convert_hierarchy(r) for r in roots]
    return result
```

Implementing convert_hierarchy

Finally, we need to implement the hierarchy conversion. We already have most of its functionality through the joint converter we've already written. The only thing it has to do is delete the original hierarchy after conversion. Let's implement convert_hierarchy inside of `charcreator.py` as follows:

```
def convert_hierarchy(node):
    result = skeletonutils.convert_to_skeleton(node)
    pmc.delete(node)
    return result
```

It's worth pointing out that the deletion of node (and implicitly, all of its descendants) only happens if the hierarchy creation completes successfully. We wouldn't want to partially convert a hierarchy and then delete the inputs, leaving the user high and dry with a corrupt scene. We'll look more at best practices for handling errors in *Chapter 3, Dealing with Errors*.

Supporting inevitable modifications

At this point, the basic character creator is done. You hook it up to a shelf or menu as explained in *Chapter 5, Building Graphical User Interfaces for Maya*, and bask in your glory.

Or not. The tool hasn't been released for a day and already you get a feature request. Animators want the joints to be larger. But because the joint display size works well for another game the code is used for, you can't just change it globally inside the `skeletonutils._convert_to_joint` function.

When you've written enough code, you tend to expect certain changes, and learn to always expect change in general. This does not mean you should build support for unneeded features *just in case*. In fact, this is one of the absolute worst things you can do. But you should keep an eye open to make sure your code will be able to change in likely ways, even if you don't add explicit support immediately.

One such inevitable modification is passing arguments from higher level functions (such as `charcreator.convert_hierarchies`) down to implementation functions (such as `skeletonutils._convert_to_joint`). However, you cannot just do this blindly. Providing an `assumePreferredAngles` parameter (a keyword argument to `pmc.joint`) to `convert_hierarchies` wouldn't make much sense and you'd end up with a bloated codebase.

One thing we can look at providing here is some sort of configuration that callers can choose from. The knowledge of this configuration can be limited to `charcreator.py`, and it can unpack its values when it prepares to call `skeletonutils`. Pay attention to the highlighted code in the revised functions inside `skeletonutils.py`.

```
def _convert_to_joint(node, parent, prefix,
                      jnt_size, lcol, rcol, ccol):
    j = pmc.joint(name=prefix + node.name())
    safe_setparent(j, parent)
    j.translate.set(node.translate.get())
    j.rotate.set(node.rotate.get())
    j.setRadius(jnt_size)
    def calc_wirecolor():
```

```
            x = j.translateX.get()
            if x < -0.001:
                return rcol
            elif x > 0.001:
                return lcol
            else:
                return ccol
        j.overrideColor.set(calc_wirecolor())
        return j


def convert_to_skeleton(
        rootnode,
        prefix='skel_',
        joint_size=1.0,
        lcol=BLUE,
        rcol=GREEN,
        ccol=YELLOW,
        _parent=None):
    if _parent is None:
        _parent = rootnode.getParent()
    j = _convert_to_joint(
        rootnode, _parent, prefix, joint_size, lcol, rcol, ccol)
    for c in rootnode.getChildren():
        convert_to_skeleton(
            c, prefix, joint_size, lcol, rcol, ccol, j)
    return j
```

All we are doing is exposing more parameters (for joint size and color) to customization. Instead of hardcoding things such as joint colors, or not even allowing the joint size to be set, we take them in as arguments and provide sensible defaults.

We can then take advantage of these newly exposed parameters in charcreator.py.

```
GREEN = 14
BLUE = 6
YELLOW = 17
PURPLE = 8
AQUA = 28

# (1)
SETTINGS_DEFAULT = {
    'joint_size': 1.0,
    'right_color': BLUE,
    'left_color': GREEN,
```

```
        'center_color': YELLOW,
        'prefix': 'char_',
    }
SETTINGS_GAME2 = {
        'joint_size': 25.0,
        'right_color': PURPLE,
        'left_color': AQUA,
        'center_color': GREEN,
        'prefix': 'game2char_',
    }


#(2)
def convert_hierarchies_main(settings=SETTINGS_DEFAULT):
    nodes = pmc.selected(type='transform')
    if not nodes:
        pmc.warning('No transforms selected.')
        return
    new_roots = convert_hierarchies(nodes, settings)
    print 'Created:', ','.join([r.name() for r in new_roots])


#(2)
def convert_hierarchies(rootnodes, settings=SETTINGS_DEFAULT):
    roots = skeletonutils.uniqueroots(rootnodes)
    result = [convert_hierarchy(r, settings) for r in roots]
    return result


# (2)
def convert_hierarchy(rootnode,  settings=SETTINGS_DEFAULT):
    result = skeletonutils.convert_to_skeleton( #(3)
        rootnode,
        joint_size=settings['joint_size'],
        prefix=settings['prefix'],
        rcol=settings['right_color'],
        lcol=settings['left_color'],
        ccol=settings['center_color'])
    pmc.delete(rootnode)
    return result
```

We've added a `settings` parameter to each function to allow the configuration of joint color, prefix, and sizes to be customized. Let's walk over the changes to the `charcreator.py` file's code:

1. Define two dictionaries that hold the configuration for different games, or characters, or whatever you want to customize.

2. Add the `settings` parameter to each function so that it can be overridden where needed.

Pass the settings into the `convert_to_skeleton` function. If you want to make the keys of the settings dictionaries match the keyword argument names in `convert_to_skeleton`, you can rewrite the line as `skeletonutils.convert_to_skeleton(node, **settings)`. It's up to you. I've chosen a more verbose way of doing things here. Check out the *Appendix*, *Python Best Practices*, for more details about using the double asterik (**) syntax if you are unfamiliar with it.

By designing the high-level `charcreator` module around a configuration concept, and making the lower-level `skeletonutils` functions explicit about what arguments they take in, we've achieved several benefits. The two modules are not coupled or tied together. We can expose more parameters in the `skeletonutils.convert_to_skeleton` function without having to change the `charcreator.convert_hierarchy` function. We can also change the way the `charcreator` functions work, and not have to change the `skeletonutils` module. The high-level character creator code has lots of assumptions built in, and the low-level skeleton library code has very few. This is a powerful methodology to take, especially in Python, where you can iterate on high-level code very rapidly.

 Another potential way to iterate on configuration quickly would be to move the `settings` dictionary out of the code and into data files such as `json` or `yaml`. Then you can modify these files by hand or even build a simple editor.

Overall, we've developed a flexible and robust system that is far more powerful than its number of lines of code would indicate!

Improving the performance of PyMEL

I hope at this point, PyMEL's superiority over `maya.cmds` has been thoroughly demonstrated. If you have any doubt, feel free to rewrite the examples in this chapter to use `maya.cmds` and see how much cleaner the PyMEL versions are.

Having said that, PyMEL can be slower than `maya.cmds`. The performance difference can usually be made up by applying one of the following three improvements.

Defining performance

For most scripts, the performance difference is too miniscule to matter. *Fast* and *slow* are relative terms. The important metric is *fast enough*. If your code is fast enough, performance improvements won't really matter. Most of the tools you will write fall under this category. For example, making a pose mirroring tool go 500% faster doesn't matter if it only takes a tenth of a second in the first place.

Refactoring for performance

In most cases where PyMEL code actually needs to be sped up, rewriting small parts can make huge gains. Is your code doing unnecessary work inside a loop? Pull the work out of the loop.

The `remove_selected` function in the following example returns a list with any selected objects filtered out of the input list. The list comprehension evaluates `pmc.selected()` for every item in the input list. This inefficiency is highlighted in the following example.

```
>>> objs = pmc.joint(), pmc.joint()
>>> def remove_selected(objs):
...      return [item for item in objs
...                 if item not in pmc.selected()]
>>> pmc.select(objs[0])
>>> remove_selected(objs)
[nt.Joint(u'joint2')]
```

Instead, we can evaluate `pmc.selected()` once, and use that value in the list comprehension. This change is highlighted in the following example.

```
>>> def remove_selected_faster(objs):
...      selected = pmc.selected()
...      return [item for item in objs if item not in selected]
>>> pmc.select(objs[0])
>>> remove_selected(objs)
[nt.Joint(u'joint2')]
```

Perhaps your code is slow because it is looking up data that can be safely cached. In that case, we can cache the data when it is first calculated and re-use that.

In the following `get_type_hierarchy` function, we want to find a MEL type's MEL type hierarchy. To do so, we need to create an instance of the node, invoke the `nodeType` method on it to get the hierarchy, delete the node, and return the hierarchy.

```
>>> def get_type_hierarchy(typename):
...     node = pmc.createNode(typename)
...     result = node.nodeType(inherited=True)
...     pmc.delete(node)
...     return result
>>> get_type_hierarchy('joint')
[u'containerBase', u'entity', u'dagNode', u'transform', u'joint']
```

Once we have the type hierarchy for a MEL type, we shouldn't need to calculate it again. To make sure we don't perform this unnecessary work, we can cache the result of the calculation, and return the cached value if it exists. This change is highlighted in the following code.

```
>>> _hierarchy_cache = {}
>>> def get_type_hierarchy(typename):
...     result = _hierarchy_cache.get(typename)
...     if result is None:
...         node = pmc.createNode(typename)
...         result = node.nodeType(inherited=True)
...         pmc.delete(node)
...         _hierarchy_cache[typename] = result
...     return result
>>> get_type_hierarchy('joint')
[u'containerBase', u'entity', u'dagNode', u'transform', u'joint']
```

Or perhaps your code is slow because it is calling a method for each item in a sequence, as the `add_influences` function is in the following example.

```
>>> j1 = pmc.joint()
>>> cluster = pmc.skinCluster(j1, pmc.polyCube()[0])
>>> def add_influences(cl, infls):
...     for infl in infls:
...         cl.addInfluence(infl)
>>> add_influences(cluster, [pmc.joint(), pmc.joint()])
```

Instead of iterating, check and see if the method can take in a list of arguments. We are fortunate that the `SkinCluster.addInfluence` method can, so let's remove the `for` loop, as highlighted in the following code.

```
>>> def add_influences(cl, infls):
...     cl.addInfluence(infls)
>>> add_influences(cluster, [pmc.joint(), pmc.joint()])
```

Nearly all of these changes will end up not just making the code faster, but simpler too.

Rewriting inner loops to use maya.cmds

Sometimes, you need to communicate with Maya inside a tight loop or heavily used function. In these cases, PyMEL may actually be too slow if it has to go through several layers of abstraction. You can rewrite the function body to use `maya.cmds` while using PyMEL types for the relevant arguments and return value.

If this type of refactoring will help improve performance, you should look at using the Maya API, which is usually even faster. Refer to *Chapter 7, Taming the Maya API*, for an introduction to the Maya API.

You should also only take this approach when you've identified that the code in question is a bottleneck, and speeding it up will yield significant overall improvement. You can use the standard library's `cProfile` module for profiling Python code. There are many resources on the Internet that explain the process in greater detail.

We should pursue high quality and composable code. But if that code takes unacceptably long to run, it matters less how clean it is. On the other hand, we cannot disregard composability and quality for the sake of performance. Code using `maya.cmds` will inevitably end up less composable and Pythonic than code using PyMEL. This is because MEL's idioms are very far from Python's. We should contain and limit code using `maya.cmds` when we cannot entirely eliminate it.

Summary

In this chapter, we learned how to write composable code. We saw examples of non-composable MEL style code, such as Maya's listing functions. We learned how to turn this legacy code into clean, composable functions, such as `head`, `tail`, `first_or_default`, and `is_exact_type`. We created a reusable library for converting a hierarchy of transforms into joints. We used that library for a configurable character creator module that can easily be called through a UI. Along the way, we learned about list comprehensions, contracts, selecting and filtering, closures, refactoring, docstrings, and improving PyMEL performance.

Writing composable code, and the topics in this chapter, are the foundation for a successful and enjoyable experience programming Python in general, and Python in Maya particularly. This is the way of the *Pythonista*.

Unfortunately, despite the composability of our functions, the care and craft of our projects, the documentation we provide, and *no matter how Pythonic our code is*, there will be problems. Mistakes will be made. Edge cases exploited. Bugs found. Dealing with these errors is the topic of the next chapter.

3
Dealing with Errors

Errors happen. Having code that can handle errors properly is essential. In this chapter, we will learn how to write code that gracefully handles errors in Maya Python. We'll start by understanding some technical basics about Python exceptions, such as the `try`/`except` statement and tracebacks. After that we will cover some golden rules for handling exceptions. We will map those guidelines to the way Maya works, and learn how to handle errors in Maya gracefully. We will use all of this knowledge to build a high-level error handler. The error handler will be an exception hook that will capture any relevant unhandled Python exception raised in Maya, and send an e-mail to us. Finally, we'll look at various ways to improve the error handler to make it useful in a production environment.

Understanding exceptions

The word **exception** is loaded. The definition seems clear: *exceptions are exceptional*. I'll say, in Python at least, this definition is simply not true. A normal Python program may handle and raise any number of exceptions as it hums along quite nicely.

Consider the Pythonic idiom we have already pointed out multiple times: *Easier to Ask Forgiveness than Permission*. It is usually expressed as follows:

```
try:
    spam.eggs()
except AttributeError:
    spam.ham()
```

The preceding code is preferred over the following code, which uses a Look Before You Leap style:

```
if hasattr(spam, 'eggs'):
    spam.eggs()
else:
    spam.ham()
```

There is nothing exceptional about exceptions in the first example. Describing them as exceptional is more accurate when describing how they behave rather than how they are used.

I prefer the following definition:

> *"Exceptions are a form of (exceptional) flow control."*

To illustrate that definition, consider the following lines of code:

```
if spam:
    for i in xrange(count):
        eggs(i)
```

We can observe in the preceding code that there are two instances of explicit flow control: the `if` statement and the `for` loop can change how the function executes. There is a hidden flow control, however, and it can occur nearly anywhere. For example, the `xrange` or `eggs` function can raise an exception for any number reasons. An exception can also be raised almost anywhere if the operating system sends a signal to Python to terminate the process. In either case, we experience an interruption that isn't handled by the code we are reading. It is a hidden and implicit flow control. This type of flow control is *exceptional* and it is handled through exceptions.

A corollary of exceptions being flow control is that exceptions are not always conceptual errors. When I use the term *error*, such as in this chapter's introductory paragraph, I mean it is as a problem the programmer did not expect or account for. Exceptions are merely the *mechanism* by which errors are usually indicated.

We don't need to be scared of exceptions any more than we should be scared of `for` loops. We just need to know when to raise an exception and how to handle an exception. Such will be the focus of this chapter.

Introducing exception types

An exception is just like any other object in Python. You can create, inspect, and see their class hierarchy as follows:

```
>>> ex = SystemError('a', 1)
>>> [t.__name__ for t in type(ex).__mro__]
['SystemError', 'StandardError', 'Exception', 'BaseException',
'object']
>>> ex.args
('a', 1)
>>> dir(ex)
['__class__', '__delattr__', ...'args', 'message']
```

One important thing to note here is that you can think of all exceptions as inheriting from the `Exception` base class. There is a history and rationale behind `BaseException` and `StandardError`, but you should treat `Exception` as the base class and ignore the latter two. If you would like more information, you can read about Python's built-in exceptions at `http://docs.python.org/2/library/exceptions.html`.

Explaining try/catch/finally flow control

Python's flow control for exceptions is nuanced. However, it is also an integral part of the language, so it is vital to understand. This section will serve as a quick primer or refresher. If you are already comfortable with exception handling, feel free to skip to the next section. If you have never encountered Python exception handling before, I suggest referring to a tutorial before proceeding. Two options are the official Python tutorial on errors at `https://docs.python.org/2/tutorial/errors.html` and the relevant chapter in the free *Dive Into Python* e-book at `http://www.diveintopython.net/file_handling/index.html#fileinfo.exception`.

The simplest form of exception handling is the basic `try`/`except` statement, demonstrated by the following code:

```
>>> try:
...     1 + 'a'
... except:
...     print 'Errored!'
Errored!
```

The naked `except` keyword should not be used because it will catch every exception, including things such as `SystemExit` which should not usually be caught. Instead, we should explicitly declare what exception types we want to catch. The change to the previous example is highlighted.

```
>>> try:
...     1 + 'a'
... except TypeError:
...     print 'Errored!'
Errored!
```

Instead of a single type after the `except` keyword, we can use a tuple to catch multiple types of exceptions with the same `except` clause. The change to the previous example is highlighted.:

```
>>> try:
...     1 + 'a'
... except (TypeError, RuntimeError):
...     print 'Errored!'
Errored!
```

We can handle different types of exceptions with unique clauses by stacking `except` statements. The first `except` expression that matches the exception type will be used.

```
>>> try:
...     1 + 'a'
... except RuntimeError:
...     print 'RuntimeError!'
... except TypeError:
...     print 'TypeError!'
TypeError!
```

We can also assign the caught exception to a variable. This allows us to use it from within the `except` clause, as demonstrated in the following code.

```
>>> try:
...     1 + 'a'
... except TypeError as ex:
...     print repr(ex)
TypeError("unsupported operand type(s) for +: 'int' and 'str'",)
```

We can reraise the original exception using a naked `raise` statement. This allows us to run custom error handling code without affecting the exception. The following code prints when the error is caught, and then raises the original error, which is caught by the interpreter and printed.

```
>>> try:
...     1 + 'a'
... except TypeError:
...     print 'Errored!'
...     raise
Errored!
Traceback (most recent call last):
TypeError: unsupported operand type(s) for +: 'int' and 'str'
```

You can also create an exception instance and raise that, as in the following code:

```
>>> try:
...     1 + 'a'
... except TypeError:
...     raise KeyError('hi!')
Traceback (most recent call last):
KeyError: 'hi!'
```

Use the `finally` keyword to provide cleanup that happens after the `try`/`except` code has been run. The code in the `finally` clause is executed "on the way out" when any other clause of the `try`/`except` statement is completed. Practically, this means the `finally` code is run whether or not an exception is raised, and it is the last clause to run.

```
>>> try:
...     1 + 'a'
... except TypeError:
...     print 'Errored!'
... finally:
...     print 'Cleaned up.'
Errored!
Cleaned up.
```

Python also provides an `else` clause that will be run if the `try` does not raise an error. No example will be shown since we do not use `try`/`except`/`else` in this book.

If any of this is still unclear, refer to one of the tutorials listed at the beginning of this section. It is very important to have some familiarity with these aspects of exception flow control because the rest of this chapter relies on it heavily.

Explaining traceback objects

A Python **traceback** (called a **stack trace** in many languages) contains the information about where an error occurred. You've probably seen a traceback similar to the one we provoke here:

```
>>> 1 + 'a'
Traceback (most recent call last):
  File "<stdin>", line 1, in <module>
  File "<stdin>", line 2, in <module>
TypeError: unsupported operand type(s) for +: 'int' and 'str'
```

The traceback records the line that raised an exception, the top-level caller, and all the calls in between the two. As we'll see later, the traceback usually also contains the contents of each line. It did not in the preceding example because our code is created from within the interactive prompt.

When a traceback is formatted into a string, the last line is the exception's representation. This is usually the exception's type name and formatted arguments.

There are many more nuances to dealing with tracebacks that we will go over as we need use them in more depth.

Explaining the exc_info tuple

The type of an exception, the exception instance, and the exception's traceback are together known as the **exc_info tuple** or **exception info**. It is known by this name because the information about the exception currently being handled is accessible by calling the `sys.exc_info()` function. In the following example, notice how we assign the exception info to the `si` variable, and can then access the exception information from outside of the `except` clause.

```
>>> import sys
>>> try:
...     1 + 'a'
... except TypeError:
...     si = sys.exc_info()
>>> print si[0]
<type 'exceptions.TypeError'>
>>> print repr(si[1])
TypeError("unsupported operand type(s) for +: 'int' and 'str'",)
>>> print si[2]
<traceback object at 0x0...>
```

We can see from this example that the `exc_info` tuple is an important part of working with exceptions in Python. It contains all the necessary information for an exception: the exception instance, type, and traceback.

You should be careful when capturing or using the `sys.exc_info()` tuple. Like most things with exceptions, there are several gotchas, such as creating circular references or garbage collection problems. We'll ignore them for this chapter since they aren't common, but keep them in mind as you go further with Python. While the exception and traceback concept may be straightforward, working with the `exc_info` tuple, traceback objects, and the `raise` statement have some rough edges.

I don't find Python 2's exception design particularly elegant or intuitive, but the good news is Python 3 has improved in this area. Despite these complaints, Python's exception handling works well enough once you learn the essential syntax and the lessons taught here.

Living with unhandled exceptions

An exception can occur in two conceptual situations. The first is when the caller expects it to happen, as we did when building `minspect._is_pymel` in *Chapter 1, Introspecting Maya, Python, and PyMEL*. An `AttributeError` being raised indicated to our algorithm that we should try a different attribute. Exceptions were being used for flow control and had no ill effects.

The second situation, which is the focus of this and the following section, is when the caller does not expect an exception. In this case, the exception bubbles up to a higher layer. If the exception bubbles all the way up to the Python interpreter (the exception is not caught by any `except` clause), it is called an **unhandled exception**. When an unhandled exception occurs, the Python process exits or some default error handler is invoked, often printing the exception information.

Failing in this catastrophic way when an unhandled exception occurs is called **failing fast**, and it is generally a good idea. We should not allow an error to go undetected and continue in an unknown state, so it is a good idea for the running code to be interrupted and for the process to die or at least complain loudly. Once we know something failed and identify the cause of the error, we can go in and fix the reason behind the failure.

We also need to be comfortable with the fact that unhandled exceptions will happen, and we shouldn't write more code than we need. For example, the exception types following the `except` keyword should be as specific as possible. This will make our code more clear and maintainable.

Handling exceptions at the application level

In nonstandard Python environments, such as Maya, the process does not exit in the case of an unhandled Python exception. The exception is handled by the application, usually printing information about the exception. In the case of Maya, this feedback is displayed in the Script Editor. Importantly, the integrity of the Maya application is preserved, along with the scene and data (hopefully).

Unfortunately, Maya does occasionally crash. Your scripts can cause Maya to get into an invalid state or corrupt memory, perhaps due to some bug in Maya itself. There's nothing Maya can do to recover, so it must crash.

The "let something else handle catastrophic errors" pattern continues outside of Python. The Autodesk Customer Error Reporting process watches Maya for unexpected termination and asks you to send an error report to Autodesk when that occurs. If the error reporting process crashes, the operating system may see it and ask you to send an error report to your operating system manufacturer. And, of course, operating systems occasionally crash!

```
A problem has been detected and windows has been shut down to prevent damage
to your computer.

The problem seems to be caused by the following file: SPCMDCON.SYS

PAGE_FAULT_IN_NONPAGED_AREA

If this is the first time you've seen this Stop error screen,
restart your computer. If this screen appears again, follow
these steps:

Check to make sure any new hardware or software is properly installed.
If this is a new installation, ask your hardware or software manufacturer
for any Windows updates you might need.

If problems continue, disable or remove any newly installed hardware
or software. Disable BIOS memory options such as caching or shadowing.
If you need to use Safe Mode to remove or disable components, restart
your computer, press F8 to select Advanced Startup Options, and then
select Safe Mode.

Technical information:

*** STOP: 0x00000050 (0xFD3094C2,0x00000001,0xFBFE7617,0x00000000)

*** SPCMDCON.SYS - Address FBFE7617 base at FBFE5000, DateStamp 3d6dd67c
```

In the next few sections we will lay down some good ideas for error handling. We'll then build an application-level error handler, so we can do more with our unhandled errors instead of having Maya just print them.

Golden rules of error handling

Programs will inevitably have errors. How we leverage our language and tools to work with that fact is of the utmost importance.

 Figuring out why an error in a program occurs is called *debugging*, and a specific discussion of debugging techniques is outside the scope of this book. However, following the guidelines for error handling here will reduce your (inevitable) time spent in debugging.

Keeping that in mind, we can establish some golden rules for dealing with errors and exceptions in Python. Adhering to these rules will make sure those errors that do occasionally occur can most effectively be learned from.

Focus on the critical path

The term **critical path** is defined as *the longest necessary path through a network of activities*. For tools and scripts in Maya, it would be something like the following:

> *"Given a scene and system configured correctly, the critical path are all the things the user must do in order to accomplish the primary purpose of the tool."*

For the character creator from *Chapter 2, Writing Composable Code*, the critical path would be "the user selects the root of the hierarchy she wants converted, clicks a button, and the hierarchy is replaced with a properly configured joint hierarchy."

Obviously, the critical path needs to work as expected. If the critical path is broken, your tool is fundamentally broken. There is never a reason or excuse to release such broken work (though I've done it and seen it done many times). More complex tools may have several critical paths.

We also need to ensure that the critical path handles edge cases gracefully. If some function is expecting one object to be selected, you must handle the case if zero or many are selected, and explain to the user why the function did not execute. We handled this in `charcreator.convert_hierarchies_main` by warning the user if nothing is selected, and converting all the unique roots if multiple objects are selected. It would not have been acceptable to raise an error if nothing is selected, or only convert the first object and not explain why. In the case of a programming error, there's nothing we can do, so we just let Maya handle the error and display some sort of error information. The critical path should be hardened against user errors or misconfiguration.

Keep the end user in mind

Almost anything is acceptable in a personal script that does not get distributed. I would encourage you to apply the best practices from this chapter and book, but no one will know if you don't.

If you are distributing a script to colleagues, the critical path should work but error handling and reporting can still be rough. You can rely on people to tell you when something breaks. You can fix the problem and get them a new version quickly. Proximity means more information, and a captive audience means you can leave some edge cases unaddressed until they come up and can be fixed.

Distributing a tool to unknown third parties is, of course, the most difficult thing to do. Sometimes people upload personal work of mediocre quality to script sharing sites, and as a dissemination of information I find it admirable. Sometimes people market personal work of mediocre quality as something more than it is, and I find it not only dishonest but potentially dangerous as well. Poorly designed scripts can cause scene or environment corruption or changes. It takes a lot of work to make something polished enough for external distribution. In *The Mythical Man-Month*, Fred Brooks observes that developing products for external customers often takes three times as much effort as developing internal products. Many software developers consider that a low estimate.

 Refer to *Chapter 9, Becoming a Part of the Python Community*, for information about distributing scripts to external audiences.

Attention must always be paid to errors. You should know when a user is hitting an error, and you should have a way to get a new build out easily. The latter topic is outside the scope of this book, but we will address the former in this chapter.

Only catch errors you can handle

After such stern warnings about the effect of errors, you may try to be very cautious and catch all errors. Do not do that. First of all, errors can happen anywhere (refer to our earlier definition of exceptions as flow control). More importantly, handling errors at too high a level obfuscates the actual problem so that fixing it becomes very difficult. It is preferable to just let the error bubble up, catch it at the application level, and preserve the full exception and stack trace. Consider how the following example hides the actual bug:

```
>>> def rename_first_child():
...     try:
...         o = pmc.selected()[0]
...         realname = o.name().split('_')[1]
...         o.getChildren()[0].rename('_' + realname)
...     except Exception as ex:
...         print 'Could not rename first child:'
...         print ex
>>> rename_first_child()
Could not rename first child:
list index out of range
```

The problem here is that there are no less than three possible places an `IndexError` can be raised: if zero objects are selected, if the selected object has zero children, or the first child has a name with no underscores. The error printout does not help at all!

What's the correct way to write this function? I don't have one; it is poorly designed. It is highly specific and doesn't make much sense. There's no way to make this clear or handle errors well. It would be better to get rid of the `try`/`except` entirely. If reporting problems to the user is important, the function should be totally rewritten to give proper feedback when a problematic condition is encountered.

Avoid partial mutations

Generally, if you catch an exception, there should be a way to roll the system back to how it was. This is normally done by having well-designed systems that are largely stateless (or at least avoid mutating arguments), and simply throwing away whatever was happening that caused the exception.

Unfortunately, Maya is a huge ball of mutable state and this approach is rarely practical. Let's look at the following code, which tries to translate three joints:

```
>>> def set_pos(objs):
...     for o in objs:
...         o.translate.set([100,50, 25])
>>> j1, j2, j3 = pmc.joint(), pmc.joint(), pmc.joint()
>>> j2.translate.lock()
>>> set_pos([j1, j2, j3])
Traceback (most recent call last):
RuntimeError: setAttr: The attribute 'joint2.translate' is locked or
connected and cannot be modified.
```

In this case, the position of `j1` would be changed, but because `j2.translate` is locked, setting the attribute value would raise an exception. The interruption would leave `j2` and `j3` in their original positions. This is quite bad! Imagine if this were a huge process that took 30 seconds and worked on hundreds of objects. A user would have to reload the scene to make sure things were not corrupted. That also means a user would have to save the scene before every use of the tool to ensure she has a known good to fall back to. We'll look at strategies to cope with this unfortunate situation in the *Dealing with expensive and mutable state* section later in this chapter.

The most common way to mitigate this issue is to use undo blocks, as we will see in the coming *Leveraging undo blocks* section. There are other techniques, such as storing and restoring state, or asking an object for permission before every mutation, but I advise against them. Use undo blocks where needed, test your tools well, and just accept that Maya is already filled with bugs. No one is going to die if your tool leaves a mutation after an error.

Practical error handling in Maya

Most of these golden rules are true in Python in general, as well as most other programming languages with exceptions. However, using Python in Maya is a different environment. There are some additional tools and constraints available. In this section, we'll go through some of the unique problems we face in Maya, and what can be done to mitigate each problem.

Dealing with expensive and mutable state

The biggest problem with error handling in Maya is that its overall design significantly constrains the choices of any system built on top of it. Consider the following script that lowercases the `fileTextureName` (`ftn`) attribute of all the file nodes in the scene:

```
>>> for f in pmc.ls(type='file'):
...     f.ftn.set(f.ftn.get().lower())
Traceback (most recent call last):
RuntimeError: setAttr: The attribute 'file2.fileTextureName' is locked
or connected and cannot be modified.
>>> [f.ftn.get() for f in pmc.ls(type='file')]
[u'ftn0', u'FTN1', u'FTN2']
```

Oops! The first file node has been renamed, but not the other two. This bug has been described in the *Avoid partial mutations* earlier in this chapter. If an error happens during the iteration, this script will leave some of the file nodes mutated (`ftn` is lowercase), and some not. This would be a bad thing! How can we avoid it?

The first strategy to address this sort of problem is to avoid mutating. However, because Maya's design works with highly mutable, complex nodes, this is not a valid answer.

The second strategy is to do a **read-copy-update** of the data. This, too, is prohibited by Maya's design. There is no way to separate the copy from the update, since when a Maya node is duplicated, the scene is changed. And an update, which means replacing the original node with the copied and mutated version, would be error prone and expensive due to hierarchies, connections, and construction histories.

 The read-copy-update pattern involves reading the value of some data, creating a copy of that data, changing that data, and updating the original value. It is commonly used as a synchronization mechanism (for example, between threads). It can also be used to ensure some data is not left partially mutated in the case of an error, by ensuring that the original data is not changed unless the entire mutation succeeds.

The third strategy is to manually roll back changes in the case of an error. This is already a tricky solution outside of Maya, but even more verbose and challenging within Maya.

```
>>> original_data = []
>>> try:
...     for f in pmc.ls(type='file'):
...         ftn = f.ftn.get()
...         f.ftn.set(ftn.lower())
...         original_data.append([f, ftn])
... except Exception:
...     for f, ftn in original_data:
...         f.ftn.set(ftn)
...     raise
Traceback (most recent call last):
RuntimeError: setAttr: The attribute 'file2.fileTextureName' is locked
or connected and cannot be modified.
>>> [f.ftn.get() for f in pmc.ls(type='file')]
[u'FTN0', u'FTN1', u'FTN2']
```

The preceding code turns a two line script into a confusing mess. We would need to apply similar logic for every mutation. You can probably create helpers to hide some of the complexity for most attribute changes, but the result would bear little resemblance to normal Maya Python programming.

This "solution" creates as many problems as it solves. No one reading your code will understand it, and your codebase will be filled with special (and error-prone) ways that people must learn in order to be "safe" while doing trivial things.

The fourth option is, finally, somewhat realistic. We can use Maya's undo system so that state is restored on an error. We will explore this strategy in the next section, *Leveraging undo blocks*.

The final strategy to the issue of handling errors in the face of expensive and mutable state is the one I often recommend. Shrug your shoulders and hope the caller can handle the partial mutation. No one is using Maya to send a person to Mars or perform surgery. Software for tasks that cannot afford errors is designed very differently than Maya. Embrace the otherwise beautiful architecture of Maya and be productive making awesome stuff and don't worry too much about this constraint.

 If you are interested in what sort of standards it takes to send someone into space, you can view NASA's Technical Standards Program here: `https://standards.nasa.gov/documents/nasa`.

Leveraging undo blocks

Maya's undo system gives us a reliable and straightforward way to preserve state in the face of an error. We will continue with the previous example, lowercasing the `fileTextureName` attribute of `file` nodes. The use of undo blocks is highlighted.

```
>>> pmc.undoInfo(openChunk=True)
>>> try:
...     for f in pmc.ls(type='file'):
...         f.ftn.set(f.ftn.get().lower())
...     pmc.undoInfo(closeChunk=True)
... except Exception:
...     pmc.undoInfo(closeChunk=True)
...     pmc.undo()
...     raise
Traceback (most recent call last):
RuntimeError: setAttr: The attribute 'file2.fileTextureName' is locked
or connected and cannot be modified.
>>> [f.ftn.get() for f in pmc.ls(type='file')]
[u'FTN0', u'FTN1', u'FTN2']
```

We start by opening a new `undo` chunk. We then perform our actions, closing the chunk when done (due to success or failure). In the case of success, we're finished, and the user can use a single undo to undo all the renaming. In the case of a failure, we call the undo ourselves, and then re-raise the error, hopefully with the original state restored by closing the undo block.

> In the next chapter, *Chapter 4, Leveraging Context Managers and Decorators in Maya*, we will look at using a context manager to write this in a less verbose way. For now, though, this will do.

The drawbacks with using `undoInfo` to handle errors are twofold.

First, undo operations are slow and you often want to turn them off entirely for complex processes. If undo is disabled for Maya, or some code being called disables undo, this approach will not work.

Second, the open-close chunk pattern can easily be broken, either by using it incorrectly yourself (something we hope to avoid through the use of a context manager in the next chapter), or in code that you don't control. Everyone has to use it correctly or the user suffers.

Dealing with Maya's poor exception design

Let's slightly redesign our script which lowercases attribute values. The attributes that fail to be set will warn the user and undo, but an error for any other reason leaves the scene corrupted so that it can be diagnosed properly. How would we go about catching an error only if the attribute setting failed? We have to look through the message of the raised exception, as highlighted in the following code:

```
>>> import sys
>>> pmc.undoInfo(openChunk=True)
>>> try:
...     for f in pmc.ls(type='file'):
...         f.ftn.set(f.ftn.get().lower())
...     pmc.undoInfo(closeChunk=True)
... except RuntimeError as ex:
...     pmc.undoInfo(closeChunk=True)
...     if ex.args[0].startswith('setAttr: The attribute '):
...         pmc.undo()
...         sys.stderr.write(
...             'Cannot set attribute, fix and try again.\\n')
...         sys.stderr.write(ex.args[0] + '\\n')
...     else:
...         raise
... except Exception:
...     pmc.undoInfo(closeChunk=True)
...     raise
Cannot set attribute, fix and try again.
setAttr: The attribute 'file2.fileTextureName' is locked or connected
and cannot be modified.
>>> [f.ftn.get() for f in pmc.ls(type='file')]
[u'FTN0', u'FTN1', u'FTN2']
```

One of the most unfortunate designs in PyMEL is that nearly everything is a `RuntimeError` with some particular message. The decision arises from the fact that PyMEL wraps Maya's command engine, which does not have typed exceptions and just uses a string. Rather than attempting to parse every error and build a massive exception type hierarchy, PyMEL merely wraps them as `RuntimeError` objects. We must parse the error message ourselves.

Parsing the error message is unavoidable in some cases. Perhaps in this example, moving the catch of the `RuntimeError` around the `f.ftn.set` statement would be a better design and avoid the need to parse the message. But in many cases there is no alternative. For example, the `maya.cmds.file` command (which PyMEL has thankfully broken up and wrapped into more digestible functions) has several dozen flags. In order to know precisely what went wrong, the error message needs to be parsed.

Leveraging the Maya application

As discussed previously, we can leverage Maya as a top-level application which provides a resilient place to handle Python errors. It is difficult (though possible) to crash Maya through Python. We will not be attempting to handle any of these hard crashes, whether due to Python or not, in this book.

We will use the Maya application for handling errors in the next section.

Dealing with the Maya application

The Maya application is something we can leverage, but it is also notoriously unstable. Occasionally, doing something routine can crash Maya reliably. If you're very unlucky, it will crash Maya randomly without easy reproduction steps. There are also things that don't work as they normally do in Python (such as the `subprocess.Popen` class), so code that works under a vanilla Python interpreter may not work in Maya.

Instability during error handling is particularly frustrating!

Leveraging Python, which is better than MEL

Let's end on a good note. It is obvious but should be made explicit. We would not be having this discussion if we were using MEL. The way to handle errors in MEL—the `catch` keyword—is clunky and does not lend itself to creating any complex programs.

Python gives us the good fortune to even be able to talk about tools and constraints. The design of our programs and how we handle errors would be so limited without a language similar to Python in Maya that we should be thankful we can even have this discussion.

Building a high-level error handler

I stated in a previous section that it's desirable to know every time a script errors. There are two ways to do this. The first is to embed some notification behavior in the tool itself using something like the following code:

```
def my_tool_main():
    try:
        do_stuff()
    except Exception:
        send_error_mail()
        raise
```

This is a fine strategy for larger programs. But what happens if you want to do this for hundreds of scripts serving dozens of artists? Embedding the error handler in each script would lead to rampant duplication and boilerplate.

Python has a solution, of course. It is `sys.excepthook` (also called the **exception hook**), described by the Python docs as follows:

"When an exception is raised and uncaught, the interpreter calls sys.excepthook with three arguments, the exception class, exception instance, and a traceback object. In an interactive session this happens just before control is returned to the prompt; in a Python program this happens just before the program exits. The handling of such top-level exceptions can be customized by assigning another three-argument function to sys.excepthook."

In keeping with the error handling frustrations specific to Maya, `sys.excepthook` does not work in Maya. We need to use an alternative, and less elegant, mechanism. First, though, let's understand how `sys.excepthook` works in standard Python.

Understanding sys.excepthook

Let's create a simple exception hook function that will print **Hello!** when an error happens, as in the following code.

```
>>> 1 + '1'
Traceback (most recent call last):
TypeError: unsupported operand type(s) for +: 'int' and 'str'

>>> import sys
>>> def ehook(etype, evalue, tb):
...     print 'Hello!'
>>> sys.excepthook = ehook
>>> 1 + '1'
Hello!
```

The first time we called `1 + '1'` we raised an error, which was caught by the Python interpreter and the traceback was printed out. After setting `sys.excepthook = ehook`, our `ehook` function handles the error instead. The `sys.excepthook` function is called for every unhandled exception before it is handled by the interpreter.

There's no way to use an exception hook to recover and hand control back to your Python script. That's what makes the exception unhandled. Though `sys.excepthook` seems to handle the exception, it is the Python interpreter that actually catches the exception and hands it off to the exception hook.

The arguments to `sys.excepthook` are the three values in the `sys.exc_info()` tuple we looked at earlier in the chapter.

The original Python `sys.excepthook` function is available via the `sys.__excepthook__` attribute. This allows us to have some custom handling and still use the default exception hook. We'll look into this in detail in a later section.

Using sys.excepthook in Maya

Unfortunately `sys.excepthook` does not work in Maya's GUI mode (it does work in mayapy, however). Instead, you must use the `maya.utils.formatGuiException` function. The `formatGuiException` function does not work in mayapy, however, so in order to test the code we are going to write, we must use the Script Editor in Maya. Follow these steps to open and use Maya's Script Editor:

1. Launch Maya.
2. Open the Script Editor.
3. In the bottom panel, type something similar to `1 + '1'`.
4. Highlight the code and press *Ctrl + Enter*.
5. In the top panel, feedback will be displayed, such as anything we print or the traceback for the error.

You can perform steps 4 and 5 repeatedly to interactively test your code. Remember to reload the module you are testing via the `reload` function.

The `sys.excepthook` example that we created in the previous section can be replicated to work in Maya as follows:

```
import maya.utils
def excepthook(tb_type, exc_object, tb, detail=2): #(1)
  return 'Hello!' #(2)
maya.utils.formatGuiException = excepthook #(3)
```

The breakdown of this function is as follows:

1. Notice that the `formatGuiException` function takes an optional `detail` keyword argument. The regular `sys.excepthook` function does not.
2. The exception hook should return what is to be printed to Maya's Script Editor. This is different from a normal `sys.excepthook` function, which doesn't return anything. You can do your custom handling here, but you also must return some string. Maya will display this string as
    `# Error: Hello! #`.
3. Assign your exception hook function to `maya.utils.formatGuiException` so that it will be called by unhandled Python exceptions in Maya.

Creating an error handler

For the rest of this chapter, we are going to build a way to catch unhandled exceptions so that you, as a script or tool author, can know when and why errors are happening. Create a file at C:\mayapybook\pylib\excepthandling.py to house this work.

 Remember, the development root you chose in *Chapter 1, Introspecting Maya, Python, and PyMEL*, may be different from what is specified here.

Go ahead and open the file in your IDE and recreate the simple exception hook function from the previous example.

```
import maya.utils
def excepthook(tb_type, exc_object, tb, detail=2):
    return 'Hello!'
maya.utils.formatGuiException = excepthook
```

This code creates a new exception hook function called excepthook that just prints the string "Hello!", and then assigns the exception hook function to maya.utils.formatGuiException.

In the Maya Script Editor, run the code 1 + '1'. You should get the following result printed at the top panel of the Script Editor:

```
1 + '1'
# Error: unsupported operand type(s) for +: 'int' and 'str'
# Traceback (most recent call last):
# File "<maya console>", line 1, in <module>
# TypeError: unsupported operand type(s) for +: 'int' and 'str' #
```

Now, run import excepthandling to install the new exception hook. Run 1 + '1' again. You should get the following result in the Script Editor:

```
1 + '1'
# Error: Hello! #
```

We now have a most basic error handler. We will add more to it over the next few sections.

Improving the error handler

Printing `Hello!` isn't a very useful way to handle an exception. Let's build something a bit more powerful. We should call the original exception hook to get a formatted exception, and add some information. Let's edit `excepthandling.py`.

```
import maya.utils

def excepthook(etype, evalue, tb, detail=2):
    s = maya.utils._formatGuiException(etype, evalue, tb, detail)
    lines = [
        s,
        'An unhandled exception occurred.',
        'Please copy the error info above this message',
        'and a copy of this file and email it to',
        'mayasupport@robg3d.com. You should get a response',
        'in three days or less.'
    return '\n'.join(lines)

maya.utils.formatGuiException = excepthook
```

The first thing our new exception hook does is invoke the original exception hook via `maya.utils._formatGuiException`. This protected function is the conceptual equivalent to the `sys.__excepthook__` function. If we were using `sys.excepthook` in standard Python, we'd just print the information out inside our exception hook. Instead, because we are using Maya, we return the string and let Maya print it out for us. In the returned string, we include a helpful message for the user explaining how to report this unhandled exception.

Execute `1 + '1'` in the Script Editor and you will see the following output:

```
1 + '1'
# Error: unsupported operand type(s) for +: 'int' and 'str'
# Traceback (most recent call last):
# File "<maya console>", line 1, in <module>
# TypeError: unsupported operand type(s) for +: 'int' and 'str'
An unhandled exception occurred.
Please copy the error info above this message
and a copy of this file and email it to
mayasupport@robg3d.com. You should get a response
in three days or less. #
```

However, this behavior is problematic. Do we want the exception hook to be called for every unhandled exception that happens in Maya? How about when the user is doing her own scripting? Should we inconvenience the user with extra error handling text? Should we tell the user to file a bug report with us if some locally installed script raises an error?

Probably not. We should filter out the exceptions that come from code that we don't care about. The difficult part of this, though, is figuring out what *care about* means. There are many ways to do this. We will look at just one way in detail, but you should choose an approach that fits your needs. You can also combine techniques if you want even more control over what you filter.

Inspecting Python code objects

The following technique involves inspecting code objects. This is less intimidating than it seems, and in fact we already dealt with this sort of thing in *Chapter 1, Introspecting Maya, Python, and PyMEL.* If we take a look at the following function, we can inspect far more than its name or the module it comes from. We can see its arguments, global and local variables, and more. And most code objects also reference other code objects.

```
>>> a = 1
>>> def spam(eggs=3):
...     b = 2
...     return a + b + eggs
>>> spam
<function spam at 0x0...>
>>> spam.func_defaults
(3,)
>>> sorted(spam.func_globals.keys())
['__builtins__', ..., 'a', ..., 'spam'...]
```

Python tracebacks are also code objects, as we can see in the following code:

```
>>> def eggs():
...     1 + '1'
>>> try:
...     eggs()
... except TypeError:
...     tb = sys.exc_info()[2] #(1)
>>> tb #(2)
<traceback object at 0x0...>
>>> tb.tb_frame #(3)
<frame object at 0x0...>
>>> tb.tb_next
<traceback object at 0x0...>
>>> tb.tb_frame.f_globals.keys() #(4)
['a', 'spam', '__builtins__', ...'tb'...]
>>> tb.tb_frame.f_code.co_filename #(5)
'<console>'
```

A breakdown of the preceding code should illuminate what we are looking at:

1. We create an error so that we can capture the traceback into the `tb` variable for inspection.

2. We see that the value of `tb` is a traceback instance.

3. The traceback is a *stack of frames*. Each frame describes a place in the code, what the value of the variables are, and so on. We can look at the traceback's frame through the `tb_frame` attribute. We can get the next frame by looking at the `tb_next.tb_frame` attribute. The traceback stored in `tb` represents the topmost frame, furthest from the error. We can walk down the stack, toward the site of the error, through the `tb_next` attribute.

4. You can access information about the frame by querying attributes on the frame, such as the globals available to that frame.

5. You can also look at the code for the frame, and see for example what file the code is defined in.

Don't worry if this seems dense. It is! There is obviously much more to code objects, and we're just scratching the surface here. Having some cursory understanding will take you far, though, and give you the ability to dig around until you find what you need.

Adding filtering based on filename

We will filter based on the names of all the files involved in the traceback. If any of the code in the traceback comes from one of our files, we care about it. This may be a good approach for a studio environment, where tools will be sourced from a known folder and some assumptions about Maya's setup can be made.

```
import os
import maya.utils

def _normalize(p): #(1)
    return os.path.normpath(os.path.abspath(p))

LIB_DIR = _normalize(os.path.dirname(__file__)) #(2)

def _handle_our_exc(etype, evalue, tb, detail): #(3)
    s = maya.utils._formatGuiException(etype, evalue, tb, detail)
    lines = [
        s,
        'An unhandled exception occurred.',
        'Please copy the error info above this message',
```

```
            'and a copy of this file and email it to',
            'mayasupport@robg3d.com. You should get a response',
            'in three days or less.']
    return '\n'.join(lines)


def _is_important_tb(tb): #(4)
    while tb:
        codepath = tb.tb_frame.f_code.co_filename
        if _normalize(codepath).startswith(LIB_DIR):
            return True
        tb = tb.tb_next
    return False


def excepthook(etype, evalue, tb, detail=2): #(5)
    if _is_important_tb(tb):
        return _handle_our_exc(etype, evalue, tb, detail)
    return maya.utils._formatGuiException(
            etype, evalue, tb, detail)


maya.utils.formatGuiException = excepthook
```

The preceding code does the following:

1. The `_normalize` function provides a common way to normalize a path, so that we can compare paths on equal ground. For example, if you want the filename comparison to be case insensitive, you would put a call to `.lower()` inside the `_normalize` function.

2. We store the normalized path to the development root (`C:\mayacookbook\pylib`) in the `LIB_DIR` variable. You may need to choose a different path for your purposes. We care about any file under this directory.

3. We pull our special error handling behavior into a function. This is a likely vector of change (and we will improve it substantially throughout this chapter), so it is good to pull it out into its own function.

4. Create a function to determine whether we care about a given traceback. We care about a traceback if any frame have code defined in a file under the `LIB_DIR` path.

5. Inside our exception hook, we check if we care about the traceback, and if so, handle it with our custom logic. If not, invoke the original `maya.utils._formatGuiException` function.

There are many other options for filtering out the stack traces we care about. One technique is to set a module level __author__ attribute on all of your files, and key off of that. In this case, all of your Python scripts would have the following line at the module level:

```
__author__ = 'rob.galanakis@gmail.com'
```

And then your traceback filterer would look as follows:

```
def is_important_tb_byauthor(tb):
    while tb:
        auth = tb.tb_frame.f_globals.get('__author__')
        if auth == __author__:
            return True
        tb = tb.tb_next
    return False
```

For the purposes of this book, we're going to continue to use the filename-based filtering. You can also combine these techniques or key off of pretty much whatever you want.

Assembling the contents of an error e-mail

Printing out some feedback is great, but what if you want to mail yourself diagnostics automatically? Why not collect information about the user's machine and scene, and automatically file a bug report via e-mail?

We will break this work into two sections. In the next section we will send the email. In the remainder of this section, we will collect information about the user's machine and environment that will make up the body of the e-mail. There are many ways in Python to gather information about a machine, even more when combined with Maya. We'll explore some of them right now.

Open up C:\mayapybook\pylib\excepthandling.py in your IDE. First we'll create our function and collect information about the Maya scene, using the following code:

```
import os
import platform
import pymel.core as pmc
import sys

def _collect_info():
    lines = []
    lines.append('Scene Info')
    lines.append('  Maya Scene: ' + pmc.sceneName())
```

Now, let's gather information about the Maya and Python executables. This will give us a high level view of what's going on, such as the Maya and Python versions, when we are trying to diagnose an error.

```python
lines.append('Maya/Python Info')
lines.append('  Maya Version: ' + pmc.about(version=True))
lines.append('  Qt Version: ' + pmc.about(qtVersion=True))
lines.append('  Maya64: ' + str(pmc.about(is64=True)))
lines.append('  PyVersion: ' + sys.version)
lines.append('  PyExe: ' + sys.executable)
```

Third, we'll gather information about the machine and OS. Even though Python and Maya are cross platform, they still have some OS-specific behavior and functionality. And of course there are platform-specific system calls available. Because of this it is useful to have information about the machine in the case of an error.

```python
lines.append('Machine Info')
lines.append('  OS: ' + pmc.about(os=True))
lines.append('  Node: ' + platform.node())
lines.append('  OSRelease: ' + platform.release())
lines.append('  OSVersion: ' + platform.version())
lines.append('  Machine: ' + platform.machine())
lines.append('  Processor: ' + platform.processor())
```

Finally, let's record information about the user's environment. This is extremely useful. Users may have configured their environment in a way that causes problems with your scripts, such as conflicting environment variables.

```python
lines.append('Environment Info')
lines.append('  EnvVars')
for k in sorted(os.environ.keys()):
    lines.append('    %s: %s' % (k, os.environ[k]))
lines.append('  SysPath')
for p in sys.path:
    lines.append('    ' + p)
return lines
```

We can simply return our list of lines to be joined with the exception information inside the _handle_our_exc function. We insert the formatted error first, then the collected info, and then the instructions to the user.

```python
import os
import platform
import pymel.core as pmc
import sys
```

```python
def _collect_info():
    lines = []
    lines.append('Scene Info')
    lines.append('  Maya Scene: ' + pmc.sceneName())

    lines.append('Maya/Python Info')
    lines.append('  Maya Version: ' + pmc.about(version=True))
    lines.append('  Qt Version: ' + pmc.about(qtVersion=True))
    lines.append('  Maya64: ' + str(pmc.about(is64=True)))
    lines.append('  PyVersion: ' + sys.version)
    lines.append('  PyExe: ' + sys.executable)

    lines.append('Machine Info')
    lines.append('  OS: ' + pmc.about(os=True))
    lines.append('  Node: ' + platform.node())
    lines.append('  OSRelease: ' + platform.release())
    lines.append('  OSVersion: ' + platform.version())
    lines.append('  Machine: ' + platform.machine())
    lines.append('  Processor: ' + platform.processor())

    lines.append('Environment Info')
    lines.append('  EnvVars')
    for k in sorted(os.environ.keys()):
        lines.append('    %s: %s' % (k, os.environ[k]))
    lines.append('  SysPath')
    for p in sys.path:
        lines.append('    ' + p)
    return lines


def _handle_our_exc(etype, evalue, tb, detail):
    s = maya.utils._formatGuiException(etype, evalue, tb, detail)
    lines = [s]
    lines.extend(_collect_info())
    lines.extend([
        'An unhandled exception occurred.',
        'Please copy the error info above this message',
        'and a copy of this file and email it to',
        'mayasupport@robg3d.com. You should get a response',
        'in three days or less.'])
    return '\n'.join(lines)
```

Sending the error e-mail

Now it is time to the write the code to send the error report e-mail. Python has the email and smtplib modules in its standard library that can be used to send e-mails.

In order to send e-mails, you need to have access to an SMTP server. If you are creating tools for use inside a business firewall, you can probably use the company's SMTP server without any special authentication and this is a relatively straightforward thing to do. You can just use the address to your server instead of 'localhost'.

If you are using e-mail for externally distributed tools, you will need another solution. There are several ways you can set this up with e-mail but they are outside of the scope of this book.

In any case, I actually suggest using a web service for reporting errors, instead of e-mail. We cover e-mail here because it should be conceptually familiar. Refer to the *Moving beyond e-mail* section later in this chapter for other ideas.

Sending an e-mail is straightforward and if you need more help or information than provided here, many tutorials are available on the Internet. Insert the following code into excepthandling.py:

```
from email.mime.text import MIMEText
import smtplib

EMAIL_ADDR = 'mayasupport@robg3d.com' # Your email here
EMAIL_SERVER = 'localhost' # Your email server here

def _send_email(body):
    msg = MIMEText(body)
    msg['To'] = EMAIL_ADDR
    msg['From'] = EMAIL_ADDR
    msg['Subject'] = 'Maya Tools Error'
    server = smtplib.SMTP(EMAIL_SERVER)
    try:
        server.sendmail(msg['From'], msg['To'], msg.as_string())
    finally:
        server.quit()
```

Again, if any of the preceding code is unclear or causing problems, a simple Internet search for Python email tutorials should set you on your way. And remember, you need an SMTP server to send e-mail, so if you are getting something similar to the following error when sending an e-mail, your server is probably not set up properly:

```
error: [Errno 10061] No connection could be made because the target
machine actively refused it
```

We need to adjust our _handle_our_exc function to send an e-mail. We will inform the user an e-mail has been sent because an error has occurred, along with the error. The diagnostic information will only go in the e-mail.

```
def _handle_our_exc(etype, evalue, tb, detail):
    s = maya.utils._formatGuiException(etype, evalue, tb, detail)
    body = [s]
    body.extend(_collect_info())
    _send_email('\n'.join(body))
    lines = [
        s,
        'An unhandled exception occurred.',
        'An error report was automatically sent to ',
        EMAIL_ADDR + ' with details about the error. ',
        'You should get a followup response in three days '
        'or less.']
    return '\n'.join(lines)
```

It would also be a good idea to handle any error that may occur while sending the e-mail, perhaps printing the body of the e-mail with instructions on how to send it manually. This is left as an exercise for the reader.

Installing the error handler

So far, our exception hook is installed (assigned to maya.utils. formatGuiException) when the excepthandling module is imported. This is a problem because it means excepthandling needs to be imported for the exception hook to be assigned. If you have a whole suite of tools, you will need to make sure excepthandling is imported early on. If you are distributing lots of separate tools, you will want to make sure each one imports excepthandling.

There is another problem, though. Imagine two people have read this chapter and created their own excepthook replacements which are assigned over maya.utils. formatGuiException. These two people then write and release some scripts. These two scripts are then installed by the same user. What would happen?

Obeying the What If Two Programs Did This rule

The *What If Two Programs Did This* rule is a technique to evaluate features and designs by asking the question: *What if two programs did this?* It comes from Microsoft programmer Raymond Chen's blog post at `http://blogs.msdn.com/b/oldnewthing/archive/2005/06/07/426294.aspx`. In the post he explains:

> ""*How do I create a window that is never covered by any other windows, not even other topmost windows?*"
>
> *Imagine if this were possible and* **imagine if two programs did this**. *Program A creates a window that is "super-topmost" and so does Program B. Now the user drags the two windows so that they overlap. What happens? You've created yourself a logical impossibility. One of those two windows must be above the other, contradicting the imaginary "super-topmost" feature.*"

In the case of `sys.excepthook` and `maya.utils.formatGuiException`, we need to store the original function and call it if it isn't the default exception hook. As long as all exception hooks adhere to this rule, every hook will be called. On the other hand, if an exception hook simply invokes `maya.utils._formatGuiException` (equivalent to `sys.__excepthook__`), we would not get this chaining effect.

In the case of `formatGuiException`, the chaining does not make total sense because `formatGuiException` is meant to return a value. However, we should dutifully do it anyway, so any side effects that do happen (like sending an e-mail) occur, even if our feedback is not printed to the user.

 We can also print the results of any chained `formatGuiException` calls, but since there's no right answer in this situation I'll choose to do the simplest thing. You can choose otherwise if it makes sense to you.

Let's go ahead and make the highlighted changes to our code:

```
_orig_excepthook = maya.utils.formatGuiException

def excepthook(etype, evalue, tb, detail=2):
    result = _orig_excepthook(etype, evalue, tb, detail)
    if _is_important_tb(tb):
        result = _handle_our_exc(etype, evalue, tb, detail)
    return result

maya.utils.formatGuiException = excepthook
```

When the module is imported, it stores the value of `formatGuiException`, which could have been the original `_formatGuiException` or something installed by another script. Then inside our hook, we call the stored exception hook, but then call our own exception hook and use that string if we care about the traceback. As long as other exception hooks are equally considerate, we should be in good shape.

Improving the error handler

There are many more things that can be done to this exception handler. How important each one is depends on your use case. I encourage you to give each one thought, but as always, release the simplest thing that works. Especially when you are dealing with error handlers, simpler is better. You don't want errors in your error handlers!

Adding a user interface

It may not be a good idea to send information about a user's machine without consent. Users should either opt in for automatic reporting (like Google Chrome automatic statistics gather), or manually approve sending the information when an error happens (like Autodesk's Customer Error Reporting system). My preference is for the latter option, which allows the user to preview the issue and submit any other information that may be helpful. The easiest way to do this is to pop up a dialog when an error happens, previewing the contents of the e-mail. This also gives you a good place to put any other customizations, such as showing a textbox to enter a description or reproduction steps, setting a window title, and providing a way to include attachments.

Obviously the dialog should only pop up when not in batch mode. When in batch mode, things should be automatically handled or ignored.

 Refer to *Chapter 5, Building Graphical User Interfaces for Maya*, to learn how to build dialogs like the one described here.

Before you collect a user's information and copy it off her computer, ensure your collection and reporting mechanisms are secure, reliable, and you have the user's consent.

Using a background thread to send the e-mail

Sending an e-mail or talking to an external server can take a while, perhaps a second in the case of success, or an unknown time if the external server is unresponsive. It would be inconsiderate to lock up a user's Maya session while the error report e-mail is being sent!

Before our error handler is ready for prime time use, make sure sending the email or communicating with any external service occurs on a background thread. Threading is outside of the scope of this book, but the change would look similar to the following code:

```
def _send_email_in_background(body):
    t = threading.Thread(
        target=_send_email, args=(body,),
        name='send_email_in_background')
    t.start()
```

You would then call `_send_email_in_background` instead of `_send_email` inside the `_handle_our_exc` function. I'd also recommend the use of a concurrency library like `gevent` rather than the standard library's `threading` module.

Moving beyond e-mail

E-mail is incredibly prolific. However, it can also be very basic and limiting. Instead of reporting through e-mail, you can also report through several other mechanisms.

If you are on a company intranet, you can log errors directly to a database or place files on a network drive. However, I'd encourage you to choose one of the other options explained in the next paragraph. They are not much more difficult but they are much more robust.

If you have a bug tracker or a task management system, whether something complex like JIRA (http://jira.com) or simple like Trello (http://trello.com), you can use their web APIs to upload exception reports there. You can also build your own web service to do this sort of thing and back it with a database.

Capturing locals

It is very useful to know what the actual values of variables are all along the stack when an exception occurs. For example, instead of just seeing `IndexError: list index out of range`, it would be great to see the actual values of both the list and the out of range index.

This is a more advanced project but it is not too difficult to *roll your own way* to capture locals and globals all the way up the stack using the `inspect` module. You can also look at the `traceback2` module at https://code.google.com/p/traceback2/.

If you want something off the shelf and the size of your project is worth it, there's the open source Sentry server (http://sentry.readthedocs.org/) and Raven client (http://raven.readthedocs.org/) system.

Attaching log files

If you have been logging to files, you can attach all the log files that currently exist to the bug reporting e-mail. It is relatively simple to collect this data, and there are many examples on the Internet of how to use attachments with e-mail. The following code will find all log files:

```
import logging
log_filenames = set() # Avoid duplicates
for logger in logging.Logger.manager.loggerDict.values():
    for handler in getattr(logger, 'handlers', []):
        try:
            log_filenames.add(handler.baseFilename)
        except AttributeError:
            pass
```

You can also echo Maya's Script Editor history to a file and include that in your e-mail. The following code will log all new output in the top pane of the Script Editor into a `.log` file in the current working directory.

```
pmc.scriptEditorInfo(
    writeHistory=True,
    historyFilename='.log')
```

Summary

In this chapter we took a close at look at how Python's exceptions work. We defined what an exception is and learned that dealing with exceptions and errors is a fact of programming life. We examined in detail the interesting `traceback` type and the `exc_info` tuple. We learned a set of best practices for handling errors, and how those best practices apply to Maya.

We spent the rest of the chapter putting together an exception hook function that will send an e-mail if any unhandled exception occurs in code we care about. We closed the chapter by covering several ways we can potentially improve our exception hook.

In the next chapter, we'll look at two relatively unique features of Python: context managers and decorators. They will help us fill in several holes while programming Maya and be more *Pythonic*.

4

Leveraging Context Managers and Decorators in Maya

Context managers and **decorators** are two Python features that open up many powerful programming patterns. Many of these end up being incredibly useful in Maya, allowing us to map the archaic, imperative style of Maya command calls onto *Pythonic* code using flexible, modern idioms.

In this chapter, we will learn what context managers and decorators are, why they are useful, how they work, and when to use one instead of the other. After that, we'll build a number of simple context managers for safely modifying scene state. Using what we've learned, we will work on two projects: a context manager for denormalizing vertex skinning, and a decorator to record metrics. We will close out the chapter by analyzing some advanced decorator topics.

Inverting the subroutine

The idea of taking code that is similar between two blocks and factoring it out into a common function (also known as a **subroutine**) is well known. We've done it several places in this book. For example, the following block of code sets up objects for left and right feet, which are just mirrored. Nearly all of the code, except for the name of the sphere and its *x* translation, is duplicated.

```
>>> leftfoot = pmc.polySphere(name='left_foot')[0]
>>> leftfoot.translate.set(5, 0, 0)
>>> # ...other code that changes left_foot
```

```
>>> rightfoot = pmc.polySphere(name='right_foot')[0]
>>> rightfoot.translate.set(-5, 0, 0)
>>> # ...same code, but for right_foot
```

We can refactor the duplicated code into the `makefoot` function.

```
>>> def makefoot(prefix, x=1):
...     foot = pmc.polySphere(name=prefix + '_foot')[0]
...     foot.translate.set(5 * x, 0, 0)
...     # ...other code that changes foot
...     return foot
>>> leftfoot = makefoot('left', 1)
>>> rightfoot = makefoot('right', -1)
```

But what happens when the code we want to take out isn't the block itself, but everything around the block? For example, what if we want the creation of the individual feet to be undo-able as a single undo? This involves duplicated code before and after calling the `makefoot` function, as in the following example.

```
>>> pmc.undoInfo(openChunk=True)
>>> try:
...     leftfoot = makefoot('left', 1)
... finally:
...     pmc.undoInfo(closeChunk=True)
>>> pmc.undoInfo(openChunk=True)
>>> try:
...     rightfoot = makefoot('right', -1)
... finally:
...     pmc.undoInfo(closeChunk=True)
```

Both context managers and decorators provide a way to make that common setup and teardown code modular and reusable. Using the context manager `mayautils.undo_chunk`, which we will build later in this chapter, we could rewrite the preceding code as follows:

```
>>> import mayautils
>>> with mayautils.undo_chunk():
...     leftfoot = makefoot('left', 1)
>>> with mayautils.undo_chunk():
...     rightfoot = makefoot('right', -1)
```

Alternatively, if we were to create a decorator, we would have something like this:

```
>>> @mayautils.chunk_undo
... def makefoot(prefix, x=1):
...     foot = pmc.polySphere(name=prefix + '_foot')[0]
...     foot.translate.set(5 * x, 0, 0)
...     # Other code that changes foot
>>> leftfoot = makefoot('left', 1)
>>> rightfoot = makefoot('right', -1)
```

Clearly, this is much nicer! Let's explore these two humble constructs that can transform the way we program.

Introducing decorators

Decorators are the single most unfortunately explained language feature of Python. An improved way to teach decorators was presented by Steve Ferg on his blog: http://pythonconquerstheuniverse.wordpress.com/2012/04/29/python-decorators/. I've adapted his suggestions for use in this section.

Decorators associate setup and teardown functionality with some callable object. In the preceding example, we associated the functionality of "each time some function is called, it can be undone as a single block" with the makefoot function. There is no way to call makefoot without this new behavior added by the decorator.

Explaining decorators

I find it easiest to explain decorators by working from very basic Python and eventually ending with the funky @ line that goes above a function.

In Python, anything with a __call__ method is known as a **callable**. Functions are one type of callable. There is basically no difference between calling something directly, and invoking its __call__ method, as the following code illustrates.

```
>>> def add(a, b):
...     return a + b
>>> add(1, 2)
3
>>> add.__call__
<method-wrapper '__call__' of function object at 0x0...>
>>> add.__call__(1, 2)
3
```

Functions in Python are *first class* objects, which among other things means they can be passed around like any other object. You can pass a function into another function, and return them as well, as we do in the following example. First we define the `nothing` function, which just returns the function passed into it. After that, we invoke `nothing` with the `add` function defined in the preceding example. Finally, we invoke `add`, returned to us from the `nothing` function.

```
>>> def nothing(func):
...     return func
>>> nothing(add)(1, 2)
3
```

As we've done earlier in this book, we can create functions inside of other functions, which we've called *closures*, *nested functions*, or *inner functions*. We can then return that nested function from its outer function. In the following example, the `makeadd` function returns the newly created `adder` nested function, which is then called to do the actual calculations.

```
>>> def makeadd():
...     def adder(a, b):
...         return a + b
...     return adder
>>> makeadd()(1, 2)
3
```

A nested function can use the argument passed into its outer function. In the following example, the caller passes the original `add` function into the `makeadd` function. Inside of the nested `inner` function, the passed in function is used, rather than doing the addition directly as in the previous example.

```
>>> def makeadd(adder):
...     def inner(a, b):
...         return adder(a, b)
...     return inner
>>> makeadd(add)(1, 2)
3
```

Inside of our nested function, we can do additional things. In the following code, we will print what we are adding, call the passed in function, and then print the result.

```
>>> def announce(adder):
...     def inner(a, b):
...         print 'Adding', a, b
...         result = adder(a, b)
```

```
...             print 'Got', result
...             return result
...         return inner
>>> announce(add)(1, 2)
Adding 1 2
Got 3
3
```

Of course, there's no reason this technique should only work for our `add` function. Let's generalize it. The following `announce` function takes in another function and defines and returns a closure. The closure prints the passed function's name, calls the function, and prints and returns the result. Instead of the `add` function we've been using, we define a `subtract` function and announce that.

```
>>> def announce(func):
...         def inner(a, b):
...             print 'Calling', func.__name__, a, b
...             result = func(a, b)
...             print 'Got', result
...             return result
...         return inner
>>> def subtract(a, b):
...         return a - b
>>> announce(subtract)(1, 2)
Calling subtract 1 2
Got -1
-1
```

To generalize further, our closure can take an arbitrary number of arguments. We can use Python's `*args` and `**kwargs` syntax to just pass the arguments through to the original function. If you are unfamiliar with this syntax, refer to the *Appendix, Python Best Practices*.

```
>>> def announce(func):
...         def inner(*args, **kwargs):
...             print 'Calling', func.__name__, args, kwargs
...             result = func(*args, **kwargs)
...             print 'Got', result
...             return result
...         return inner
>>> def add3(a, b, c):
...         return a + b + c
>>> announce(add)(1, 2)
```

```
Calling add (1, 2) {}
Got 3
3
>>> announce(add3)(1, 2, 3)
Calling add3 (1, 2, 3) {}
Got 6
6
```

Also, instead of calling our returned closure immediately, we can assign it to a variable. In the following code, we assign the result of calling the announce function to the loud_add variable. We can then call that variable as we would a normal function.

```
>>> loud_add = announce(add)
>>> loud_add(1, 2)
Calling add (1, 2) {}
Got 3
3
```

Instead of creating the loud_add variable, we can just reassign over add, so that whenever it is called it will have the print behavior imbued into it through announce.

```
>>> add = announce(add)
>>> add(1, 2)
Calling add (1, 2) {}
Got 3
3
```

This last example is all the @ decorator syntax is short form for. Using @announce is the same as calling it with our function and reassigning over the function. In the following code, we decorate the divide function with announce by using the decorator syntax above the divide declaration:

```
>>> @announce
... def divide(a, b):
...     return a / b
>>> divide(10, 2)
Calling divide (10, 2) {}
Got 5
5
```

What is seen by outsiders and newcomers as a bizarre syntax or obscure feature proves itself to be elegant, straightforward, and surprisingly useful. Decorators give us a way of *inverting the subroutine* and factoring out setup and teardown code into something reusable.

Let's look at an example of where we can use decorators in Maya.

Wrapping an exporter with a decorator

More than once in my career I've had to use an exporter or other middleware that
operates on the current selection instead of a collection of objects. This is a pet peeve
of mine but alas, the practice abounds among plugin writers, and occasionally inside
of Maya itself.

We can create a `preserve_selection` decorator that will store the selection, call the
function being decorated, and then restore the selection.

```
def preserve_selection(func):
    def inner(*args, **kwargs): #(1)
        sel = list(pmc.selected()) #(2)
        result = func(*args, **kwargs) #(3)
        pmc.select(sel, replace=True) #(4)
        return result #(5)
    return inner #(6)
```

The code works as follows:

1. Inside of our decorator, define a closure named `inner` that takes any
    positional and keyword arguments.
2. Store the current selection.
3. Invoke the passed function `func` and store the result. Invoking this
    function may change the current selection.
4. Restore the original selection.
5. Return the value the passed function returned.
6. Return the closure, which will replace the decorated function.

We can use our decorator as follows. The `superExporter` function is a pretend
exporter that will export selected objects. The `export_char_meshes` function must
change the selection before it calls `superExporter`. It uses the `preserve_selection`
decorator to make sure the selection is restored after export.

```
@preserve_selection
def export_char_meshes(path):
    objs = [o for o in pmc.ls(type='mesh')
            if '_char_' in o.name()]
    pmc.select(objs)
    pmc.superExporter(path)
```

The decorator works well here because the fact that `export_char_meshes` changes
the selection is an **implementation detail** of the function. Callers should not expect
that an export function would change the selection. You can hide this behavior with
the `preserve_selection` decorator, so selection preservation happens every time
`export_char_meshes` is called.

But what if we want to factor out setup and teardown code like selection preservation, but don't want it to be associated with a function? What if we want to be able to use it at arbitrary points in our code? To do this we can use a **context manager**.

Introducing context managers

Context managers are explained in detail in **PEP 343: The "with" statement** (`http://www.python.org/dev/peps/pep-0343/`). You shouldn't bother reading it unless you really care about the intricacies of Python itself. In simple terms, it adds the `with` keyword to Python, so statements like the following are possible:

```
>>> with open('myfile.txt') as f:
...     text = f.read()
```

These two lines open a file for reading, and assign the contents of the file to the `text` variable. It uses the `open` function as a context manager. It is almost equivalent to these three lines:

```
>>> f = open('myfile.txt')
>>> text = f.read()
>>> f.close()
```

This naive code harbors a potential problem. If calling `f.read()` raises an exception, the file's `close` method is never called. The file may be opened and locked by Python until the process dies. Ideally, we'd want to make sure the file is closed if an error happens. We can use the `with` statement, like we did in the first example, to make sure the file gets closed when we're done with it.

> Generally, the `close` method will be called when f is **garbage collected** (its memory is freed), which happens some point after f cannot be used (falls out of scope). In **CPython** (the standard implementation of Python and what Maya uses), the issue of an open file hanging around is not a problem, because it uses **reference counting** for garbage collection and f will be freed immediately. In other Python implementations (for example, **IronPython**, which is used by **Autodesk 3ds Max**), a **generational garbage collector** may be used which makes no guarantees about when f would be freed. It would occur at the next collection, which can occur whenever.
>
> This is highly technical stuff and you can avoid having to deal with it if you just stick to using best practices.

Using `with` and the `open` context manager expands to something like the following. Note that any exception that occurs will still be bubbled up after the file is closed.

```
# open can fail,
# so make sure the variable is referenced
>>> f = None
>>> try:
...     f = open('myfile.txt')
...     text = f.read() # only happens if open succeeds
... finally:
...     if f: # If open failed, f is still None
...         f.close()
```

An object is considered a context manager and can be used by the `with` statement if it has the following two methods:

```
def __enter__(self):
    ...

def __exit__(self, exc_type, exc_value, exc_tb):
    ...
```

The `__enter__` method should return what is assigned from the `with`. For example, the `open` context manager returns the file object from its `__enter__` method, which we assigned to the variable `f`. The `__exit__` method takes the expanded `exc_info` tuple. We will look at these two methods in more detail throughout this section.

To create context managers, we'll need to use custom classes. If you're not familiar with **object oriented programming,** don't worry. This is very lightweight stuff and odds are if you have gotten this far in the book you can follow along. If you get lost, we discuss custom Python classes in *Chapter 7, Taming the Maya API.*

The pattern to safely open a file that was demonstrated earlier can be implemented with the following class (and this is basically how `open` as a context manager can be thought of):

```
>>> class safeopen(object):
...     def __init__(self, *args, **kwargs):
...         self.args = args
...         self.kwargs = kwargs
...         self.f = None
...     def __enter__(self):
...         self.f = open(*self.args, **self.kwargs)
...         return self.f
...     def __exit__(self, *exc_info):
...         if self.f:
...             self.f.close()
```

We can use this new type just like the open builtin.

```
>>> with safeopen('myfile.txt') as f:
...     text = f.read()
```

Note that we return the opened file object from the __enter__ method. This allows it to be assigned as the target of the with statement. Let's build a context manager that will more precisely demonstrate when all of these methods are called and how they behave.

```
>>> class demo(object):
...     def __init__(self):
...         print 'init' #(1)
...     def __enter__(self):
...         print 'entered' #(2)
...         return 'hello!' #(3)
...     def __exit__(self, *exc_info):
...         print 'exited. Exc_info:', exc_info #(4)
```

Let's look at this code in detail. We will see an example usage next.

1. When an instance of demo is created, the string 'init' is printed.

2. When the context manager is entered, the string 'entered' is printed.

3. The string 'hello!' is returned from __enter__.

4. When the context manager is exited, we print 'exited' and the exception information.

When we use the demo context manager, we see the following printed:

```
>>> with demo() as d:
...     print 'd is', d
init
entered
d is hello!
exited. Exc_info: (None, None, None)
```

If we raise an error while under the context manager, we see different feedback:

```
>>> with demo() as d:
...     raise RuntimeError('hi')
init
entered
exited. Exc_info: (<type 'exceptions.RuntimeError'>,
RuntimeError('hi',), <traceback object at 0x0...)
Traceback (most recent call last):
RuntimeError: hi
```

The arguments to __exit__ are all None if there was no exception under the context manager, as in the first example. If there was an exception, the arguments will be filled in appropriately, as in the second example.

It is relatively rare to handle exceptions inside of the __exit__ method. There are other details to its behavior, such as special return values, that will not be covered. Just think about it as you would a finally block.

We'll now use context managers to implement two different ways to handle undo. The first will wrap a series of commands in an undo block via the undo_chunk context manager. After that, we will look at the __exit__ method in more detail and create an undo_on_error context manager.

There is also a contextlib module that has a contextmanager decorator that can turn a function into a context manager. This form ends up being much more convenient than the explicit __enter__ and __exit__ methods on a custom class. However it is also more magical so I've chosen not to present it here. If you find yourself writing a significant number of context managers, you should learn how to use it. It can really streamline your code, especially for simple cases.

Writing the undo_chunk context manager

As we saw in *Chapter 3*, *Dealing with Errors*, the undoInfo command is a perfect use case for a context manager. It has setup and teardown code, and it must be called correctly or undo queue mayhem may ensue. Not every good use case has so many similarities with Python's open function, but when something does, it is usually a good candidate to be wrapped with a context manager.

Go ahead and create a mayautils.py file in your development root. In our case, we're creating C:\mayapybook\pylib\mayautils.py. Open it up in your IDE and add the following code to create a context manager that will open an undo chunk when entered, and close it on exit.

```python
import pymel.core as pmc

class undo_chunk(object):
    def __enter__(self):
        pmc.undoInfo(openChunk=True)
    def __exit__(self, *_):
        pmc.undoInfo(closeChunk=True)
```

We can then use it in our code wherever we need to open and close an undo chunk. In the following code, note that both joints are removed when we call the undo function.

```
>>> with mayautils.undo_chunk():
...     pmc.joint(), pmc.joint()
(nt.Joint(u'joint1'), nt.Joint(u'joint2'))
>>> pmc.ls(type='joint')
[nt.Joint(u'joint1'), nt.Joint(u'joint2')]
>>> pmc.undo()
>>> pmc.ls(type='joint')
[]
```

That's all there is to it! You now have a way to wrap a block of code into a single undo, and ensure chunks will be opened and closed properly.

Writing the undo_on_error context manager

Going back to the usage of undo as an error handling mechanism from last chapter, we can actually extract a useful context manager from the code we wrote. Let's review the original code and behavior.

```
>>> pmc.undoInfo(openChunk=True)
>>> try:
...     for f in pmc.ls(type='file'):
...         f.ftn.set(f.ftn.get().lower())
...     pmc.undoInfo(closeChunk=True)
... except:
...     pmc.undoInfo(closeChunk=True)
...     pmc.undo()
...     raise
Traceback (most recent call last):
RuntimeError: setAttr: The attribute 'file2.fileTextureName' is locked
or connected and cannot be modified.
>>> [f.ftn.get() for f in pmc.ls(type='file')]
[u'FTN0', u'FTN1', u'FTN2']
```

This code is creating and closing an undo chunk, and calling undo in the case of an error. It is a way to *roll back* a failed operation. We can extract this behavior into a new context manager in mayautils.py:

```
class undo_on_error(object):
    def __enter__(self):
        pmc.undoInfo(openChunk=True)
```

```
def __exit__(self, exc_type, exc_val, exc_tb):
    pmc.undoInfo(closeChunk=True)
    if exc_val is not None:
        pmc.undo()
```

In the `__exit__` method, we check if `exc_val` is `None` as a way of determining if an error occurred. Recall that it will be `None` if no error occurred, and set to the exception instance if an error did occur. We can hook this context manager up to the original code and see how it is simplified but keeps the rollback behavior.

```
>>> with mayautils.undo_on_error():
...     for f in pmc.ls(type='file'):
...         f.ftn.set(f.ftn.get().lower())
Traceback (most recent call last):
RuntimeError: setAttr: The attribute 'file2.fileTextureName' is locked
or connected and cannot be modified.
>>> [f.ftn.get() for f in pmc.ls(type='file')]
[u'FTN0', u'FTN1', u'FTN2']
```

Contrasting decorators and context managers

The difference between context managers and decorators is that context managers associate the setup and teardown with the **caller**; decorators associate it with the **callee**. For example, consider the difference between using `undo_chunk` as a context manager:

```
def makearm(prefix, xaxis=1):
    ...
with undo_chunk():
    leftarm = makearm('left', 1)
```

Compared to using it as a decorator:

```
@undo_chunk
def makearm(prefix, xaxis=1):
    ...
leftarm = makearm('left', 1)
```

The `makearm` function definition is the callee, and the invocation of `makearm('left', 1)` is the caller. If you want the setup and teardown to happen *every time* something is called, you should prefer to use a *decorator*. If you want the caller to control the setup and teardown (as we would expect for undo), use a *context manager*.

When to choose a decorator and when to choose a context manager is not always clear cut and often comes down to: *how can this functionality be used most conveniently?* In the case of undo_chunk, a context manager seems to make the most sense. It is usually up to the caller to decide whether something is a single undo block.

In the end, though, it comes down to whatever is more convenient and will result in better code. Actual programming is always blurry and full of compromises, much more than examples in a book can be. Use your judgment.

There may also be reasons to have the same functionality as both a context manager and decorator. We will only use one or the other in this book, but various third-party libraries and frameworks (such as mock and django) have objects that can be used as either. The following code illustrates how the mock.patch function can be used as a context manager or decorator.

```
>>> import mock, sys
>>> with mock.patch('sys.executable'):
...     print sys.executable
<MagicMock name='executable' id='...'>
>>> @mock.patch('sys.executable', mock.MagicMock())
... def foo():
...     print sys.executable
>>> foo()
<MagicMock id='...'>
```

Context managers for changing scene state

One frustrating aspect of Maya's design, from a coding perspective at least, is the single global scene and application state. To ensure state is changed and restored effectively, we can use context managers. There are a few common or interesting areas where we may want to apply them.

You can put all of the context managers we create in the following sections into mayautils.py. For the most part, their usage follows the same patterns we've already seen, so I've chosen not to clutter the chapter with demonstrations. The code files with this book include tests you can run to see them in action.

Building the set_file_prompt context manager

One often overlooked flag on the bloated `maya.cmds.file` command is the `prompt` keyword. Using `False` disables most file prompts. However, this flag is not a customization flag that is used when the `file` command is invoked. It is a stateful flag that must be set separately from other calls to `file`. To safely call `file` with prompting on or off requires four lines: store the existing `prompt` value, turn `prompt` on or off, use the `file` command, and restore the original `prompt` value. We should combine these into a single context manager.

```
class set_file_prompt(object):
    def __init__(self, state):
        self.state = state
        self.oldstate = None
    def __enter__(self):
        self.oldstate = cmds.file(q=True, prompt=True)
        cmds.file(prompt=self.state)
    def __exit__(self, *_):
        if self.oldstate is not None:
            cmds.file(prompt=self.oldstate)
```

It's usually a good idea to leave `prompt` enabled in a Maya GUI session. For example, we usually want a user to know if there is an error exporting a file. Use a context manager to ensure `prompt` is set back to its old value if you end up needing to temporarily suppress prompts in your scripts.

There are two other important things to note that will show up in other context managers in this chapter.

First, we set `self.oldstate = None` in the object's __init__ method, and then check if it is `None` inside of the __exit__ method. This is because it is possible that the setting of `oldstate` inside of the __enter__ method can fail for some exceptional reason. We only want to restore `oldstate` if we were able to query it successfully inside of __enter__. We will use this pattern for Boolean values repeatedly.

Second, we do not bother listing the arguments to __exit__. We use `*_` as a convention that says *we are ignoring the exception information*. You can certainly have the three `exc_info` arguments every time, but I find it cleaner to just use `*_` when I am ignoring them in __exit__.

Building the at_time context manager

There can be only one current time in Maya. And sometimes, a command must affect a particular time and not the current time. Use the following context manager to temporarily change the current time.

```
class at_time(object):
    def __init__(self, t):
        self.t = t
        self.oldt = None
    def __enter__(self):
        self.oldt = pmc.getCurrentTime()
        pmc.setCurrentTime(self.t)
    def __exit__(self, *_):
        if self.oldt is not None:
            pmc.setCurrentTime(self.oldt)
```

While Maya's built-in commands are usually flexible enough to allow the caller to specify the time, sometimes a third-party script or plugin is not. This sort of limitation is unfortunately common. Using a context manager will allow you to wrap a bad interface into something more *Pythonic*.

Building the with_unit context manager

Similar to time, there can be only one current unit in Maya for each type of unit: linear, angular, and time. We can create a context manager to preserve and restore all of them while we temporarily change one of the units.

```
class with_unit(object):
    def __init__(self, *args, **kwargs):
        self.args = args
        self.kwargs = kwargs
        self.oldlin, self.oldang, self.oldtim = None, None, None
    def __enter__(self):
        self.oldlin = pmc.currentUnit(q=True, linear=True)
        self.oldang = pmc.currentUnit(q=True, angle=True)
        self.oldtim = pmc.currentUnit(q=True, time=True)
        pmc.currentUnit(*self.args, **self.kwargs)
    def __exit__(self, *_):
        if self.oldlin is not None:
            pmc.currentUnit(linear=self.oldlin)
        if self.oldang is not None:
            pmc.currentUnit(angle=self.oldang)
        if self.oldtim is not None:
            pmc.currentUnit(time=self.oldtim)
```

The same rationale and design for `at_time` also applies to `with_unit`. The implementation is slightly more complex because we store and reset every unit.

Building the set_renderlayer_active context manager

The following context manager will temporarily set a given render layer active.

```
class render_layer_active(object):
    def __init__(self, renderlayer):
        self.renderlayer = renderlayer
        self.orig_layer = None
    def __enter__(self):
        self.orig_layer = pmc.nodetypes.RenderLayer.currentLayer()
        self.renderlayer.setCurrent()
    def __exit__(self, *_):
        if self.orig_layer is not None:
            self.orig_layer.setCurrent()
```

We should note both how obvious this pattern should seem by now, and more importantly, the benefits of PyMEL. We do not have to worry about what the command is for setting a render layer active. We can just use the `setCurrent` method on the PyMEL `RenderLayer` instance.

Building the set_namespace_active context manager

Use the following context manager to make a namespace active for a block of code. It will ensure that the previously active namespace is restored when the code finishes, even in the case of error.

```
class set_namespace_active(object):
    def __init__(self, ns):
        if ns == '':
            # This would be too ambiguous, so prohibit it
            raise ValueError('argument cannot be an empty string')
        self.ns = ns
        self.oldns = None
    def __enter__(self):
        self.oldns = pmc.namespaceInfo(currentNamespace=True)
        pmc.namespace(setNamespace=self.ns)
```

```
def __exit__(self, *_):
    if self.oldns is not None:
        oldns = ':' + self.oldns.lstrip(':')
        pmc.namespace(setNamespace=oldns)
```

Namespaces have traditionally been a nasty area of Maya programming so there are a few things to note.

First, while we've made the decision to use PyMEL objects throughout this book, PyMEL generally uses Unicode strings for namespaces, even though it has a `Namespace` type. So `pmc.namespace(set=ns)` works with a string or `Namespace` instance, and `PyNode.namespace()` (a method on all `PyNode` instances) returns a Unicode string instead of a `Namespace` instance. I'm not sure of the reason for the choice.

 Refer to *Appendix, Python Best Practices*, for a brief introduction to Unicode strings.

Second, and for an equally confounding reason, the root namespace (`':'`) cannot be represented as a PyMEL `Namespace` instance. It is easier to make a consistent exception here and use strings for namespaces than it is to try to use PyMEL `Namespace` objects.

Third, `PyNode.namespace()` will actually return an empty string if the `PyNode` is in the root namespace. This is bizarre. An empty string should not be a valid namespace (perhaps it could be said to represent the *current* namespace, sort of like the current working directory on the OS, but that design isn't presented consistently). So when we create our context manager, we check explicitly for the very ambiguous empty string and do not allow it. We could also assume an empty string is the root namespace (so the same as `':'`), but I feel it is better to be explicit.

It is worth commenting that this ambiguity about what a string means is precisely the type of thing that using PyMEL objects instead of strings removes. Using PyMEL for namespaces would also remove the concept of relative and absolute namespace strings. A namespace simply is and can be interpreted and used much more easily. You would not pass relative or absolute namespaces. You would just pass a namespace. In short: prefer PyMEL, except when it's so strange that even PyMEL doesn't use PyMEL.

And finally, we've made the decision here to deal with absolute namespaces only. Inside of the `__exit__` method, we trim off any leading colons and re-root the original namespace. There may be some issues with this implementation depending on your use case. This code works for absolute namespaces, including the root namespace. If you need to deal with relative namespaces, you may need a different implementation. Your mileage may vary.

Improving on future versions of Maya

We've looked at context managers for working with various gnarly places in the Maya commands system. It is likely there are others. In future versions of Maya there will undoubtedly be new problem areas. Occasionally, due to Autodesk or PyMEL developers, problem areas will be fixed. The same patterns we've applied here will continue to apply everywhere we find an imperative, non-Pythonic MEL command system wrapped with Python.

And even when you're programming Python outside of Maya, you can use these lessons to wrap any non-Pythonic system behind something more enjoyable to use.

Creating the denormalized_skin context manager

In this and proceeding sections, we'll build a context manager that will temporarily denormalize a skin cluster.

Most skin clusters are normalized and support a limited number of influences. A skin is normalized when the sum of all influence weights equals 1.0 for each vertex. This ensures the skin deforms in a predictable way. Limiting the number of vertex influences is generally useful when doing things like painting skin weights. It can also be a technical constraint (for example in the case of many video games), or a useful way to simplify the skinning process (you don't need to worry about culling low influences repeatedly).

Even though normalized skin and limited influences are useful for interactive work, they can be a pain for scripting. Sometimes we want to set the values of influences explicitly, and normalize and cull influences at the end. We will build a context manager to facilitate this.

The lessons here can be applied to wherever you have a context manager or decorator that changes the state of one or several Maya nodes.

Safely swapping vertex influences

Let's start by building a simple way to turn normalization and maximum influences off. The code follows the now-familiar pattern of save state, change state, reapply changed state. Let's put this code into a new `skinutils.py` file in the development root.

```
class denormalized_skin(object):
    """Turns off skin cluster normalization and maintaining
```

```
            max influrnces."""
        def __init__(self, skinCl):
            self.skinCl = skinCl
            self.maxInfl, self.norm = None, None
        def __enter__(self):
            self.maxInfl = self.skinCl.maintainMaxInfluences.get()
            self.norm = self.skinCl.setNormalizeWeights(q=True)
            self.skinCl.maintainMaxInfluences.set(False)
            self.skinCl.setNormalizeWeights(0)
        def __exit__(self, *_):
            if self.maxInfl is not None:
                self.skinCl.maintainMaxInfluences.set(self.maxInfl)
            if self.norm is not None:
                self.skinCl.setNormalizeWeights(self.norm)
```

An example use would be retargeting vertex weights from one influence to another, like in the case of mirroring skinning between left and right sides of a character. It is useful to denormalize the skin cluster so a single influence can be swapped without affecting the other influences. The following code will swap two influences on a given vertex using the denormalized_skin context manager.

```
    def swap_influence(skinCl, vert, inflA, inflB):
        """For a given vertex,
        swaps the weight between two influences."""
        valA = pmc.skinPercent(skinCl, vert, q=True, t=inflA)
        valB = pmc.skinPercent(skinCl, vert, q=True, t=inflB)
        with denormalized_skin(skinCl):
            pmc.skinPercent(skinCl, vert, tv=[inflA, valB])
            pmc.skinPercent(skinCl, vert, tv=[inflB, valA])
```

If we do not denormalize before swapping, we could have subtle bugs. In between the last two skinPercent calls, the weight of other influences can change. This can wreak havoc with maintaining max influences, rounding errors, and rigid weights (a weight of 1.0 to a single influence). So we denormalize before swapping, and renormalize when swapping is complete, to make sure we don't run into issues.

See this chapter's accompanying code for examples. You would use it as follows:

```
    >>> swap_influence(
    ...     skinCluster,
    ...     plane.vtx[0],
    ...     jointleft,
    ...     jointright)
```

Addressing performance concerns

Even though the preceding code works, it will be very slow when used in production. As written, if we wanted to swap 1000 vertices, we would need to make 6000 calls to setNormalizeWeights and maintainMaxInfluences, instead of just the six we'd ideally use. We have two options:

1. Move the context manager out of the function and into the caller. The function docstring should mention that it requires the skin cluster to be denormalized via denormalized_skin. This is a valid approach, especially for internal code, where you can better control how things are called. It isn't ideal though, since it requires the caller to do extra work.

2. Skip the denormalization if a skin cluster is already denormalized. This is a better options since the optimization is transparent to the caller.

Let's go with the second approach. We can implement it by adding a cache inside the denormalized_skin context manager.

```
_denormalized_skins = set() #(1)
class denormalized_skin(object):
    """Turns off skin cluster normalization and maintaining
    max influrnces."""
    def __init__(self, skinCl):
        self.skinCl = skinCl
        self.maxInfl, self.norm = None, None
    def __enter__(self):
        if self.skinCl in _denormalized_skins: #(2)
            return
        _denormalized_skins.add(self.skinCl) #(3)
        self.maxInfl = self.skinCl.maintainMaxInfluences.get()
        self.norm = self.skinCl.setNormalizeWeights(q=True)
        self.skinCl.maintainMaxInfluences.set(False)
        self.skinCl.setNormalizeWeights(0)
    def __exit__(self, *_):
        _denormalized_skins.discard(self.skinCl) #(4)
        if self.maxInfl is not None: #(5)
            self.skinCl.maintainMaxInfluences.set(self.maxInfl)
        if self.norm is not None:
            self.skinCl.setNormalizeWeights(self.norm)
```

Let's walk through the code and analyze the changes:

1. The `_denormalized_skins` collection acts as our cache to keep track of what skin clusters are currently denormalized. A `set` instance in Python stores unique values, like the keys of a dictionary. We can simply test if something is in a set, just like we can check if a key exists in a dictionary. It is a very fast operation. Prefer to use a `set` instance to a `list` instance when storing unique values and the order of those values does not matter.

2. If the skin cluster is in our cache, it means it is already denormalized, and we can just return and not bother storing the existing normalization and max influence state. The context manager becomes a **non-operation** (in programmer parlance that's often called a **no-op** or **noop**).

3. We add the skin cluster to the cache and denormalize it.

4. When the context manager exits, we remove the skin cluster from our cache using the `_denormalized_skins.discard` method. If the cluster has already been removed, `discard` is a no-op.

5. Finally, we check if we need to turn normalization and max influences back to their original values. If the context manager was a no-op, both of the original values will be None and the functions will not be called.

Now our `swap_influences` function can have correct behavior when called in isolation, but not have performance problems when called thousands of times. We get the best of both worlds.

This is generally a good thing. And if you find that using the cached context manager is still not fast enough for your uses, you can always create a `swap_influences_fast` function with additional caveats in the docstring, as we have in the following example. Callers that need more speed can use the simpler, faster function.

```python
def swap_influence(skinCl, vert, inflA, inflB):
    """For a given vertex,
    swaps the weight between two influences."""
    with denormalized_skin(skinCl):
        swap_influence_fast(skinCl, vert, inflA, inflB)


def swap_influence_fast(skinCl, vert, inflA, inflB):
    """For a given vertex,
```

```
swaps the weight between two influences.
`skinCl` should be denormalized before calling this function.
See `denormalized_skin`.
"""
valA = pmc.skinPercent(skinCl, vert, q=True, t=inflA)
valB = pmc.skinPercent(skinCl, vert, q=True, t=inflB)
pmc.skinPercent(skinCl, vert, tv=[inflA, valB])
pmc.skinPercent(skinCl, vert, tv=[inflB, valA])
```

Creating a decorator to record metrics

A popular thing to do in professional studios is to record how long something takes
and how often it happens. This sort of profiling can be useful for tracking things
like program startup time, how long it takes to export meshes, or who is using
that deprecated tool that should have been killed a long time ago. We will build a
decorator to time how long a function takes to execute.

Generally this sort of recording has the following pattern:

1. Get a unique key for a callable item.

2. Record the time it takes to invoke the callable item.

3. Report the time taken to some other system, identifying the callable through
   the unique key.

This is perfect for a decorator. We use a decorator instead of a context manager
because the fact that a function is profiled is an aspect of the function itself, and not
something left up to the caller.

The use of the finished decorator will look something like the following:

```
@profiling.record_duration
def export_scene():
    # do stuff
```

We'll tackle each of the three steps—creating a key, recording time, and reporting
results—separately.

Getting a unique key

Begin by creating a file under your development root named `profiling.py`. First we'll implement the `_getkey` function, which will return the unique key for our callable. You may recall that when we implemented `minspect._py_to_helpstr` back in *Chapter 1, Introspecting Maya, Python, and PyMEL*, we wrote some code to check if an object was a method or function. The `_getkey` function will return a unique key for methods and functions, and raise a `TypeError` for any other type of argument.

```python
import types


def _getkey(func):
    if isinstance(func, types.FunctionType):
        return '%s.%s' % (func.__module__, func.__name__)
    if isinstance(func, types.MethodType):
        return '%s.%s.%s' % (func.__module__,
                             func.im_class.__name__,
                             func.__name__)
    raise TypeError('%s must be a function or method' % func)
```

We can now use this unique key to identify every function throughout our entire codebase.

Recording duration

Next we will create our `record_duration` decorator function. Start by stubbing out a simple decorator that simply passes everything through.

```python
def record_duration(func):
    def inner(*args, **kwargs):
        return func(*args, **kwargs)
    return inner
```

Next, we can hook up the recording of start and end time. Before and after we invoke `func` we store the result of `time.clock()`. Use `time.clock` when profiling code. The `time.clock` function is the preferred way to record how long something takes in Python. After the function runs, print out how long it took. In the next section, we will create a way to report the duration.

```python
import time


def record_duration(func):
    key = _getkey(func)
    def inner(*args, **kwargs):
```

```
        starttime = time.clock()
        result = func(*args, **kwargs)
        endtime = time.clock()
        duration = endtime - starttime
        print '%s took %ss' % (key, duration)
        return result
    return inner
```

Let's see a simple example using the `record_duration` decorator as it currently is:

```
>>> @record_duration
... def expensive_func():
...     time.sleep(.1)
...     return 'whew'
>>> result = expensive_func()
__main__.expensive_func took 0.0991245s
>>> result
'whew'
```

Reporting duration

Now comes the only tricky part: recording the duration. I've used databases, middleware, web services, and various other mechanisms. We are going to go very low-tech and simply write to a file in the current directory. In production environments, you would want something more robust.

To report our data, we'll just open a file, and append a line to the end of it with the key (function or method name) and current time. Let's create our reporting function.

```
def _report_duration(key, duration):
    with open('durations.txt', 'a') as f:
        f.write('%s: %s\n' % (key, duration))
```

The second argument to the `open` function, `'a'`, opens the file in append mode so we keep adding to it. Make sure the call to `write` includes a newline character (\n) or all metrics will end up on the same line!

We can easily hook up the `_report_duration` function in the `record_duration` function.

```
def record_duration(func):
    key = _getkey(func)
    def inner(*args, **kwargs):
        starttime = time.clock()
```

```
        result = func(*args, **kwargs)
        endtime = time.clock()
        duration = endtime - starttime
        _report_duration(key, duration)
        return result
    return inner
```

Handling errors

It would be dangerous to not think about errors here. The `record_duration` decorator is extra code that is associated with a function, so we need to handle errors intelligently. Imagine if the file recording metrics weren't writable: a user's program would be broken, or at least significantly slower, because metrics couldn't be saved. Clearly this is undesirable.

Writing the report file can fail for any number of reasons. The most common will be if the file is locked for writing by another process that is recording metrics at the same time. In this case, we will just print that we have skipped the reporting. This is non-critical data so dropping a few pieces is not a big deal.

If the writing fails for any other reason, we will just disable the recording of metrics entirely and print out the entire error. It could slow down a program considerably if we try and fail to record metrics for every call. We'll make a few important changes to our code.

```
import errno #(1)
import traceback #(2)


_reporting_enabled = True #(3)


def _report_duration(key, duration):
    global _reporting_enabled
    if not _reporting_enabled: #(4)
        return
    try:
        with open('durations.txt', 'a') as f:
            f.write('%s: %s\n' % (key, duration))
    except OSError as ex: #(5)
        if ex.errno == errno.EACCES: #(6)
            print 'durations.txt in use, cannot record.'
```

```
    else:
        _reporting_enabled = False #(7)
        traceback.print_exc()
        print 'Disabling metrics recording.'
```

This code introduces a number of new things so let's go through it point by point.

1. Import the `errno` module. This module contains many common system error codes mapped to Python constants. We will use it to figure out what sort of error we hit when writing to the file.

2. Import the `traceback` module. This module is used for printing exception tracebacks, or all the information about an error.

3. Store whether reporting is enabled in a variable on the module. We will turn this off when we hit an unexpected error.

4. Before we report anything, we check to make sure reporting is still enabled. If not, we return early. Note the use of Python's `global` keyword to indicate that when we assign `_reporting_enabled` later on, we want to set the variable on the module, not create a new variable in the function's scope.

5. We catch any `OSError` that occurs while writing our file. On Windows machines, this will be a `WindowsError`, which is a subclass of `OSError`.

6. If the error's errno (error number) equals `errno.EACCES` (an access error, perhaps due to a locked file), we print a warning and do nothing else.

7. If the error is due to anything else, we disable reporting by setting `_reporting_enabled` to `False`. This ensures we won't keep hitting this error, since future reporting will be a no-op. We also print the traceback via `traceback.print_exc`, and then print that we are turning off metrics recording.

While appending metrics to a text file may be too rudimentary to be of much use in a studio environment, hopefully this code serves as a useful blueprint for more advanced versions. For example, if you were using HTTP to post metrics to a web service, you could use this same pattern of turning the reporting off in the case of an error.

I hope this simple project shows you how decorators can be used in interesting ways, and how flexible and powerful Python can be. If this sort of project inspires you, keep going with it! Sometimes the abilities and expressiveness of a language can be enough to provoke ideas that less exciting languages would not.

Advanced decorator topics

Let's go over a few pieces of advice concerning decorators that did not fit into earlier sections.

Defining decorators with arguments

Decorators with arguments are an advanced topic. They can be implemented as types with a __call__ method, or as a triple-nested function. For example, the following two pieces of code behave the same.

```python
def deco_using_func(key):
    def _deco(func):
        def inner(*args, **kwargs):
            print 'Hello from', key
            return func(*args, **kwargs)
        return inner
    return _deco


class deco_using_cls(object):
    def __init__(self, key):
        self.key = key
    def __call__(self, func):
        def inner(*args, **kwargs):
            print 'Hello from', self.key
            return func(*args, **kwargs)
        return inner
```

Either one would be hooked up as follows. Note that the decorator is called with arguments.

```python
>>> @deco_using_func('func deco')
... def decorated_func1():
...     return
>>> decorated_func1()
Hello from func deco
>>> @deco_using_cls('class deco')
... def decorated_func2():
...     return
>>> decorated_func2()
Hello from class deco
```

If you don't understand the code, that's fine. It can be difficult enough to understand decorators, and decorators with arguments can seem exponentially more complex. When you're getting started with decorators, avoid creating them with arguments until you are comfortable. But once you are, there is plenty of power to unleash.

Decorating PyMEL attributes and methods

Something very relevant to Maya is decorating PyMEL. It is also quite difficult, since so many PyMEL calls are dynamically dispatched. You will need to use the reassignment pattern of decoration, decorating and replacing methods, as in the following example:

```
DagNode.setTranslation = announce(DagNode.setTranslation)
```

To make things extra difficult, decorating methods is more complex than decorating functions. You'll need to read up on it if you run into trouble. My suggestion is to avoid decorating PyMEL entirely.

Stacking decorators

Decorators can be stacked. Here is some demonstration code. Note how `func` is decorated by both the `deco1` and `deco2` decorator functions.

```
>>> def deco1(func):
...     def inner():
...         print 'deco1'
...         return func()
...     return inner
>>> def deco2(func):
...     def inner():
...         print 'deco2'
...         return func()
...     return inner
>>> @deco1
... @deco2
... def func():
...     print 'inside func'
>>> func()
deco1
deco2
inside func
```

The decorator stack is applied from the bottom up and executed from the top down. The non-decorator version of the preceding code should make this behavior more clear. The decorators are applied right-to-left, and called left-to-right. The function returned by deco2 is passed to deco1, and the function returned by deco1 is what we call when func2() is invoked.

```
>>> def func2():
...     print 'inside func2'
>>> func2 = deco1(deco2(func2))
>>> func2()
deco1
deco2
inside func2
```

Stacking decorators is not commonly used, but it is useful to know it exists in case you see it or have a use case for it.

Using Python's decorator library

Because decorators are so convenient and composable, it's easy to reuse them. The *Python Wiki* has a page full of decorator recipes that you may find useful. The *Python Decorator Library* is located at https://wiki.python.org/moin/PythonDecoratorLibrary. There are also many decorator libraries available on the **Python Package Index**. Check out *Chapter 9, Becoming a Part of the Python Community*, for more information about the Python Package Index.

Doing decorators the right way

Before finishing this chapter, it behooves me to point out that the techniques presented here for creating decorators are perhaps overly simplistic for external code. Decorating a function in the way presented destroys much of the function's metadata, such as its name and argument information. To do decorators the right way, refer to Graham Dumpleton's wrapt library, available from https://pypi.python.org/pypi/wrapt. He also has a wonderful series of blog posts about decorators, which you can find at http://blog.dscpl.com.au/search/label/decorators.

That said, the simple techniques in this chapter are often good enough.

Summary

In this chapter, we saw how Python decorators and context managers invert the subroutine and allow us to factor out common setup and teardown code. We learned how both of these techniques work, and when to apply them. We implemented several context managers that make programming Python in Maya a better experience. We closed by exploring some potential uses for decorators, and advanced topics for future investigation.

Context managers and decorators are two powerful features that will come up again and again throughout this book and as you program Python. It is well worth understanding what they have to offer, and we've only just scratched the surface in this chapter. As convenient as they are for mapping Maya's problems onto Pythonic idioms, they are just as useful when designing systems from scratch. Web frameworks in particular have been able to use decorators for amazing things.

In the next chapter we will change topics and look at creating graphical user interfaces for Maya. We will keep building on what we've learned so far to make the process and code beautiful, simple, and *Pythonic*.

5

Building Graphical User Interfaces for Maya

If you have been a bit confused about building **graphical user interfaces (GUIs)** in Maya, you are not alone. What's the difference between PySide and PyQt? Do you build GUIs by hand or with a WYSIWYG designer application? What about using Maya's UI commands? The GUI landscape in Maya has been rapidly changing for the past few years. Fortunately it seems like it is calming down, and from the turmoil we can establish best (and worst) practices for the future.

In this chapter, we will start by gaining a basic understanding of PySide's concepts, including bindings, widgets, layouts, windows, and signals. We will also learn about PySide's relationship to Qt and PyQt. Then, we will lay down some principles for building GUIs that will allow them to be decoupled from Maya and faster to develop. We will learn how to install PySide and PyQt, and write code that will run with either framework.

After that, we will create a GUI that runs outside of Maya, and see the benefits that developing code this way can bring. Then we will learn how to integrate the GUI with Maya so that they can interact with each other. We will wrap up the chapter by learning how to use PySide with Maya's menu and shelf systems.

Introducing Qt, PyQt, and PySide

Let's start by going over some terminology and history to clear up the confusion surrounding the Maya user interface ecosystem.

There is a C++ framework called **Qt**. While the Qt user interface classes are the most widely known, Qt is actually an entire application framework. For this book, we'll limit ourselves to the user interface classes in the QtGui namespace, with occasional uses of the QtCore namespace which contains some base functionality.

By the way, Qt is officially pronounced *cute*, not *cue-tee*. However, I doubt anyone will call you out for using the latter, and it is how most people pronounce it anyway.

Maya began using Qt in the 2011 version. Before that, it was using a proprietary system for its UI. The change was mostly under the hood, and Maya's scripting interface for working with UI did not change. However, it did allow developers to create Qt extensions that are usable in Maya.

We are able to use Qt from Python by using **bindings** for C++ classes. A binding allows us to call C++ objects from Python. There is a Qt binding called **PyQt** that allows Qt classes to be called from Python. A few years ago, Qt and PyQt were involved in a licensing drama. The gist of it is that Qt itself switched its Open Source license to the less restrictive LGPL, while the company that controls PyQt refused to change its license from GPL.

As an outcome of this controversy, PySide was created as an LGPL alternative to PyQt. When Autodesk announced that Maya 2014 would ship with PySide available, a number of lawyers suddenly had less work and in many development circles there was much rejoicing.

PySide and PyQt are in most ways identical. Where they are different, we will support them both through the qtshim.py file included with this book. See the section *Supporting PySide and PyQt* later in this chapter. When I use the term PySide for the rest of this chapter, I will usually mean your current Qt bindings, whether they are PySide or PyQt.

With that history lesson out of the way, let's go over some key concepts for working with PySide. The information in the following sections apply to both general PySide use and when writing Maya GUIs. We'll use these concepts to build several GUIs later in this chapter.

Introducing Qt widgets

In Qt, a widget is a user interface control. A slider is a widget (QSlider), a textbox is a widget (QTextEdit), and even an empty widget is a widget (QWidget). A complete interface is usually composed of several widgets. Every widget has a parent widget, or None in the case of top-level windows.

Qt uses **type hierarchies** to grow functionality of widgets. For example, a checkbox widget (the QCheckBox class) has basic button functionality because it inherits from the QAbstractButton class. The QAbstractButton class has basic widget functionality because it inherits from the QWidget class. A button (the QPushButton class) is also an QAbstractButton (which is, as just mentioned, a QWidget). This is very similar to the way PyMEL uses type hierarchies, as we saw in *Chapter 1, Introspecting Maya, Python, and PyMEL*. While it is not vital to understand object-oriented programming to begin working with Qt, it will quickly become more important as you build your own GUIs and custom widgets.

Introducing Qt layouts

Every widget has a **layout**, which is an instance of the QLayout class. An interface with three buttons stacked on top of each other would be some sort of container widget that has a QVBoxLayout layout, and the three buttons are part of that layout.

It is important to note that the concept of parent and layout are distinct. Widget A can be part of the layout of Widget B without being a child of Widget B. Many GUI frameworks, including Maya's UI commands, combine the two concepts into one. We'll rarely get a case when a widget's parent is not equal to the owner of the layout it is a part of, but we should keep the distinction in mind. Simply parenting a widget does not add it to the parent's layout; they are two distinct concepts. Getting comfortable with this design is important for working with Qt effectively.

Understanding Qt main windows and sorting

Every Qt GUI application has at least one top-level window. In the case of Maya, that is the Maya window itself. We want our tool windows to sort just like Maya's own windows, such as the Script Editor. They never disappear behind the main window. To do this, we will use the main window as the parent of tool windows. If a tool window has no parent, it will sort as if it is a window from another process with no relation to Maya.

While technically a window can be made from any widget without a parent, one usually uses an instance of QMainWindow, or QDialog for dialogs. The main Maya window itself is a QMainWindow subclass. There is also the QMessageBox class for displaying customizable message boxes. By the end of this chapter, you should have the skills to use the QMessageBox class as a much more powerful alternative to Maya's message box commands like promptDialog and confirmDialog.

Introducing Qt signals

In Qt, a **signal** is an event that can be listened to, and listeners are notified when the event happens. A listener **connects** to a signal with a **callback**. A callback is just a function that is invoked when the signal **emits**. A listener can stop listening by disconnecting. It is very important to become familiar with these terms, as we will use them extensively once we start programming with Qt signals.

This simple concept ends up being incredibly powerful. It allows us to have all Maya code outside of the user interface. The GUI and Maya functionalities become completely self-contained, meaning each can be developed and tested in isolation. We'll see later how this simplifies GUI development.

Establishing rules for crafting a GUI

There are several ways to build GUIs in Maya. In this book, we will take the approach described in this section. While this is not the only approach one can take, I certainly think it is the most productive in both the short and long term. Once you are able to execute on the concepts in this chapter, you will want to use them for all your user interfaces. In my experience, the approach presented here has proved valuable time and time again.

Prefer pure PySide GUIs where possible

Build your GUIs in pure Python, runnable completely outside of Maya. Then from inside of Maya, connect to signals that are emitted from your GUI. Likewise, the GUI can connect through an intermediary to signals that are emitted from Maya. By doing this, your GUIs will be more abstract (they will not contain Maya code) and much faster to develop (you do not need to build them in Maya or run Maya to test them).

There are exceptions to this rule that are covered in the second rule.

Use command-style UI building where necessary

Though Qt's widget library is rich, applications like Maya often have higher-level widgets that are composites of several simpler widgets. Maya menu and shelf systems are examples of this. Consider the options box associated with Maya menu items, which is not part of normal Qt menu items.

Rather than reinvent the wheel, we will use Maya's commands (through PyMEL, of course) to work with Maya's menus and shelves. We can then interact with their underlying Qt objects. The sections *Working with menus* and *Working with Maya shelves* demonstrate this approach.

We can also use commands to get the Qt objects underlying well-known Maya widgets like the Script Editor or Outliner if we want to customize or interact with them.

Avoid the use of .ui files

When Maya first supported Qt GUIs, scripters everywhere rejoiced. They could finally use the **Qt Designer**, which is a **What-You-See-Is-What-You-Get** (**WYSIWYG**) program for building GUIs. You visually build your interface, save its definition into a .ui file, and dynamically load the file in Python to create the GUI at runtime. In a future version of the same universe, however, everyone who needed to work with these auto-generated GUIs was lamenting their fate.

WYSIWYG-created interfaces are generally poorly designed from a technical and aesthetic standpoint. They are difficult to extend and maintain because the auto-generated code is a bloated mess of spaghetti. Objects are poorly named and organized, and filled with useless attributes. In some languages and frameworks, such as **WinForms** and **Windows Presentation Foundation** for the .NET framework, WYSIWYG designers are a valid to way to combat overly verbose syntax, clunky APIs, or slow iteration speed. With Python and Qt, there is absolutely no need. The Qt framework is elegant and Python does not require any substantial boilerplate. With a minimal amount of training, you can build better GUIs cleaner and faster with code than with a WYSIWYG designer.

Feel free to use the Qt Designer for getting a better grip on how Qt works, such as what widgets are available and how different layout values behave. It is also useful to create mockups to show users. But under no circumstances should it be used for production code.

Installing PySide

To run the code in this chapter, you will need PySide or PyQt available in Maya. The instructions below focus on PySide, since it is the framework of choice. If you are using PyQt at this point, you probably know what you're doing and do not need the instructions in this section.

If you are using Maya 2014 or above, you are all set. PySide should already be available.

If you are using Maya 2010 or below, you cannot use Qt.

For all other Maya versions, you can follow the instructions in *Chapter 9, Becoming a Part of the Python Community*. For Maya 2011, 2012, or 2013 on OS X, or Maya 2011 or 2012 on Windows, you can use a binary distribution from `https://pypi.python. org/pypi/PySide`. If you are using Maya 2013 on Windows, you can download compatible binaries from `http://www.robg3d.com/maya-windows-binaries/`.

Supporting PySide and PyQt

For the purposes of this book, there are two differences between PySide and PyQt. We will use the `qtshim.py` file to swap between the two depending on what is available. When the module is imported, it will choose between PySide and PyQt implementations, depending on what is available.

The `qtshim.py` module contains four attributes:

- The `QtCore` and `QtGui` namespaces, pulled from the imported implementation.
- The `Signal` class, which just aliases the `PySide.QtCore.Signal` or `PyQt4. QtCore.pyqtSignal` class.
- The `wrapinstance` function which takes a pointer to a Qt object and returns the Qt object it points to. A pointer here is a long integer that refers to the memory location of the underlying Qt object. There is a significant difference between the implementation of `wrapinstance` between PySide and PyQt due to how their supporting libraries (`shiboken` and `sip`, respectively) work.

I'd suggest using a shim like `qtshim` to allow easy switching between implementations, and also because the provided shim improves on the default `wrapinstance` function interface.

The contents of `qtshim.py` follow. I've removed the comments, and we will not go into any details, since the code uses advanced topics that aren't relevant to this chapter.

```
try:
    from PySide import QtCore, QtGui
    import shiboken
    Signal = QtCore.Signal
```

```
    def _getcls(name):
        result = getattr(QtGui, name, None)
        if result is None:
            result = getattr(QtCore, name, None)
        return result
    def wrapinstance(ptr):
        """Converts a pointer (int or long) into the concrete
        PyQt/PySide object it represents."""
        ptr = long(ptr)
        qobj = shiboken.wrapInstance(ptr, QtCore.QObject)
        metaobj = qobj.metaObject()
        realcls = None
        while realcls is None:
            realcls = _getcls(metaobj.className())
            metaobj = metaobj.superClass()
        return shiboken.wrapInstance(ptr, realcls)
except ImportError:
    from PyQt4 import QtCore, QtGui
    Signal = QtCore.pyqtSignal
    import sip
    def wrapinstance(ptr):
        return sip.wrapinstance(long(ptr), QtCore.QObject)
```

Creating the hierarchy converter GUI

In this section we'll create a PySide user interface for the character creator/hierarchy converter we worked on in *Chapter 2, Writing Composable Code*. The GUI will respond to the user changing selection, and when the user interacts with the GUI, it will update the Maya scene. This project will teach us the fundamental concepts that allow the decoupling of Maya and PySide components. This decoupling allows an ever-more-complex set of interactions while still keeping the code maintainable.

Creating the window

Our GUI will be a Python script like any other. Let's make a file hierarchyconvertergui.py in our development root C:\mayapybook\pylib. Open it up in your IDE and write:

```
from qtshim import QtGui, QtCore, Signal
```

This will import the two main PySide modules into your file, allowing you to use GUI classes (through `QtGui`) and core library classes (through `QtCore`), as well as the `Signal` class. Most of the time you will only use `QtGui` classes, but in this example we'll need a few things off of the `QtCore` module, as well as signals.

The next step is to write the code that creates our actual GUI. Note that there are many ways this can be done. The function-based approach here is only one technique. See *Considering alternative implementations* later in this chapter for other approaches. The following code will create a new Qt window:

```
def create_window():
    win = QtGui.QMainWindow()
    return win
```

Finally, we need to run the `create_window` function and then show the window. These five lines of code are actually quite dense and we'll go over the concepts behind them in the next few sections.

```
if __name__ == '__main__':
    app = QtGui.QApplication([])
    win = create_window()
    win.show()
    app.exec_()
```

Running a Python file as a script

The `if __name__ == '__main__'` line in the preceding code is a Python idiom that means *if this is the script being run*. The code nested under that expression will not execute if the module is imported. It will only execute if the module is run directly, such as from the command line.

To test this out, let's make a file `C:\mayapybook\pylib\scratch.py` that you can delete after this section. Inside, write:

```
print 'Hello, you are in', __name__
if __name__ == '__main__':
    print 'Running main'
print 'Finishing'
```

Use the `mayapy` interpreter to run the file from the command line. Calling `mayapy` with a path to the Python file will run it as a script.

```
> mayapy C:\mayapybook\pylib\scratch.py
```

You should see the following output:

```
Hello, you are in __main__
Running main
Finishing
```

Now, again from the command line, we'll import this module instead of running it. Calling `mayapy` without any arguments will open up an interactive prompt where we can import the file and see what it prints.

```
> mayapy
>>> import scratch
Hello, you are in scratch
Finishing
```

We can see that the __name__ variable is set to the string "__main__" when a file is run as a script, and the name of the file when it is imported.

Introducing the QApplication class

That brings us to the line `app = QtGui.QApplication([])`. What does it mean?

Every program that uses Qt widgets has a single instance of the `QtGui.QApplication` class. In fact this object must be created before any widget is created. So the pattern we see in the `hierarchyconvertergui` main block is:

1. Ensure the application exists.
2. Create the `QMainWindow` instance.
3. Show the window.
4. Call `exec_` on the `QApplication` which will pump the event loop until all windows are closed. The program will then exit. We look at the event loop in the next section.

Understanding the event loop

We usually think of code executing sequentially: there is a start and an end. With interactive programs such as GUIs, however, there must be an event loop (also called a message pump) that polls for input and events. The `exec_()` method we used previously is a loop that just *pumps messages*. The call to `exec_` will block until the event loop is told to not pump any more messages. Even though this call is blocking, Python code still executes in response to events like button clicks.

The exec_ method can be thought of like the following.

```
def exec_():
    while should_keep_going(): #(1)
        message = get_next_message() #(2)
        process_message(message) #(3)
```

Let's go over the preceding pseudocode.

1. Inside exec_ is a while loop. On each cycle, it checks whether it should still be looping. For example, it may stop looping because it received a quit message. Once the loop is broken, the exec_ method returns.

2. The get_next_message function is a blocking call that checks a queue for a message. A message can be something like a button being clicked, a window asking to be redrawn, or any number of things.

3. The message is processed. If there is Python code set up to run when a button is clicked, the process_message function would eventually run that code. In essence, this is what allows the program execution to look blocked in the call to exec_(), but still run code in response to user interaction.

While you can do most of your GUI programming without understanding how the event loop works, I find it's useful to have some basic understanding. This terribly simplified information is applicable to all GUI frameworks, not just Qt.

Running your GUI

Now that this most basic of code is written, we can run our GUI. Don't bother opening up Maya! We're going to use mayapy to run our code instead. A standard Python 2.6 or 2.7 install with PySide would also work. To test our GUI we run mayapy with our Python file path from the command line like so:

```
> mayapy.exe C:\mayapybook\pylib\hierarchyconvertergui.py
```

You should see a window pop up onscreen, but you can't do anything with it yet. When you close it, the Python process should exit.

Congratulations! You've created a GUI purely with PySide.

Designing and building your GUI

Now that the boilerplate is out of the way and you have a general understanding of how things work, we can do the fun (or excruciating, depending on your interests) work of actual GUI design and programming. I always suggest starting with a rough sketch of how the finished product should look. I usually do these with pen and paper, but you can use an image editor, WYSIWYG designer, or GUI mockup tool. Just don't get bogged down by the technology. Simpler is better.

The following is the mockup I created for the hierarchy converter tool.

The basic elements of the finished tool are apparent in the sketch:

- A labeled textbox to enter the prefix for the new joints.

- A button to convert the hierarchy.

- A status bar to report the currently selected items.

We'll start with the textbox since it is the most straightforward and will allow us to introduce several new Qt concepts.

Defining control, container, and window widgets

Before we create our textbox, we need a place to put it. There are three basic categories of widgets in Qt:

- **Controls**, such as textboxes, buttons, spinners, and labels. Basically, controls are the actual interactive widgets. Generally these are the most granular widgets, and they usually do not have children.

- **Containers**, which hold controls or other containers. For example, a scroll area can hold many buttons, as well as another container which itself contains a text field. Importantly, it is usually only containers which need to worry about layout. A container's layout must specify whether its child widgets are laid out top to bottom, left to right, or whatever is appropriate.

- **Windows,** which have many special features, such as menu bars and status bars. They have a single widget, almost always a container, which is called its central widget. Windows do not worry about their layout. They delegate it to their central widget.

Note that these categories are my terms as I'm not aware of any official terminology. I've tried to be precise with vocabulary here because it can otherwise get overwhelming. Keeping a clear distinction between these categories and using widgets as intended will make your GUI code understandable and usable.

In the following code, we create one of each category in order to add our textbox to the window:

```
def create_window():
    window = QtGui.QMainWindow() #(1)
    container = QtGui.QWidget(window)
    textbox = QtGui.QLineEdit(container)

    layout = QtGui.QHBoxLayout(container) #(2)
    container.setLayout(layout)
    layout.addWidget(textbox) #(3)
    window.setCentralWidget(container) #(4)

    return window
```

Let's walk through the preceding code.

1. Create three widgets: a window (the QMainWindow), a container (the QWidget), and a control (the QLineEdit). The parent of the control is the container, the parent of the container is the window, and the window has no parent.
2. Create one layout. It belongs to the container.
3. The textbox is added to the container's layout.
4. Finally, set the container as the window's central widget.

Many of these things could happen in a different order. Some people put the layout code after all widgets are created, as we do in the preceding example, and some interleave it with widget creation. It doesn't really matter. Use the style that seems clearest to you.

If you run `mayapy` with the `hierarchyconvertergui.py` file path, a window similar to the one in the following image will appear. The window will have a textbox that we can type in.

Adding the rest of the widgets

Let's add the rest of our widgets. We follow the same pattern we have already used for the textbox. We also call `window.setWindowTitle` to give our GUI a title, instead of the name of the process (**mayapy** in the preceding figure).

```
def create_window():
    window = QtGui.QMainWindow()
    window.setWindowTitle('Hierarchy Converter')

    container = QtGui.QWidget(window)
    label = QtGui.QLabel('Prefix:', container)
    textbox = QtGui.QLineEdit(container)
    button = QtGui.QPushButton('Convert', container)

    layout = QtGui.QHBoxLayout(container)
    container.setLayout(layout)
    # Add them to the layout, first widget added is left-most
    layout.addWidget(label)
    layout.addWidget(textbox)
    layout.addWidget(button)
    window.setCentralWidget(container)

    return window
```

Run `mayapy` with the path to `hierarchyconvertergui.py` again. The window that appears should look like the following image. It is close to the initial sketch:

Now that our controls are in place, let's add some interactivity into our user interface.

Hooking up the application to be effected by the GUI

We want to make our GUI interactive so that when we press the **Convert** button, the hierarchies of the selected objects in Maya are converted to joints. In traditional GUI programming, you may put the call to the charcreator module directly into the button's click handler. This technique, however, would make the GUI depend on Maya, which we have agreed not to do. It may seem simpler to take a shortcut, but the long term cost of tying your GUI to Maya will quickly outweigh any short-term benefits.

Instead, we will create a signal on our window that will be emitted when **Convert** is pressed. For testing, we can connect a callback that will print some text. Later, when we hook up the GUI in Maya, we will connect the charcreator call that will convert selected hierarchies.

 See the *Introducing Qt signals* section earlier in this chapter if you need a refresher on signals.

We need to create custom classes to work with signals. Because of some deep PySide magic, you cannot just assign a Signal instance to an object. For example, writing window.convertClicked = qtshim.Signal() would not result in a working signal. You must define a subclass of a Qt class. Fortunately, you can get by if you just copy what's provided here until you get more comfortable creating your own types. You can use this same pattern for your own projects.

The highlighting in the following code demonstrates how to use a signal to allow the caller to define what happens when **Convert** is pressed, rather than hard coding the reaction.

```
class ConverterWindow(QtGui.QMainWindow): #(1)
    convertClicked = Signal(str)

def create_window():
    window = ConverterWindow()
    window.setWindowTitle('Hierarchy Converter')

    container = QtGui.QWidget(window)
    label = QtGui.QLabel('Prefix:', container)
    textbox = QtGui.QLineEdit(container)
    button = QtGui.QPushButton('Convert', container)
```

```
    def onclick(): #(2)
        window.convertClicked.emit(textbox.text())
    button.clicked.connect(onclick) #(3)

    layout = QtGui.QHBoxLayout(container)
    container.setLayout(layout)
    layout.addWidget(label)
    layout.addWidget(textbox)
    layout.addWidget(button)
    window.setCentralWidget(container)

    return window

if __name__ == '__main__':
    def onconvert(prefix): #(4)
        print 'Convert clicked! Prefix:', prefix
    app = QtGui.QApplication([])
    win = create_window()
    win.convertClicked.connect(onconvert) #(5)
    win.show()
    app.exec_()
```

Let's go over the changes in more detail. This pattern of using signals is essential to successful PySide GUI programming.

1. Define the `ConverterWindow` class, which is a `QMainWindow` subclass. Give it an attribute named `convertClicked` that is an instance of `qtshim.Signal`. We pass the `str` type into the `Signal` initialization, which does two things. First, it tells Qt that the signal must be emitted with a single argument. Second, it indicates to the programmer that the argument to `emit` should be a string.

2. Create a nested function `onclick` that emits the window's `convertClicked` signal with the contents of the textbox. Recall that the `convertClicked` signal emits a single string argument (see point 1).

3. Connect the **Convert** button's `clicked` signal to the `onclick` callback. When the button is pressed, the `clicked` signal will be emitted, and `onclick` will be invoked.

4. In our testing code, create a nested callback function `onconvert`. The function will print out the contents of the textbox, which the `convertClicked` signal is emitted with (see point 2).

5. Also in our testing code, connect the window's `convertClicked` signal to call the `onconvert` callback. When the **Convert** button is pressed, the `convertClicked` signal will be emitted, which will invoke the `onconvert` function (see points 2 and 3).

Run `mayapy` with the `hierarchyconvertergui.py` file path and press the **Convert** button. You should see the contents of the textbox printed to the console. The GUI behavior and application behavior have been successfully decoupled.

Instead of creating the `convertClicked` signal, you may be tempted to have the testing code connect to the button's `clicked` signal and query the contents of the textbox. The approach we took in this section is superior. It presents a much cleaner set of contracts to callers. A caller can connect to the highly specific `ConverterWindow.convertClicked` signal on the top-level window, rather than having to connect to the generic `QPushButton.clicked` signal on the button instance. This sort of abstraction is a key to writing decoupled GUIs that are easy to maintain, and one place WYSIWYG tools can fall short.

Hooking up the GUI to be effected by the application

In the last section, the application (test code) connected to signals on the GUI, so when the GUI changed, the application responded. We will now use a similar technique so that when the application state changes, the GUI is updated. We will eventually want to monitor Maya for selection changes. We'll abstract this behavior so we can develop and test our GUI without requiring Maya.

The abstraction will be handled by a controller, which will be responsible for alerting the GUI itself (the **view**) that changes have occurred in the Maya scene (the **model**). This is a version of the **model-view-controller (MVC)** pattern of implementing user interfaces. The specifics of MVC are less important than the idea that there is an abstraction between Maya and our GUI that is mediated by a controller.

The following code creates a very simple controller with a single signal that will be emitted when Maya's selection changes. We will fake a selection change by emitting the signal ourselves when developing outside of Maya. The controller is a Python class that has a single signal attribute. The controller inherits from the `QtCore.QObject` class so it can define a `Signal` attribute.

```
class HierarchyConverterController(QtCore.QObject): #(1)
    selectionChanged = Signal(list)
```

```
class ConverterWindow(QtGui.QMainWindow):
    convertClicked = Signal(str)

def create_window(controller): #(2)
    window = ConverterWindow()
    window.setWindowTitle('Hierarchy Converter')
    statusbar = window.statusBar() (3)

    container = QtGui.QWidget(window)
    label = QtGui.QLabel('Prefix:', container)
    textbox = QtGui.QLineEdit(container)
    button = QtGui.QPushButton('Convert', container)

    def onclick():
        window.convertClicked.emit(textbox.text())
    button.clicked.connect(onclick)

    def update_statusbar(newsel): #(4)
        if not newsel:
            txt = 'Nothing selected.'
        elif len(newsel) == 1:
            txt = '%s selected.' % newsel[0]
        else:
            txt = '%s objects selected.' % len(newsel)
        statusbar.showMessage(txt)
    controller.selectionChanged.connect(update_statusbar) #(5)

    layout = QtGui.QHBoxLayout(container)
    container.setLayout(layout)
    layout.addWidget(label)
    layout.addWidget(textbox)
    layout.addWidget(button)
    window.setCentralWidget(container)

    return window
```

Let's walk through the highlighted changes in more detail:

1. Create the `HierarchyConverterController` class definition with a `Signal` attribute named `selectionChanged`. The signal will be emitted with a single `list` argument.

2. Add a `controller` parameter to the `create_window` function. The caller is responsible for creating a controller and passing it into this function.

3. Call the `window.statusBar()` method to create the status bar that will display how many items are selected. The status bar will be empty initially.

4. The `update_statusbar` callback function will update the status bar text to tell the user what is selected.

5. Connect the `update_statusbar` callback to the controller's `selectionChanged` signal so the callback will be invoked when the selection is changed.

Now we need to adjust our test application code (the code under `if __name__ ==` `'__main__'`) to create a controller and simulate some events.

Simulating application events

In order to test our GUI outside of Maya, we need to simulate a selection changing. As a convenience, we will fake the selection change whenever the **Convert** button is pressed. You can also use a timer or background thread for this. Let's update our test application code to the following:

```
def _pytest(): #(1)
    import random #(2)

    controller = HierarchyConverterController() #(3)
    def nextsel(): #(4)
        return random.choice([
            [],
            ['single'],
            ['single', 'double']
        ])

    def onconvert(prefix):
        print 'Convert clicked! Prefix:', prefix
        controller.selectionChanged.emit(nextsel()) #(5)

    app = QtGui.QApplication([])
    win = create_window(controller) #(6)
    win.convertClicked.connect(onconvert)
    win.show()
    app.exec_()

if __name__ == '__main__':
    _pytest() #(1)
```

The changes to support simulating the selection are as follows:

1. Move the test code into a `_pytest` function as a convenience.

2. Import the `random` module.

3. Create an instance of the controller class.

4. Define the `nextsel` function. The function will return a list that will act as our fake selection.

5. Inside the already-existing `onconvert` callback, emit the controller's `selectionChanged` signal to simulate the selection change.

6. Pass the controller into the window creation function.

Run `mayapy` with the `hierarchyconvertergui.py` file path from the command line. Each time you press **Convert**, not only will text be printed to the console like before, but the status bar text will update depending on what the fake selection is.

Considering alternative implementations

I should point out that this implementation is only one potential way of separating Maya from your GUI code. In particular, we made the following choices, and each of them has some alternatives:

- **Functions versus classes**: I used functions for building the GUI because I didn't want to introduce any heavy use of custom classes and object-oriented programming. In production code, however, I'd almost always use classes. Functions are in some ways cleaner, but classes allow you to override functionality easily. It is worth writing all but the most trivial projects with classes for GUI code. To see an example of this alternative strategy, consult basically any PySide programming tutorial.

- **Specific versus general controller**: In our example, we created a custom `HierarchyConverterController` with a `selectionChanged` signal for this particular project. This specific controller has the benefit that as the interactions between the GUI and Maya get more complex, the interface stays clear because it is in one place (the controller). However, because creating signals for Maya events is so common, you may want to create a general Maya controller class that can be passed into your user interfaces. With the specific controller approach, you would need to hook Maya's selection changed callback into each controller. With a general controller, you would only need to hook up Maya's selection changed callback once. Try both and choose. I prefer the specific approach since controllers created by the general approach can easily get hijacked by less rigorous programmers and bloated with non-general code.

- • **Complete test setup**: I am sure that some people will find the amount of testing code in the `_pytest` function superfluous, and argue that it is easier to iterate in Maya than build test setups. There's a simple answer here: do not take shortcuts, especially if you are not familiar with this technique. There is much written on the topic of software lifecycles, testing, and maintenance. Far too much to lay out a complete and compelling argument here. If you are an experienced programmer and normally practice Test Driven Development and you just need to write a one-off GUI, go ahead and ignore this advice (not that you need my permission!). However, if you are struggling with some of the concepts we've gone over, I would implore you to get comfortable with them instead of falling back to what you already know.

The biggest benefit of having decoupled code and a complete test harness is that anyone can run our file and see how the GUI is supposed to work. There is no mental or material burden of using Maya. There is no test scene that needs to be loaded. There are no restrictions on the development tools that can be used. I've seen veteran technical artists learn the techniques in this chapter and experience a doubling or tripling of productivity. In the end, you will be able to do more interesting tools and features at a higher quality in a shorter time.

Integrating the tool GUI with Maya

It's finally time to hook together Maya and the hierarchy converter tool GUI. This will consist of a few steps. First, we need to get the GUI to simply appear and behave properly with the Maya window. Then, we must get Maya to emit the `selectionChanged` signal on the controller when Maya's selection changes. Finally, we hook up Maya to respond to the `convertClicked` signal on our GUI and perform the actual hierarchy conversion.

Opening the tool GUI from Maya

In this section, we will set up our GUI to open from a Maya shelf button. Let's start by creating a new Python file which will hold the Maya-specific code which will glue Maya to the controller. Go ahead and create a `hierarchyconvertermaya.py` file in your development root with the following text:

```
import hierarchyconvertergui as hierconvgui

_window = None
def show():
    global _window
```

```
if _window is None:
    cont = hierconvgui.HierarchyConverterController()
    _window = hierconvgui.create_window(cont)
_window.show()
```

The preceding code creates new `HierarchyConverterController` and `ConverterWindow` instances only the first time the `hierarchyconvertermaya.show` function is called. The setup and creation of the GUI should only be done once. The function will be called repeatedly (it is about to be hooked up to a shelf button), but we only want to create one instance of the controller and window. Subsequent calls to `show` will just bring the existing window to the foreground.

Note that unlike the tester function, we don't need to worry about any `QApplication` stuff. That's already handled by Maya. If you need access to the `QApplication` instance Maya creates, you can use the `QApplication.instance()` method.

The next step is to create a shelf button that can invoke the `hierarchyconvertermaya.show()` function when it is pressed. In Maya's script editor, type the following:

```
import hierarchyconvertermaya
hierarchyconvertermaya.show()
```

Highlight this text and middle-click drag it to the shelf to automatically create a shelf button. Press this button, and the GUI should appear. You'll notice that the appearance of the window is different than it was in pure Python. It now matches Maya's dark style. I will warn you, though, that occasionally what worked fine in a standard Python process will look broken in Maya. This is common when you use certain Unicode characters or hard-coded colors.

Now, make sure the hierarchy converter tool window is in front of the main Maya window. Then, click anywhere in the Maya window. The tool window has probably moved behind the main Maya window. In the next two sections, we will make the tool window behave like normal Maya child windows and stay on top of the main Maya window.

Getting the main Maya window as a QMainWindow

A Qt window, like other widgets, can have a parent. Child windows will never be behind their parent. Windows without parents will compete, and the window with focus will be on top, just like how your OS treats windows from different applications. To fix the sorting issue, we need to make our hierarchy converter window a child of the main Maya window.

We're going to write a utility function that returns the QMainWindow instance that represents Maya's main window. Open C:\mayapybook\pylib\mayautils.py and put the following code inside of it.

```
from qtshim import wrapinstance
import maya.OpenMayaUI as OpenMayaUI


def get_maya_window():
    """Return the QMainWindow for the main Maya window."""

    winptr = OpenMayaUI.MQtUtil.mainWindow()
    if winptr is None:
        raise RuntimeError('No Maya window found.')
    window = wrapinstance(winptr)
    assert isinstance(window, QtGui.QMainWindow)
    return window
```

First, we use the maya.OpenMayaUI.MQtUtil class to get the pointer to the main Maya window. We raise a RuntimeError if the pointer is None, which would happen if no window exists. I use an exception in this function because I feel it should never be called if there is no Maya GUI. We then return our pointer, wrapped/converted to a true Qt object by calling the qtshim.wrapinstance function. Before we return the QMainWindow instance, we assert that our result is the expected type.

Making a Qt window the child of Maya's window

With the Qt object representing Maya's main window, we can fix our sorting issue. Open up hierarchyconvertergui.py and change the definition of create_window so that it takes in an optional parent and passes it to the creation of the ConverterWindow instance. The following is the updated definition and first line of the create_window function.

```
def create_window(controller, parent=None):
    window = ConverterWindow(parent)
    # ...
```

If the parent argument is None, we will get the same behavior we have been getting, so our test environment does not change at all. If parent is a window, our sorting problems will be fixed.

Let's verify our solution by opening `hierarchyconvertermaya.py` and changing the two highlighted lines:

```
import hierarchyconvertergui as hierconvgui
import mayautils


_window = None


def show():
    global _window
    if _window is None:
        cont = hierconvgui.HierarchyConverterController()
        parent = mayautils.get_maya_window()
        _window = hierconvgui.create_window(cont, parent)
    _window.show()
```

You will need to reload your changes or restart Maya. Then click the shelf button to see the fixed sorting behavior.

Using Python's reload function with GUIs

In *Chapter 1, Introspecting Maya, Python, and PyMEL*, we looked at Python's built-in `reload` function. While I discourage the use of `reload` most of the time, for GUI programming it is indispensable. Maya has a significant startup time, and restarting Maya for every change is simply not fast enough.

When I use `reload` for GUIs in Maya, I follow a simple routine. I create a **Python** tab that contains the code for reloading. The code imports and reloads one module per line. It is very important the modules are listed from general at the top to specific at the bottom. To reload, I make sure the GUI is closed, highlight the tab's code, and execute it using *Ctrl + Enter*. Finally, I reopen the GUI, which should have picked up the changes. If the code wasn't updated properly, I just restart Maya.

Working in this way ensures that the code for a single tool is cohesive enough that no more than a handful of modules need to be reloaded at a time. If you need to reload your entire codebase as you work, you should structure your code so you only need to make changes in a few files at once.

It should be noted that reloading a module will not preserve module state. In other words, the module-level `_window` variable that is on the `hierarchyconvertermaya` module will be reset back to `None`. A new controller and window will be created the next time the `hierarchyconvertermaya.show` function is called. This can potentially cause a problem if we have many callbacks registered. We will ignore this problem since there is no single good solution.

And finally, it's worth reiterating that reloading should not become a way of life, but a necessary convenience for an unfortunate reality. If you find yourself worrying about reloading, writing utilities to facilitate it, or sharing import/reload scripts, I'd suggest that you are using the wrong solution to your iteration speed problem.

Armed with this knowledge, create a new **Python** tab in the Script Editor and into it type:

```
import hierarchyconvertergui
reload(hierarchyconvertergui)
import hierarchyconvertermaya
reload(hierarchyconvertermaya)
```

Verify the sorting behavior is fixed if you haven't already. Close your hierarchy converter GUI if it's open, highlight the tab's code, press *Ctrl + Enter*, and click the shelf button to open the hierarchy converter GUI again.

Emitting a signal from Maya

Now that the tool window that sorts properly, we will move on to hooking up Maya to emit the `selectionChanged` signal on the controller.

There are two ways to have Maya call your code when it does something: script jobs and Maya API callbacks. Script jobs are handled through the `scriptJob` command. They are a MEL construct and, in my opinion, not well suited to a Python world. Callbacks are a complex topic and script jobs are an abstraction that is difficult to use and full of holes. With Python, we have access to Maya's API, which I feel provides a much better interface into Maya callbacks. We will not be using script jobs in this book, and unless you already have an affinity for them, I suggest you avoid them. Certainly they have served many scripters very well for a long time, and it's possible you have successfully used and loved script jobs. However, for the style of code in this book, they are not as good a fit as Maya API callbacks.

We are going to make our first foray into the Maya API. We'll explore it much more in *Chapter 7, Taming the Maya API*. For now, we only need to use it to register a callback to be invoked when the selection changes. Open `hierarchyconvertermaya.py` and change its contents to the following:

```
import maya.OpenMaya as OpenMaya
import pymel.core as pmc
import hierarchyconvertergui as hierconvgui
import mayautils

_window = None
```

```
def show():
    global _window
    if _window is None:
        cont = hierconvgui.HierarchyConverterController()
        def emit_selchanged(_): #(1)
            cont.selectionChanged.emit(
                pmc.selected(type='transform'))
        OpenMaya.MEventMessage.addEventCallback( #(2)
            'SelectionChanged', emit_selchanged)
        parent = mayautils.get_maya_window()
        _window = hierconvgui.create_window(cont, parent)
    _window.show()
```

There are two important changes we made to hook up the callback:

- The `emit_selchanged` function is the callback that Maya will invoke. This callback will emit the controller's `selectionChanged` event, which will in turn update the GUI. Ignore the underscore (_) parameter. It will be explained in *Chapter 7, Taming the Maya API*, when we look at more API methods.

- Hook the `emit_selchanged` function into Maya using the `OpenMaya. MEventMessage.addEventCallback` method. Maya will invoke `emit_ selchanged` when its selection changes.

Now, if you reload all your code and open the GUI, you should notice the status bar text updates as you change the selection. You should add a few nulls to your scene to help you test it out. Use **Create** | **Empty Group** or *Ctrl+G* to create nulls.

Connecting Maya to a signal

Let's hook up Maya to run the hierarchy conversion on selected objects when the **Convert** button is pressed. The changes are highlighted in the following code:

```
import maya.OpenMaya as OpenMaya
import pymel.core as pmc
import hierarchyconvertergui as hierconvgui
import mayautils
import charcreator #(1)

_window = None

def show():
    global _window
```

```
        if _window is None:
            cont = hierconvgui.HierarchyConverterController()
            def emit_selchanged(_):
                cont.selectionChanged.emit(
                    pmc.selected(type='transform'))
            OpenMaya.MEventMessage.addEventCallback(
                'SelectionChanged', emit_selchanged)
            parent = mayautils.get_maya_window()
            _window = hierconvgui.create_window(cont, parent)
            def onconvert(prefix): #(2)
                settings = dict(
                    charcreator.SETTINGS_DEFAULT,
                    prefix=unicode(prefix)) #(3)
                charcreator.convert_hierarchies_main(settings)
            _window.convertClicked.connect(onconvert) #(4)
        _window.show()
```

Let's walk through the changes:

- Import the `charcreator` module we built in *Chapter 2, Writing Composable Code*.

- Create the `onconvert` callback function that will be invoked when **Convert** is pressed. It will create a copy of the default hierarchy converter settings, and supply the prefix from the GUI. The `charcreator.convert_hierarchies_main` function will be invoked with these settings.

- Depending on the Qt implementation, the value of prefix may be a Python string or a QString instance. Convert it to a Unicode string just in case.

- Finally, connect the window's `convertClicked` signal to call the `onconvert` callback.

Notice that we didn't need to go into `charcreator` to make any changes. In fact, I wrote that code well before starting this chapter, without knowing it'd be hooked up to a GUI. I didn't need to change the code at all. You'll recall that we built the library in a chapter titled *Writing Composable Code*. That is what good programming is all about! Well written code, using clear interfaces and standard, extensible techniques.

Verifying the hierarchy converter works

If you try out the hierarchy converter tool now, you should make sure of the following:

- The tool's appearance in Maya is consistent with Maya's theme, but has the OS's appearance when running it from pure Python or mayapy.

- The window sorts properly with Maya and Maya's other windows, such as the Script Editor and Hypershade.

- The status bar text updates when the selection changes.

- Any selected transform nodes are converted when the **Convert** button is clicked.

- You have a small amount of GUI-only code that is easy to maintain because it is easily testable outside of Maya, and decoupled from any Maya logic.

Congratulations! Even though this GUI is relatively simple, you've built it using techniques that will scale up well to much more complex systems.

Working with menus

Working effectively with Maya's menu system involves marrying Maya UI commands with PySide to get the best of both worlds. Maya's menus are an abstraction of standard Qt widgets, and we should use that same abstraction, through UI commands, rather than creating our own. However, we may still want to work with the controls in more sophisticated ways than Maya allows, requiring us access to the actual Qt object.

For the next few sections, we'll create a way to highlight menu items as new until the first time they are clicked.

Creating a top-level menu

Maya's UI commands work just like its other commands. A UI object is represented by a pipe-delimited hierarchical path, such as 'MayaWindow|DemoMenu|menuIt em254'. When we use a command to create a UI object, such as a menu, we need to know the path to its parent.

In the case of creating an entry on Maya's menu bar alongside **File**, **Edit**, and **Help**, we need to know the path to the main Maya window. We can do this through the following function. Place the code into the `mayautils.py` file that should already exist in your development root.

```
import pymel.core as pmc


def get_main_window_name():
    return pmc.MelGlobals()['gMainWindow']
```

To create the top level menu, open the Script Editor, and type and execute the following:

```
import mayautils
import pymel.core as pmc
menu = pmc.menu(
    'DemoMenu', parent=mayautils.get_main_window_name())
```

You should now have a menu named **DemoMenu** just to the left of the **Help** menu.

Getting the Qt object from a Maya path

Let's use PyMEL's `menuItem` command to create a menu item under the new **DemoMenu** menu. Enter the following code into the Script Editor and execute it:

```
def callback(_):
    print 'Hello, reader!'
menuitem = pmc.menuItem(
    parent=menu, label='Greet', command=callback)
```

If you click on the **DemoMenu** menu there should be a single entry under it that has the text of **Greet**. When the **Greet** menu item is clicked, `Hello, reader!` should be printed into the top Script Editor pane.

If we look at the value of `menuitem` by printing it from the Script Editor, we can see it's a PyMEL object that has a path, just like a regular node. Your exact path may differ.

```
print repr(menuitem)
ui.SubMenuItem('MayaWindow|DemoMenu|menuItem254')
```

We are going to convert this path into a Qt object. This is actually quite simple due to some helpers Maya gives us and the `wrapinstance` function in the `qtshim` module. Add the following code into the `mayautils.py` file:

```python
def uipath_to_qtobject(pathstr):
    """Return the QtObject for a Maya UI path to a control,
    layout, or menu item.
    Return None if no item is found.
    """
    ptr = OpenMayaUI.MQtUtil.findControl(pathstr)
    if ptr is None:
        ptr = OpenMayaUI.MQtUtil.findLayout(pathstr)
    if ptr is None:
        ptr = OpenMayaUI.MQtUtil.findMenuItem(pathstr)
    if ptr is not None:
        return wrapinstance(ptr)
    return None
```

We use the `maya.OpenMayaUI.MQtUtil` class to get the pointer for the object a path is referring to. The `uipath_to_qtobject` function will search controls, layouts, and menus looking for the specified object. If the object is found, it's pointer is converted into a Qt object by calling the `qtshim.wrapinstance` function. If nothing is found, the function returns `None`.

Changing the font of a widget

We can use this new `mayautils.uipath_to_qtobject` function to make the font of a menu item bold. Execute the following code from the Script Editor:

```python
reload(mayautils)
action = mayautils.uipath_to_qtobject(menuitem) #(1)
font = action.font() #(2)
font.setBold(True) #(3)
action.setFont(font) #(4)
```

This block of code introduces us to changing the appearance of Qt widgets.

1. First, we get the `QWidgetAction` that represents our menu item. A `QWidgetAction` is a type of `QAction`, which Qt commonly uses to represent menu items. It is not a widget itself so we cannot manipulate it like we would other widgets. For example, it has no palette or color information to control its styling. But it does have a font we can manipulate.

2. Get the font for the `QWidgetAction` representing our menu item. The font is an instance of `QFont`, which contains the font settings for a widget. Note that a copy of the action's font is returned from the `action.font()` method. Mutating it does not affect the font of the action.

3. Make the font bold by calling the `setBold(True)` method.

4. Reassign the updated font instance back to the action, which will update the appearance of the menu item.

After this code is run, the **Greet** menu item under the **DemoMenu** menu should have a bold font. Now that we know how to change a menu item's appearance, we can generalize this code for reuse. In the next section, we will create a way to mark menu items as new, and unmark them when they are clicked for the first time.

Marking menus as new

Let's take the code we wrote in the previous section and put it into a reusable function. The function will take a PyMEL menu item or path string, get the Qt object for it, and set its font to bold. Create a file named `newmenumarker.py` in your development root with the following code:

```
import pymel.core as pmc
import mayautils
from qtshim import QtGui

def register_menuitem(menuitem_path):
    action = mayautils.uipath_to_qtobject(menuitem_path)
    font = action.font()
    font.setBold(True)
    action.setFont(font)
```

In order to test the preceding function, we need to reset the font of the **Greet** menu item. We can do this by creating a new `QFont` instance and assigning it to the action. The new `QFont` will be set to all the Maya-defined defaults. Run the following from the Script Editor, and the font of **Greet** should revert back to its non-bold default.

```
from qtshim import QtGui
action.setFont(QtGui.QFont())
```

We can re-register the menu item, making its font bold, using the function we just wrote.

```
import newmenumarker
newmenumarker.register_menuitem(menuitem)
```

After running the preceding code, **Greet** should again have a bold font.

The next step is to make it so that when the menu item is clicked, the font is set back to its default. Make the highlighted changes to the `register_menuitem` function:

```
def register_menuitem(menuitem_path):
    action = mayautils.uipath_to_qtobject(menuitem_path)
    font = action.font()
    font.setBold(True)
    action.setFont(font)
    def setdefault():
        action.setFont(QtGui.QFont())
    action.triggered.connect(setdefault)
```

We create a `setdefault` callback function, and connect it to the `action`'s `triggered` signal. The `triggered` signal is emitted when the menu item is clicked.

Let's see this in action. We'll need to reset our font and then re-register the item. Run this from the Script Editor.

```
action.setFont(QtGui.QFont())
reload(newmenumarker)
newmenumarker.register_menuitem(menuitem)
```

Our menu item should now have a bold font. After we click it, the font should return to normal.

While the current code serves as a demonstration for customizing menus, it still needs some work to be functional enough for non-demonstration use. Let's go ahead and set up a more complex use case, and add a persistence layer so that the menu items remember whether they are marked or not between Maya sessions.

Creating a test case

Let's add a test function to the bottom of the `newmenumarker.py` file:

```
def make_test_items():
    menu = pmc.menu(
        'DemoMenu', parent=mayautils.get_main_window_name())
    def makeitem(ind):
        def callback(_):
            print 'Item', ind
        item = pmc.menuItem(
```

```
            parent=menu, label='Item %s' % ind, command=callback)
        register_menuitem(item.name())
    for i in range(5):
        makeitem(i)
```

When we call this function, a menu named **DemoMenu** and five menu items will be created for us. Each menu will have the name `Item X`, where `X` is 0 through 4.

You will need to restart Maya for this to work, since the menu creation will fail if **DemoMenu** already exists. In a new Maya session, run the following:

```
import newmenumarker
newmenumarker.make_test_items()
```

You should now have a **DemoMenu** menu with five menu items that have a bold font.

Adding a persistence registry

Finally, we can put everything together by creating a way to persist the state of no-longer-new menu items between Maya sessions. When a registered (bold) menu item is clicked, it will revert its font and mark itself as no longer new in some persisted registry. The next time the menu item is registered, the font will not be changed.

The registry, persistence, and hookup to the `register_menuitem` function are all included in the following code. We will go through it in-depth after the listing.

```
import json #(1)
import os

_REG_FILENAME = os.path.join( #(2)
    os.environ['MAYA_APP_DIR'],
    'newmenumarkingsystem.json')

def _loadregisry():
    try:
        with open(_REG_FILENAME) as f: #(3)
            return json.load(f)
    except IOError: #(4)
        return {}

def _saveregistry(registry):
    with open(_REG_FILENAME, 'w') as f: #(5)
        json.dump(registry, f)
```

```
def register_menuitem_3(menuitem_path):
    if menuitem_path in _loadregisry(): #(6)
        return
    action = mayautils.uipath_to_qtobject(menuitem_path)
    font = action.font()
    font.setBold(True)
    action.setFont(font)
    def setdefault():
        action.setFont(QtGui.QFont())
        registry = _loadregisry() #(7)
        registry[menuitem_path] = None
        _saveregistry(registry) #(8)
    action.triggered.connect(setdefault)
```

Let's walk through this code step-by-step. There are a number of new concepts.

1. Import the `json` module. JSON is the **JavaScript Object Notation** file format. The specifics are not important to us. The important thing is that it is a human-readable format that can serialize simple Python types (numbers, strings, lists, dictionaries), save them to a file, and deserialize (load) them from a file. We could have used another format, such as `pickle`, but because JSON is human-readable and only supports basic types, I prefer it for what we are doing here.

2. Decide where to store the persisted registry. I have chosen to put it in the Maya application directory. You can change this location to anywhere the user has write access.

3. Use the built-in `open` function to read the registry's `.json` file. We used the `open` function in *Chapter 3, Dealing with Errors*. We pass only the registry filename to `open`, which opens the file in `read` mode so we can load from it.

4. Pass the value returned from `open` into `json.load`, which will return the contents of the file loaded as Python objects.

5. If the call to `open` raises an `IOError`, we catch it and return an empty `dict` as the default registry. We can get this error if the registry file does not yet exist.

6. To save the file, call `open` but pass it a second argument of `'w'`, which means write mode. Save the passed-in registry into the file. Saving and loading basic Python objects to a file is really easy.

7. Inside the `register_menuitem` function, check if the menu item path is already in the registry. Its presence means the menu has already been clicked and should not be marked.

8. Inside the callback that is fired when the menu item is clicked, load the registry and add the menu item so it won't be marked bold the next time it is registered. We use a `dict` with `None` as the value of every key as the registry because JSON does not support serializing Python `set` objects.

9. Finally, save the newly updated registry.

It's worth pointing out that we don't store the registry for any long period of time. We load it from disk when registering the menu item to check if the item is already in the registry, and we load the registry from disk right before updating it. The main reason for this is that other Maya processes will be using the same registry file. If the registry were loaded once, and stored throughout the entire session, then the last Maya to write would have its version of the registry saved, but other ones would not. Though file accesses are not free and should usually not be scattered around like this, it is conceptually important here that the registry doesn't hang around in memory.

There is also the possibility that a Maya process will read the registry file while it is being written, or write to it at the same time as other processes, causing exceptions or inconsistencies. We will ignore this possibility to avoid confusing the implementation too much.

Verifying the new menu marker works

Restart Maya and run `newmenumarker.make_test_items()`. Click on the items named **Item 1** and **Item 2**. If you look at the `_REG_FILENAME` file (on my Windows machine, it is at `C:\Users\rgalanakis\Documents\maya\newmenumarkingsystem.json`), it should have some contents.

Now shut down and restart Maya again. Run `newmenumarker.make_test_items()`, and notice that **Item 0**, **Item 3**, and **Item 4** have bold text but **Item 1** and **Item 2** do not. If you were to shut down Maya, delete the registry file, restart Maya and run `newmenumarker.make_test_item()` yet again, you'd see all the test items have a bold font. Deleting the file resets the registry.

Using alternative methods to style widgets

Styling in Qt is an advanced topic. You can style through code, or Qt Style Sheets, which is a CSS-like language for styling GUIs. In either case, you should generally avoid hard-coding things like colors. The Qt documentation includes lots of good information about styling best practices.

However, I generally discourage significant styling for tools. It is easy to sink many hours into making things look just right, rather than improving how something works. An exception would be icons; I wish people used custom icons more and didn't just use text or the default!

If you are building an application, it may be important to make it look a certain way. But if you are extending an application by creating your own windows and widgets, as we do for Maya, you should prefer to depend on the already-styled application to achieve consistency and reduce effort.

Working with Maya shelves

Like menus, Maya's shelves are an abstraction above plain Qt. Working with them at the Qt level allows you to do things like place arbitrary widgets into a shelf, as in the following image:

You can work with shelves using most of the same techniques we used for menus. However, there is one major problem. We can create custom menus directly using Qt because users do not customize their menu setup heavily. Users do customize their shelves, however, and expect these customizations to persist across sessions. Nearly every aspect of a shelf and its buttons can be customized. Shelves are persisted as MEL files, though, so any custom Python and Qt widgets or behavior we hook up dynamically is lost. This presents a dilemma.

One solution is to completely recreate shelves when Maya starts up. This may be acceptable in a controlled studio environment. However, if you want users to have control over your custom shelf buttons, you're limited to what Maya already provides and should avoid customizing. You will have to decide if the power of Qt and Maya shelves is worth the complexity or restrictions it imposes. Hopefully Autodesk will add some ways to do custom shelf styling and more complex widgets in future versions of Autodesk Maya.

Summary

In this chapter, we learned all about using PySide to build graphical user interfaces. First, we went over some important concepts and strategies for building GUIs with PySide. Then we saw how writing your interface with Qt is superior to using a WYSIWYG editor or Maya commands. Our main project was building a GUI frontend for the hierarchy converter library we built in *Chapter 2, Writing Composable Code*. We developed and tested the GUI totally outside of Maya, including mocking up how it responds to user interaction. We then hooked it up for actual use in Maya with a minimal amount of code. Finally, we did some work with Maya's menu system, creating a system to mark menu items as new, and revert their styling the first time they are clicked.

If this chapter was all about improving how humans interact with Maya, the next chapter is the total opposite. We will explore ways to control Maya in a totally automated fashion so that it can be scripted to perform complex tasks orchestrated from outside of Maya itself.

6

Automating Maya from the Outside

Most of the programming we do in Maya is about *automation*. There's little that can be accomplished with code that cannot otherwise be done by hand. We create code to run inside of Maya, during a user's session, to get them faster from point A to point B. We speed up what takes too long to be pleasant or practical.

In this chapter, though, we will do programming that isn't directly about speeding what a user normally does. We're going to develop a system that will allow us to control and automate Maya in arbitrary ways. The controlling code will not run inside of Maya, but in its own Python process. We will not control Maya using an application-specific feature like the command port, but a general request-reply system that could be at home in another application. Automating Maya from the outside will open up totally new possibilities for designing tools and pipelines.

We will start by learning about the request-reply pattern for client and server communication, and how to implement it using the powerful ZeroMQ library. After that, we will figure out how to build the automation system, and enumerate important design considerations like error handling, timeouts, and handshakes. We will build the system in a series of steps, incrementally adding functionality. Along the way, we will learn about subprocesses, Maya's startup routine, environment configuration, and how to execute arbitrary code in Python. Finally, we look at some ways to leverage the automation system, and improvements that can be made.

Controlling Maya through request-reply

There is a plethora of documentation on the **request-reply** (often called **request-response**) pattern, since it is the pattern that most of HTTP works with. In simple terms: a *client requests* something from a server and the *server replies*. That's it! Our automation system will be a very basic implementation of this pattern pattern. We are not, for example, implementing a web browser. We will be using monogamous clients and servers, sharing a common protocol, with synchronous behavior, and residing on the same machine. The extent of our required request-reply knowledge is minimal.

So that's all you need to know about request-reply right now: the client requests something from the server, and the server replies. Rinse and repeat.

Using a Python client and Maya server

Our implementation of request-reply will be using a **Python client** and **Maya server**. The term *server* here is used in the sense that Maya will be the thing receiving requests and sending replies; this is your plain Maya, running on whatever computer and OS you want. Think of server as a *conceptual* role, not a machine or special process.

Our plan is taking shape: the client will tell Maya what to do, and Maya (our server) will do it and send the result.

 Astute readers may have already figured out that Maya, by virtue of hosting Python, can also be a client that talks to another Maya (or even itself!) as a server. This is a fun implementation possibility, but it helps to not think about it. The fact that it would be Maya hosting a Python client, and not another application or standard Python process, is irrelevant.

Controlling Python through exec and eval

Fortunately there's an easy way to dynamically tell Python what to do. We can send a string from the client to the server and have the server interpret the string as code. This is a wonderful aspect of dynamic languages like Python.

We will primarily use the exec statement to **execute** code and control Maya. We will use the eval function to **evaluate** an expression when we need a result back from Maya. We'll look at exec and eval in much more detail when we implement our request-reply system.

Handling problems with IPC

When doing any **inter-process communication (IPC)**, there are several things that must be considered. Doubly so when communicating with Maya, as we are using an often fragile application in a way that its designers never intended.

One problem is the **monogamy** or **pairing** of the server and client process. Usually a server listens on a predefined port. HTTP servers use port 80, for example. We cannot run multiple Maya servers all using the same port, so how can we dynamically allocate ports for our server and client pairs?

Another problem is **availability**. What happens if the server goes down? We will put a **timeout** mechanism into place so the client doesn't hang indefinitely.

Yet another complication is **process lifetime**. We have a server and client that are tightly coupled. One client, one server. The client needs to manage the process lifetime for the server, so the server is killed if the client process exits.

Finally, we need a graceful way to **handle errors**. Dealing with errors between processes can involve considerable complexity. We must be careful about how we handle errors, so our server is resilient to bad client requests and the client can understand what happened when something goes wrong on the server.

Our design must address all of these considerations. But first, we'll set up ZeroMQ and explore a simple example program.

Installing ZeroMQ

To run the code in this chapter, you will need to have the **PyZMQ** Python package installed. PyZMQ provides Python bindings to the included **ZeroMQ** asynchronous messaging library. It is relatively easy to install PyZMQ. It provides binary distributions for Windows and OS X on its Python Package Index page at `https://pypi.python.org/pypi/pyzmq/`. Refer to *Chapter 9*, *Becoming a Part of the Python Community*, for instructions on how to install third-party packages like PyZMQ that contain C code.

Demonstrating request-reply with ZeroMQ

Creating a request-reply client and server in Python is easy, and well covered in the excellent *ZMQ- The Guide* located at `http://zguide.zeromq.org/py:all`. Here is a very simple implementation of the request-reply pattern explained previously. Save the following code to a scratch file like `C:\mayapybook\pylib\reqrepdemo.py` to use for testing. Feel free to delete this file after going through these examples.

```
import sys
import zmq

if sys.argv[-1] == 'client':
    print 'Client is going to send.'
    reqsock = zmq.Context().socket(zmq.REQ)
    reqsock.connect('tcp://127.0.0.1:5555')
    reqsock.send('Hello from client!')
    recv = reqsock.recv()
    print 'Client received', recv, 'exiting.'
else:
    print 'Server is listening.'
    repsock = zmq.Context().socket(zmq.REP)
    repsock.bind('tcp://127.0.0.1:5555')
    recv = repsock.recv()
    print 'Server received', recv
    repsock.send('Hello from server!')
    print 'Server sent, exiting.'
```

To see this example in action, open up two command line prompts. In the first, we'll run the server. Enter the first line from the following example and the second line will print into the console.

```
> mayapy C:\mayapybook\pylib\reqrepdemo.py
Server is listening
```

In the second prompt, we will run the client. Run the first line and the lines following it will be printed.

```
> mayapy C:\mayapybook\pylib\reqrepdemo.py client
Client is going to send
Client received Hello from server! exiting.
```

If you go back to the first (server) prompt, some additional lines were printed.

```
Server received Hello from client!
Server sent, exiting.
```

The server process starts, prints, then binds to a port. Ports, binding, and connecting is described in the next section. The call to a `recv` method blocks, so when the client or server calls `recv`, the Python process will wait there until there is something to receive. Then the client process starts, prints, connects, and calls the `send` method to send a message to the server. The server prints that it received the message, sends its reply, prints again, and exits. The client receives the reply, prints, and also exits.

Notice how directly the Python code maps to the request-reply pattern. You don't need to understand how TCP works, you don't need to know what an ACK or packet is, you barely need to know anything about network programming at all, and you can still have the totally awesome request-reply Maya automation system we're going to develop in this chapter.

I would encourage you, of course, to learn about what is actually going on, but it is by no means required. If you would like to learn more about ZeroMQ you should read some of *ZeroMQ- The Guide*. To learn about networks and network programming in general, see the excellent *Foundations of Python Network Programming by John Goerzen* and *Brandon Rhodes*.

Explaining connection strings, ports, bind, and connect

Most of the previous example should be abstract enough that you can take it for granted. The exceptions are **connection strings**, **ports**, **binding**, and **connecting**.

A port is a numbered resource on a computer, between 1 and 65535. Computers (and processes on the same computer) can talk to each other by sending and receiving data over ports. There is a lot more to the topic of ports that we do not need to cover here. We just need to know that port 5555 is used in the example, but we could have chosen nearly any port number. Later on, we'll stop using predefined ports, and start using randomly chosen open ports.

Sockets can bind or connect to a port. For our purposes, a request socket will always use the `connect` method, and a reply socket will always use the `bind` method. When you tell the reply socket to bind, it *locks* that port so no other socket can bind to it. When a request socket connects, however, you're telling it what port the listening server is bound to. The sending of data will happen on whatever port ZMQ chooses.

Both binding and connecting takes a **connection string** like `"tcp://127.0.0.1:5555"`. In that connection string, `5555` is the port, and `tcp` is the protocol for sending data between client and server. We will forgo a discussion of protocols in this book and just use `tcp`. The string `127.0.0.1` is an IP address which indicates we are using our local computer as the server machine. We will use `127.0.0.1` for our connection strings for the entire chapter. For those interested, the *Supporting control from a remote computer* section later in the chapter has more information on using the automation system with remote machines.

Because of our limited use case, the previous example and these definitions cover pretty much all the network programming topics we'll need. However, just because our request-reply system doesn't require much network programming skill doesn't mean it is simple. There is a good deal of complexity our system will need to handle.

Designing the automation system

With some understanding of how ZeroMQ and request-reply systems work, we will now design the automation system. We'll start by going over some design considerations and use cases.

Pairing one client and one server

Normally, a server deals with many clients, usually concurrently. It can do this because of the design of most servers: all state changes, like withdrawing money from a bank account, happen in something like a database. The server processes themselves are stateless. The web server translating a web request to a database call does not remember anything relevant about the transaction. Databases are designed to allow multiple readers and writers to work simultaneously on shared state.

We do not have this luxury in Maya. Maya is not a database and we cannot design as if it were one. When a client asks the server to create a sphere, the client expects the sphere to remain there until the client deletes it. It does not expect the state of the Maya scene to be changed by any other client. We must have *monogamous* (paired) clients and servers. They must also behave **synchronously**. That is, the client blocks while waiting for the server, and the server does not reply to the client until it is done processing. When we write code to be used in the automation system, we still want to write *normal looking* Maya code.

This paired client/server requirement leads us to our next design consideration.

Bootstrapping the server from the client

Bootstrapping comes from the phrase "pulling yourself up by your own bootstraps." There are several uses of it in computer science (it's where the phrase "booting the computer" comes from). Generally it means "starting a more complex process from a simpler process" and that is the definition here.

Because our client and server are paired, we need the client process to start up (bootstrap) the server process, and eventually kill the server process as well. This creates a pretty complex problem that needs to be solved if we hope to have multiple clients connected each to its own server.

The client-server handshake

The fact that we'll need multiple clients bootstrapping their own servers means hard-coding a port like we did with 5555 earlier cannot work. This is because each server needs to bind to its own port (recall that only a single socket can bind to a given port). Nor can the client simply find an open port, start the server process, and tell it to use that number. By the time the server starts up, the port that was open can be bound by another process. There would be a **race condition** between the server and any other process binding to the port.

So we need to perform a **handshake**, illustrated in the following diagram.

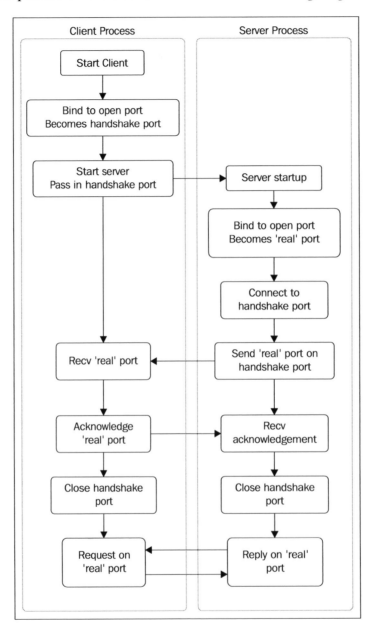

Let's follow along with the image, starting from the top left.

1. Create a client.

2. The client binds to any open port, which we'll call the **handshake port**. No other process can use this port once the client binds. The client binding means that, during the handshake process, our client will reply and our server will request. This is an inversion of their final roles.

3. The client starts the server process, telling it the handshake port. We will pass the handshake port number from the client to the server using a command line argument.

4. The server process starts up, and binds to a different open port. We'll call this the **application port**, or **app port** for short. Once the handshake is over, all of the work will happen over the application port.

5. The server process connects to the handshake port, and sends a **request** to the client, telling the client to use the application port for further communication.

6. The client sends a **reply** back to the server, acknowledging it has received the application port. We need synchronization at this point. If the server were to not wait for an acknowledgment, it could possibly send its data before the client is ready to receive it.

7. The client and server each close their sockets accessing the handshake port. The handshake is complete.

8. The client connects to the application port.

9. The client is now in its role as *requester* and the server in its role as the *replier*, and all further communication happens over the application port.

The key part of the handshake is that, for the handshake itself, roles are reversed. The server is the client, sending a request that includes the application port number. The client is the server, receiving the application port number. Once the handshake is done, both actors revert to their proper roles, with client as the requester and server as the replier.

Defining the server loop

All servers, at their core, run a loop that just calls `recv` on a socket and operates on what is received. Our server will look essentially like this:

```
sock = zmq.Context().socket(zmq.REP)
sock.bind('tcp://127.0.0.1:5555')
while True:
    request = sock.recv()
    response = process_request(request)
    sock.send(response)
```

There are, of course, many differences between this and a real server loop, such as error handling and timeouts. This is fundamentally, though, the design of our server loop.

Serializing requests and responses

We'll need to send more than ASCII strings between client and server. We can use a **serializer** to convert data into bytes that can be sent across the network. We will use the `json` module from the Python standard library for this task. Our previous server loop example with serialization support added looks like the following:

```
sock = zmq.Context().socket(zmq.REP)
sock.bind('tcp://127.0.0.1:5556')
while True:
    request = json.loads(sock.recv())
    response = process_request(request)
    sock.send(json.dumps(response))
```

The same pattern will occur on the client as well. The `json.loads` function will be called on what is received, and `json.dumps` will be called on what is being sent.

> In *Chapter 5, Building Graphical User Interfaces for Maya*, we used `json.dump` and `json.load` to save to and load from a file. Here, we use `json.dumps` and `json.loads` (notice the trailing s character) to save Python objects to bytes and read Python objects from bytes. Use dump and load when working with files (or any *file-like object*, in the parlance of Python), and dumps and loads when working with in-memory byte strings.
>
> We could also use the `send_json` and `recv_json` methods on the ZMQ socket, but I've chosen to be explicit here.

Choosing what the server does

In the preceding example, we did not specify what data the `request` variable refers to. We'll use a very simple design: the client will send a list of two items to the server. The first item will tell the server what to do, and the second item will be the arguments for it. We are just choosing this as an arbitrary convention. You are free to design your own convention for what data is sent between the client and server.

Instead of calling a mysterious `process_request` function as in our previous example, let's put the request processing code inside of our loop. We will add or subtract the two values in the second item depending on whether the first item is the + or - character.

```
sock = zmq.Context().socket(zmq.REP)
sock.bind('tcp://127.0.0.1:5557')
while True:
    request = json.loads(sock.recv())
    func, args = request
    a, b = args
    if func == '+':
        response = a + b
    elif func == '-':
        response = a - b
    sock.send(json.dumps(response))
```

This design is a rudimentary way for the client to specify a **remote procedure call (RPC)** to execute on the server.

However, what if `func` is not + or -, or the arguments cannot be added or subtracted? The server would raise an exception.

Handling exceptions between client and server

As we saw in *Chapter 3, Dealing with Errors*, exception handling is a complex topic. The complexity is greatly increased when dealing with exceptions across processes. There are two main types of exceptions in a server and client environment.

The first type of exception is due to a logical bug on the server. These should raise a fatal exception, bring down the server process, and potentially notify the people maintaining the code. A faulted server may cause the client to hang and timeout. However, these exceptions should happen very rarely. The server code is actually quite small and straightforward, since most of it is simply responding to client requests. We will not handle this type of error in this chapter.

The second type of exception happens when the server is fulfilling the client's request, such as adding two numbers. If the client wants to add a string and a number, the server should, of course, not crash. The server should indicate to the client that an exception occurred, along with the traceback and any other diagnostic information.

This second type of error can occur for a number of reasons.

- The client's request cannot be deserialized on the server. Perhaps the client has serialized and sent a Python object that the server does not know about, or has used a different serializer than the server. For example, if the server uses json and the client pickle, the server will not know how to deserialize client requests.

- The client's request causes an error. For example, if the client sends ['+', (1, 'a')], trying to add an integer and string would raise an exception. This is the most common type of error.

- The result of the client's request cannot be serialized. For example, if the client's request causes the server to try to serialize a PyMEL object, an error would be raised because PyMEL nodes cannot be serialized.

- The client asks the server to do something it does not recognize. In the preceding example, if the client sent * instead of + or -, the server would not know what to do.

You may want to handle each of these errors in a distinct manner. For the sake of simplicity, we will not distinguish between the first three. The last one will be handled explicitly, however.

In order to tell the client there was a problem, we will use **status codes**. Conceptually, this is just like the HTTP status codes you may be familiar with, such as 200 OK or 404 Not Found. We will use three status codes: 1 to indicate success, 2 to indicate an *invalid method* (the last type of error listed previously), and 3 for all other errors. The response will be a two-item list of [<status code>, <response>].

Here is the updated server code with exception support:

```
import traceback # (1)
while True:
    recved = sock.recv()
    try:
        func, args = json.loads(recved)
        a, b = args
        if func == '+':
            response = a + b
```

```
        code = 1 #(2)
    elif func == '-':
        response = a - b
        code = 1 #(2)
    else: #(3)
        code = 2
        response = 'Invalid method: ' + func
    pickled = json.dumps([code, response])
except Exception: #(4)
    code = 3
    response = ''.join(traceback.format_exc())
    pickled = json.dumps([code, response])
sock.send(pickled)
```

Let's walk through the changes in the preceding code:

1. Import the `traceback` module, which we will use to get information about the error which we can send back to the client.

2. If the server fulfills the client request (adds or subtracts) successfully, set the status code to 1 and `response` to the value the request computed.

3. If the server does not recognize the request, set the status code to 2 and `response` to a message indicating what happened.

4. If there's an exception anywhere, set the status code to 3, and `response` to the current `traceback` formatted as a string. This should give the client some information about what went wrong, albeit in a pretty opaque form. We cannot send the exception itself because it may not be serializable by the server or deserializable by the client.

There are many ways to handle errors on our server. This is just the absolute minimum of functionality. As you build on and improve this chapter's code, you should also improve the error handling.

Understanding the Maya startup routine

Most of our design so far has been Maya agnostic. We will now switch gears and focus on Maya, understanding how Maya starts up and how we can use Python to control the startup routine. We'll start with a brief digression to look at Maya's batch and GUI modes. Then we'll understand how Maya starts up and some of its configuration options. Finally, we'll step back and take a higher-level view of how we want to control the startup, so that we know what sort of code to write when we actually implement our automation system.

Using batch mode versus GUI mode

Maya can run in either its normal **GUI mode**, or in **batch mode**, which is Maya without any GUI. Code can query which mode is active by calling `pmc.about(batch=True)`. Almost every Maya or PyMEL command will work in batch mode, though you may run into some that only work in GUI mode.

Most usage of the Maya server will probably be in batch mode. There are many legitimate uses for a GUI version of Maya running the automation server, however, such as setting up two-way communication between Maya and another application like a game editor, Adobe Photoshop or Autodesk MotionBuilder. We will not support a GUI mode server in this chapter for the sake of simplicity. Should you want to try on your own, the changes are straightforward. See the section *Running a server in a Maya GUI session* later in this chapter.

In order to run Maya in batch mode, you will need to run `mayabatch.exe` instead of `maya.exe` on Windows, or pass in the `-batch` command line flag to the `maya` executable on OS X and Linux. See the coming *Using command line options* for more information.

Choosing a startup configuration mechanism

Maya's startup mechanisms are pretty standard. Maya is configured by passing in **command line options** and by using **environment variables**. Once Maya goes through its startup process and is fully initialized, it runs a series of **user-defined scripts**. We will look at the former two mechanisms in the next sections. We will not deal with user-defined scripts, such as `userSetup.mel`, in this chapter.

I should note that many of the principles of Maya's startup apply to other programs as well, and serve as a good example of how to design user-customizable applications.

Using command line options

To see the complete list of Maya's command line options, see the *Start Maya from the command line* section of the Autodesk help. We are interested in the `-command` flag.

The `-command` flag allows us to pass a string containing MEL code that Maya will execute after it starts. We can use this string to execute Python code that will launch our server, in addition to any additional startup logic. We can do this with the `python` MEL function. For example, we could launch Maya with `maya -command 'python("import mymodule;mymodule.runserver()")'` to have Maya import the `mymodule` module and invoke its `runserver` function after Maya is finished initializing. We will use this technique to run our actual reply server.

Another relevant command line option is –batch. As mentioned previously, on OS X and Linux you will need to use the -batch flag to launch Maya in batch mode, instead of using mayabatch.exe as we use in this chapter's code.

Using environment variables

There are many parts of Maya that can be customized by changing environment variables. For more documentation about environment variables, including how to work with them from your operating system's shell or terminal, you should refer to your operating system's documentation. Using Python, we can change environment variables in a cross-platform way using the os.environ dictionary or the os.getenv and os.putenv functions.

When we start our Maya process, it will inherit the environment variables from its parent process, which is the process starting Maya. As long as we are launching Maya from a *compatible interpreter*, whether mayapy or vanilla Python, environment variables should not pose a problem. A compatible interpreter would be using Python 2.6 x64 with Maya 2012 64bit, for example. An interpreter using a different Python version, architecture, or compiler would be incompatible. If you need to launch a process with a different Python interpreter, you will need to clean and adjust the environment before launching the process.

We will not deal with environment variables in this chapter since we can just use the mayapy executable and its matching maya (or mayabatch) executable. If you need to change environment variables before launching a child process, you should look at the env argument of the subprocess.Popen class. You can take a copy of the current environment variables in os.environ, modify them, and feed them into the new process.

Building the request-reply automation system

Finally, we can begin putting theory into practice, and build our request-reply Maya automation system.

We'll start by learning how Python packages work, how to bootstrap Maya from another process, and how process pipes work. After that, we will set up a bare bones client and server. Once that is working, we will add support for exec and eval, exceptions, timeouts, and more.

Creating a Python package

Before writing our code, we need to create some files. Because these files are all closely related, we can put them in a folder and create a Python package.

Start by creating a `mayaserver` directory in your development root. For this book, that is `C:\mayapybook\pylib\mayaserver`. Inside, create three empty files: `__init__.py`, `client.py`, and `server.py`.

The `__init__.py` file is what turns this folder in a package. It allows us to do things like import `mayaserver`, which would import the `__init__.py` file, and import `mayaserver.client` and import `mayaserver.server`, which import the `client.py` and `server.py` files, respectively. Code that is common between the client and server goes into the `__init__.py` file. In our case, that will be just a few values that we will define later.

Using Python packages is an essential tool for keeping files organized and code cohesive.

Launching Maya from Python

Launching an application by wrapping it in a Python script is a very powerful pattern. It allows us to configure everything about an application's environment before it starts up. For example, if we need to set Maya's environment variables like `MAYA_SCRIPT_PATH`, which need to be set *before* Maya starts, we can use a Python launch script to do that.

The script we are creating will be rather limited. It will make many assumptions, and support only what we need to have Maya start up and run our reply server. However, this code can be expanded to create a startup routine for a regular Maya. It could do things like custom menu and shelf creation, in addition to or instead of running the reply server.

Let's start by writing just enough code to launch and kill a Maya process. Open up `C:\mayapybook\pylib\mayaserver\client.py` and put in the following code. I have hard-coded paths to the Maya executable on my Windows system. You must replace this with whatever is appropriate for your machine, or calculate it dynamically.

```
import os
import subprocess

#(1)
MAYAEXE = r'C:\Program Files\Autodesk\Maya2014\bin\mayabatch.exe'
```

```
def kill(process): #(2)
    if os.name == 'nt':
        os.system('taskkill /f /pid %s' % process.pid)
    else:
        process.terminate()

if __name__ == '__main__':
    import time
    proc = subprocess.Popen([MAYAEXE]) #(3)
    # proc = subprocess.Popen([MAYAEXE, '-batch'])
    time.sleep(5) #(4)
    kill(proc) #(5)
```

Let's walk through this script.

1. Define the path to your `mayabatch.exe` file.

2. Define a function named `kill`. This function takes in a `subprocess.Popen` instance, which we create later in the script, and kills it. Normally, you could just use `Popen.terminate()` to kill the process, but it does not work reliably on Windows. So we use the `taskkill` system call on Windows to kill the process. On most other operating systems, the `terminate()` method will kill the process.

3. Use the `subprocess.Popen` class to start Maya. The first argument is a list of arguments that you would pass on the command line to start the process. On Windows, we are not passing Maya any arguments so it is a list with just the path to the executable. On OS X and Linux you must pass the `-batch` argument to `maya` to use Maya in batch mode.

4. Sleep for five seconds. This will allow us to observe what Maya prints out before it exits.

5. Finally, kill the process.

If you run the `mayaserver/client.py` file, a new Maya process will start up, and after five seconds, the client will kill the Maya server process and exit. You should see something like the following in the Python window you used to run `mayaserver/client.py`:

> **mayapy mayaserver/client.py**
Result: untitled

Where did this `Result: untitled` text come from?

It was printed by Maya when it started up. The Maya process is a **child process** of the **parent process** that launched it. We know that a child process inherits the environment variables of its parent. It also inherits the parent's **file handles**, so what is printed in the child process will also print in the parent process. You can change this behavior by supplying values to the `stdout` and `stderr` parameters of `subprocess.Popen`, but we will just allow the Maya server process to print into the client process that launches it.

Automatically killing the server

Instead of explicitly killing our Maya server process, we can instead have it killed automatically when the client process exits. We will use the `atexit` module to register an **exit handler**. The exit handler will run and kill the server process just before the client process exits. Make the highlighted changes to the `mayaserver/ client.py` file:

```
import atexit

def start_process():
    process = subprocess.Popen([MAYAEXE])
    atexit.register(kill, process)

def kill(process):
    if os.name == 'nt':
        os.system('taskkill /f /pid %s' % process.pid)
    else:
        process.terminate()

if __name__ == '__main__':
    import time
    start_process()
    time.sleep(5)
```

Register the exit handler by calling `atexit.register(kill, process)`. The `atexit` module takes care of running code when the process exits, and will call `kill(process)`.

This feature is important because if the client process does not kill the server process, the server may stay alive and have to be killed manually. Now, no matter what, your server process will die when your client process exits.

No matter what? Of course not! There are several circumstances that can cause the exit handler not to run, including:

- The client process crashes due to some interpreter error or is killed by the operating system.

- The client process does not work properly with the `atexit` module (or more precisely, the `sys.exitfunc` behavior it relies on). This is common where the interpreter is embedded in another application. In fact, `atexit` is broken in many versions of Maya!

- Another exit handler, run before ours, forcibly terminates the client process, causing our exit handler to not be run.

- An error occurs in our exit handler or the `kill` function.

There are ways we can mitigate these issues, but none of them are clean or elegant. Generally you can have some sort of *process watcher* that will kill the server process once the client is dead, or you can start a *kill timer* in the server so that it will shut down if it goes a certain amount of time without hearing from the client. You should consider adding this functionality as needed.

Creating a basic Maya server

Next we'll create the server loop that will run in Maya. For now, it will reply to the client with a hard-coded response. The following code goes into the `mayaserver/server.py` file.

```
import json #(1)
import zmq

def runserver(): #(2)
    sock = zmq.Context().socket(zmq.REP)
    sock.bind('tcp://127.0.0.1:5454') #(3)
    while True: #(4)
        recv = json.loads(sock.recv())
        sock.send(json.dumps('Pinged with %s' % recv))
```

Let's walk through the preceding code.

1. Import the `json` and `zmq` modules.

2. Create the `runserver` function. This function contains a loop that calls `recv` indefinitely. Rather than break out of the loop, we rely on the client to terminate the server process.

3. Create a reply socket and bind it to a hard-coded port, like we did in the example earlier in this chapter.

4. Inside of the `while True` loop, the server calls the `sock.recv()` method to receive requests from the client and then `sock.send` to send a reply. The code uses the `json` module to serialize and deserialize requests and responses.

The code in `mayaserver/server.py` will run inside of the Maya server process. Now let's see how to tell Maya to execute this code when it starts up.

Running code at Maya startup

In order to have Maya run code when it starts up, we can use the `-command` command line argument. As explained in the *Using command line options* section earlier in this chapter, we will use MEL's python function to run some Python code. The Python code will import the `mayaserver.server` module and call its `runserver` function. We also need functions to create a request socket and handle sending and receiving of requests and responses. The following is the new and changed code in `mayaserver/client.py`.

```python
COMMAND = ('python("import mayaserver.server;'
           'mayaserver.server.runserver()");') #(1)


def start_process():
    process = subprocess.Popen(
        [MAYAEXE, '-command', COMMAND]) # (2)
    atexit.register(kill, process)
    return process


def create_client(): #(3)
    socket = zmq.Context().socket(zmq.REQ)
    socket.connect('tcp://127.0.0.1:5454')
    return socket


def sendrecv(socket, data): #(4)
    socket.send(json.dumps(data))
    unpickrecved = json.loads(socket.recv())
    return unpickrecved


if __name__ == '__main__':
    proc = start_process()
    sock = create_client()
    got = sendrecv(sock, 'Ping') #(5)
    print 'Got: %r. Shutting down.' % got #(6)
```

If we run this code, the following should be printed to the console:

```
> mayapy mayaserver/client.py
Got: u'Pinged with Ping'. Shutting down.
```

Let's take a closer look at how this code works.

1. Create a string that is the MEL command Maya will run. Maya will import the `mayaserver.server` module and then call `mayaserver.server.runserver()`, which will run the code we just wrote in `mayaserver/server.py` and keep Maya in an endless loop.

2. Call the Maya executable with the `-command` flag and the MEL command string. Maya will know to run that MEL command after it starts up and finishes initializing.

3. The `create_client` function creates the request socket, hardcoded to connect to the same port the server will bind to.

4. The `sendrecv` function sends requests and receives responses, using `json` to serialize and deserialize, just like the server.

5. After starting the process and creating the client socket, send a request to the server. The server sends back a response acknowledging the request.

6. Print the response into the console and exit.

We now have a working client and server with all of the basic pieces in place. The rest of this chapter will be adding features make it useful and robust. The most important piece to implement is support for the `eval` and `exec` of arbitrary code strings, so the client can do what it wants on the server.

Understanding eval and exec

You may be familiar with the concept of `eval` and `exec` from other dynamic languages. They allow the construction of code in the form of strings that can then be **evaluated** or **executed**, as if it were normal code.

There are some important differences between `eval` and `exec`. The most important difference is that `eval` returns the value of an **expression** and `exec` executes a **statement**. An expression represents a value. The expression $1 + 1$ represents the value 2. A statement does something. For example, the `assert` statement may raise an `AssertionError`. Statements never return a meaningful value (they always return `None`).

As the following code demonstrates, we get two different behaviors whether we eval or exec the string `"1 + 1"`. Also note that eval is a function and is thus called with parenthesis, while exec is a statement, like print, and is not called with parenthesis.

```
>>> eval('1 + 1')
2
>>> exec '1 + 1'
```

The call to eval returned 2 while the call to exec returned None (and thus the interactive interpreter did not print a value). But what happens if we eval and exec a print statement instead of an expression?

```
>>> exec 'print 1'
1
>>> eval('print 1')
Traceback (most recent call last):
  ...
  File "<string>", line 1
    print 1
          ^
SyntaxError: invalid syntax
```

The call to exec printed the value successfully, but eval raised a SyntaxError. This is because print is a statement and eval can only evaluate an expression.

Another common statement is assignment. We can use exec to assign some value to a variable, and then use eval to evaluate the name of the variable and get back the value.

```
>>> exec 'b = 1 + 1'
>>> eval('b')
2
```

The preceding pattern works because the **execution scope** of code at the interactive prompt is all global. What if we were to hide the exec call from the previous example away in a function, thus changing the execution scope of the exec call?

```
>>> def exec2(s):
...     exec s
>>> exec2('c = 2 + 2')
>>> eval('c')
Traceback (most recent call last):
NameError: name 'c' is not defined
```

The preceding code raises a NameError because the variable c, created in the exec2 function, is not accessible in the scope where eval was called.

For our request-reply server, we want the ability for code to refer to variables assigned in earlier exec statements. We can do this by providing some additional arguments for exec and eval to override their execution scope.

```
>>> def exec3(s):
...     exec s in globals(), globals()
>>> exec3('d = 3 + 3')
>>> eval('d', globals(), globals())
6
```

Both eval and exec take two optional arguments that define the dictionaries to use for global and local variables. The globals() function returns a dictionary of the names and values of variables in the global (module-level) scope. Calling exec will mutate this dictionary when an assignment is done (just like regular Python code would), and the variable assigned to will then be available in the eval function. The following code demonstrates this behavior.

```
>>> 'e' in globals()
False
>>> e = 1
>>> 'e' in globals() # Normal assignment puts e in globals
True
>>> 'f' in globals()
False
>>> exec 'f = 1'
>>> 'f' in globals() # Assignment in exec puts f in globals
True
```

Execution scope can be a complicated topic, but fortunately we don't need to fully understand how it works in order to leverage it.

Adding support for eval and exec

Armed with this information, we can add support for eval and exec into the automation system. At the bottom of the mayaserver/client.py file, we will send a request to test each. Instead of just sending a string to the server, like 'Ping' in our previous client example, we will send a tuple of (function name, code string). This is the same way the demonstration server we built earlier in this chapter works, except here we will use the strings 'eval' and 'exec' instead of '+' and '-'.

```
if __name__ == '__main__':
    proc = start_process()
    sock = create_client()
```

```
goteval = sendrecv(sock, ('eval', '1 + 1'))
print 'Got Eval: %r' % goteval
sendrecv(sock, ('exec', 'a = 3'))
sendrecv(sock, ('exec', 'a *= 2'))
gotexec = sendrecv(sock, ('eval', 'a'))
print 'Got Exec: %r' % gotexec
```

Now in `mayaserver/server.py`, we can choose a different method based on whether the client asks for `eval` or `exec`. The required changes are highlighted in the following code:

```
def runserver():
    sock = zmq.Context().socket(zmq.REP)
    sock.bind('tcp://127.0.0.1:5454')
    while True:
        func, arg = json.loads(sock.recv())
        if func == 'exec':
            exec arg in globals(), globals()
            tosend = None
        elif func == 'eval':
            tosend = eval(arg, globals(), globals())
        sock.send(json.dumps(tosend))
```

If you run `mayaserver/client.py` from the command line, you should see the following output:

```
> mayapy mayaserver/client.py
Got Eval: 2
Got Exec: 6
```

There is a latent bug here. If the client sends a function name that is not `eval` or `exec`, a `NameError` will be raised on the server because the `tosend` variable will not be assigned. Exception handling will be added in the next section so this situation can be managed gracefully.

Adding support for exception handling

Handling exceptions involves changes to our server and client. The server will need to catch exceptions that may happen as a result of client requests and send back a status code and response. The client must key off of this status code and raise an exception in the case of an unsuccessful request. We will replicate what we did in the *Handling exceptions between client and server* section earlier in this chapter.

First we will declare our status codes in the `mayaserver/__init__.py` file.

```
SUCCESS = 1
INVALID_METHOD = 2
UNHANDLED_ERROR = 3
```

Next, inside of `mayaserver/server.py`, add a `try/except` around all the code that handles a client request, and add support for setting the status code.

```
import json
import traceback #(1)
import zmq
import mayaserver #(1)


def runserver():
    sock = zmq.Context().socket(zmq.REP)
    sock.bind('tcp://127.0.0.1:5454')
    while True:
        recved = sock.recv()
        try: #(2)
            func, arg = json.loads(recved)
            code = mayaserver.SUCCESS #(3)
            response = None
            if func == 'exec':
                exec arg in globals(), globals()
            elif func == 'eval':
                response = eval(arg, globals(), globals())
            else:
                code =  mayaserver.INVALID_METHOD #(4)
                response = func
            pickled = json.dumps([code, response])
        except Exception: #(5)
            pickled = json.dumps([
                mayaserver.UNHANDLED_ERROR,
                ''.join(traceback.format_exc())])
        sock.send(pickled)
```

Let's go through the highlighted changes in more detail:

1. Import the `traceback` and `mayaserver` modules. The `mayaserver` module contains the status codes defined in the `mayaserver/__init__.py` file.

2. Create a `try/except` around the request handling code.

3. Set the default code and response. The `exec` statement always returns `None`, but `eval` returns the value to use as the response.

4. If the client sends a function name that is not `eval` or `exec`, the status code is set to `mayaserver.INVALID_METHOD` and the response is the requested method's name.

5. If an exception occurs, the status code is set to `mayaserver.UNHANDLED_ERROR` and the response is set to the traceback string.

Finally, inside of `mayaserver/client.py`, check the status code of the response and behave accordingly.

```python
import mayaserver #(1)

def sendrecv(socket, data):
    tosend = json.dumps(data)
    socket.send(tosend)
    recved = socket.recv()
    code, response = json.loads(recved) #(2)
    if code == mayaserver.SUCCESS: #(3)
        return response
    if code == mayaserver.UNHANDLED_ERROR: #(4)
        raise RuntimeError(response)
    if code == mayaserver.INVALID_METHOD: #(5)
        raise RuntimeError('Sent invalid method: %s' % response)
    raise RuntimeError('Unhandled response: %s, %s' % (
        code, response)) #(6)

if __name__ == '__main__':
    proc = start_process()
    sock = create_client()
    try:
        sendrecv(sock, ('spam', '')) #(7)
    except RuntimeError as ex:
        print 'Got intended error!', ex
    try:
        sendrecv(sock, ('eval', 'a = 1')) #(8)
    except RuntimeError as ex:
        print 'Got intended error!', ex
```

Let's first go over the highlighted changes in the `sendrecv` function:

1. Import `mayaserver` to access the status codes.

2. Unpack the server's response into `(code, response)`.

3. If the request was a success, just return the response.

4. If the server encountered an error while handling our request, raise a `RuntimeError` containing the traceback string. This isn't the most beautiful way of signaling to the client what caused the error, but it's usually enough.

5. If the request was for an invalid method, raise a `RuntimeError` containing the invalid name. You may also just want to take down the entire Python process, as this should never happen except due to a coding error.

6. Finally, if the response code is unrecognized, raise a `RuntimeError`. This should also never happen except due to a coding error.

Instead of the overuse of `RuntimeError`, you may want to define and raise custom error types, such as `RequestError`, `InvalidMethodError`, and `UnknownStatusCodeError`. We will use the more naive `RuntimeError` implementation in this chapter, though.

In the test code under `if __name__ == '__main__'`, we have two tests:

1. Ensure that sending an invalid method name (`'spam'`) causes the client to raise a `RuntimeError`.

2. Ensure that sending an invalid request, such as trying to `eval` the string `'1/0'` (which would cause a `ZeroDivisionError`), causes the client to raise a `RuntimeError`.

If you run the `mayaserver/client.py` file, you should get something like the following:

```
> mayapy mayaserver/client.py
Got intended error! Sent invalid method: spam
Got intended error! Traceback (most recent call last):...
```

Even though we've covered the places we expect an exception to be raised, what about the *unexpected* places? What if Maya crashes, is accidentally killed by the user, or there is some logical bug we haven't uncovered? The server process would die or lock up indefinitely, and the client would be forever waiting for a response.

Adding support for timeouts

It is not acceptable for a client to wait forever for a response it will never receive. The user would have to kill the client process manually, which is not just inconvenient but can also result in lost work. We can get around this by **timing out** and raising an error inside of the client's `sendrecv` function.

The good news is that timeouts only involve work on the client side, and we will not have to deal with the server for this feature. The bad news is that however you cut it, timeouts add complexity. Make the highlighted changes to add support for timeouts into the `mayaserver/client.py` file.

```python
import time #(1)

def sendrecv(socket, data, timeoutSecs=10.0): #(2)
    socket.send(json.dumps(data))
    starttime = time.time() #(3)
    while True: #(4)
        try:
            recved = socket.recv(zmq.NOBLOCK) #(5)
            break #(6)
        except zmq.Again: #(7)
            if time.time() - starttime > timeoutSecs: #(8)
                raise
            time.sleep(.1) #(9)

    code, response = json.loads(recved) #(10)
    # ...same code as before...
```

The new code is quite nuanced so let's go over it step-by-step.

1. Import the `time` module.

2. Add a `timeoutSecs` keyword argument to the `sendrecv` function. This new argument defines the number of seconds the client should wait for a response from the server before timing out.

3. After we send but before we recv, record the current time in seconds by calling the `time.time()` function.

4. Create a `while True` loop that will loop until we explicitly break out of it.

5. Pass the `zmq.NOBLOCK` argument to the `socket.recv` method. Instead of waiting indefinitely for a response, the call to `socket.recv` will immediately raise the `zmq.Again` error if there is no response from the server waiting.

6. If there *is* a response waiting, break out of the `while` loop and continue processing the response (see point 10).

7. Catch the `zmq.Again` error. This is a special error that is raised when `socket.recv(zmq.NOBLOCK)` is called and there's nothing to receive (see point 5).

8. If the current time is greater than our start time plus timeout, re-raise the exception. This is the *timeout*.

9. Otherwise, sleep for 0.1 seconds and try again (go back to point 5). You may want to handle your *sleep duration* differently, or avoid sleeping altogether. Sleeping just pauses the current thread for the provided number of seconds. Since we only have one thread, sleeping will pause the client process.

10. The code from here — response deserialization and processing — is the same as it was.

Let's test the new timeout functionality by putting the following code at the bottom of the `mayaserver/client.py` file and running it through the mayapy interpreter:

```
if __name__ == '__main__':
    start_process()
    sock = create_client()
    sendrecv(sock, ('exec', 'import time')) #(1)
    try:
        sendrecv(sock, ('exec', 'time.sleep(5)'), .1) #(2)
    except zmq.Again:
        print 'Timed out successfully!'
        sock = create_client() #(3)
    sendrecv(sock, ('eval', '1 + 1')) #(4)
    print 'And recovered successfully!'
```

Let's go through how the preceding test code works.

1. The client will instruct the server to import the time module so it can be used for the next call (see point 2). Refer to the *Understanding eval and exec* section earlier in this chapter for an explanation of execution scope and why this works.

2. Tell the server to sleep for 5 seconds, but only use a timeout of 0.1 seconds. The client will time out waiting for the server.

3. If a ZeroMQ socket does not receive successfully, it cannot be used to send again. Recall that in the case of a timeout, the `socket.recv` method raises an error and does not complete. To recover from the timeout, we must create a *new socket* to use. This is an unfortunate but important implementation detail. If we try to reuse the old socket, an error will be raised the next time the `socket.send` method is called because the socket will be in an invalid state.

4. To demonstrate that we can recover from the timeout, we send and receive a final `eval` request using the new socket.

Running `mayaserver/client.py` should result in the following printed to the console:

```
> mayapy mayaserver/client.py
Timed out successfully!
And recovered successfully!
```

Adding support for the client-server handshake

Finally, we get to the key remaining component of the automation system. Review *The client-server handshake* section earlier in this chapter if you need a reminder as to how the handshake is supposed to work. This will require adding quite a bit more code and removing the hard-coded connection strings.

First we will add the handshake code to the `mayaserver/server.py` file. This involves changing all the code before the `while True` loop, as shown in the following listing:

```
def runserver(handshake_port):
    sock = zmq.Context().socket(zmq.REP)
    appport = sock.bind_to_random_port('tcp://127.0.0.1')

    handshakesock = zmq.Context().socket(zmq.REQ)
    handshakesock.connect('tcp://127.0.0.1:%s' % handshake_port)
    handshakesock.send(str(appport))
    handshakesock.recv() # acknowledgement
    handshakesock.close()
    # ... server loop is the same ...
```

The first thing to note is that the `runserver` function takes in the handshake port number as an argument. Before starting the handshake, bind a new reply socket to a random port. This bound port is the *application port* and will be used for the application's client/server communication. This takes the place of the hard-coded port used previously. Then create a request socket and connect to the *handshake port*. We send the application port number from the server to the client over the handshake port, wait for the client to send an acknowledgment, and close the handshake port. From this point, we can use the same exact server loop we had previously.

The client code has much more substantial changes.

```
COMMAND = ('python("import mayaserver.server;'
          'mayaserver.server.runserver(%s)");') #(1)


def start_process(): #(2)
    handshakesock = zmq.Context().socket(zmq.REP) #(3)
    handshakeport = handshakesock.bind_to_random_port(
        'tcp://127.0.0.1')
    command = COMMAND % handshakeport #(4)
    process = subprocess.Popen(
        [MAYAEXE, '-command', command]) #(5)
    atexit.register(kill, process)
    appport = int(handshakesock.recv()) #(6)
    handshakesock.send('')
    handshakesock.close() #(7)
    return appport #(8)


def create_client(port): #(9)
    socket = zmq.Context().socket(zmq.REQ)
    socket.connect('tcp://127.0.0.1:%s' % port)
    return socket
```

Let's go over the preceding code, which is almost all new.

1. The command string has changed because the handshake port number must be provided as part of the string. The COMMAND variable now acts as a *template* that we will customize with the handshake port.

2. Before the Maya process starts, initiate the handshake. Create the handshake socket and bind it to a random port. Recall we did the same, but for the application port and socket, on the server.

3. Create a *concrete* command string, formatting it with the handshake port number.

4. Use the concrete command string as the value of the -command argument for a new Maya process. Use the atexit module to kill the server when the client dies, just like we were doing already.

5. Wait for the server to send the client the application port number by receiving on the handshake socket.

6. Acknowledge that the application port was received by sending an empty string. Close the handshake socket. The handshake is over.

7. Return the application port number. The `start_process` function cannot return a socket because we may need to recreate sockets to the same server in the case of a timeout, as in the previous section.

8. Change the `create_client` function so it takes in a port and uses that instead of the hard-coded port it used previously.

Let's test out the handshake by starting up two clients and servers simultaneously. Place the following code at the bottom of `mayaserver/client.py`.

```python
if __name__ == '__main__':
    def start_and_get_pid():
        appport = start_process()
        sock = create_client(appport)
        sendrecv(sock, ('exec', 'import os'))
        return sendrecv(sock, ('eval', 'os.getpid()'))
    srv1Pid = start_and_get_pid()
    srv2Pid = start_and_get_pid()
    print 'Client proc %s started Maya procs: %s, %s' % (
        os.getpid(), srv1Pid, srv2Pid)
```

If you run this code in a new mayapy interpreter, you should get something like the following:

```
> mayapy mayaserver/client.py
Result: untitled
Result: untitled
Client proc 8056 started Maya procs: 4448, 6264
```

The `Result: untitled` line was printed twice because two Maya processes were started. With hard-coded ports, we could only start up one Maya process. Now we can create any number of client and server pairs from any number of Python processes.

At this point, our automation system is fully functional and ready for use. While there are still improvements to make (aren't there always?), the rest of this chapter will look into some use cases and improvements for the automation system.

Practical uses and improvements

We will close out the chapter by describing various uses for our automation system, as well as a few improvements.

Batch processing using Maya

The most obvious application for the automation system is batch processing. The following simple script will go through all files in the current directory, delete all unknown nodes, and save the file to a new path. It will print out the result of the processing for each file, and skip over errors.

```python
import os
import mayaserver.client as mayaclient

execstr = """import pymel.core as pmc
pmc.openFile(%r, force=True)
for item in pmc.ls(type='unknown'):
    if item.exists():
        pmc.delete(item)
pmc.system.saveAs(%r)"""

def process(socket, path):
    newpath = os.path.splitext(path)[0] + '_clean.ma'
    mayaclient.sendrecv(
        socket, ('exec', execstr % (path, newpath)))

if __name__ == '__main__':
    sock = mayaclient.create_client(mayaclient.start_process())
    paths = [p for p in os.listdir(os.getcwd())
             if p.endswith(('.ma', '.mb'))]
    for p in paths:
        if p.endswith(('.ma', '.mb')):
            print 'Processing', p
            try:
                process(sock, p)
                print 'Success!', p
            except RuntimeError:
                print 'Failed!', p
```

While it is nice that the processing happens in a separate process, we can do much better. The following is some additional code to **parallelize** the batching. Multiple Maya instances will be processing files simultaneously.

```python
def process_files(paths):
    sock = mayaclient.create_client(mayaclient.start_process())
    for path in paths:
        print 'Processing', path
        try:
            process(sock, path)
            print 'Success!', path
        except RuntimeError:
            print 'Failed!', path


if __name__ == '__main__':
    import threading
    paths = [f for f in os.listdir(os.getcwd())
             if f.endswith(('.ma', '.mb'))]
    threads = []
    num_procs = 4 # Or number of CPU cores, etc.
    for i in range(num_procs):
        chunk = [paths[j] for j in
                 range(i, len(paths), num_procs)]
        t = threading.Thread(target=process_files, args=[chunk])
        t.start()
        threads.append(t)
    for t in threads:
        t.join()
```

The preceding parallelization code will ultimately start four threads. Each thread will process about a quarter of the total Maya files. The processing happens in a function which will start a Maya process, and ask it to process each file in the thread's list of files. Finally, the code waits for all threads to complete their work.

Because the processing happens on a number of threads, and the actual computation takes place outside of the current Python process (in Maya), the work occurs mostly in parallel. Threading is outside of the scope of this book so we will not go into more detail. A cursory understanding of the Python standard library's threading module should make the behavior of the preceding code clear. This technique is a great way to make batch processing go much faster while adding very little new code.

Running a server in a Maya GUI session

There are two changes we need to make in order to run the automation server in a Maya session that has a GUI.

The first is to run the server loop on a background thread. If we run the server on the main thread, the **event loop** will never be pumped, causing the GUI to be locked up.

 Refer to *Chapter 5, Building Graphical User Interfaces for Maya*, for an explanation of the event loop.

The second change is to use `maya.utils.executeInMainThreadWithResult` instead of invoking `exec` or `eval` directly. The `executeInMainThreadWithResult` function takes a function and its arguments, and will schedule the function to be called in the main thread when it is idle.

We must do this because the server loop runs outside of the main thread, but the client request may need to interact with the Maya scene. You should only interact with the Maya scene from the main thread. The following code demonstrates the necessary changes. The code that hasn't changed is edited out.

```
import threading
from maya.utils import executeInMainThreadWithResult

def runserver(handshake_port):
    threading.Thread(
        target=_runserver, args=[handshake_port]).start()

def _eval(s):
    return eval(s, globals(), globals())

def _exec(s):
    exec s in globals(), globals()

def _runserver(handshake_port):
    ...
        if func == 'exec':
            executeInMainThreadWithResult(_exec, arg)
        elif func == 'eval':
            response = executeInMainThreadWithResult(
                _eval, arg)
    ...
```

There are few things to take note of in the preceding code. First, the `_runserver` function, which contains the server loop, executes in a thread so it does not block the main Maya thread. The old `runserver` function just starts this thread.

Second, there are now `_eval` and `_exec` functions wrapping the underlying calls to `eval` and `exec`. This makes the `maya.utils.executeInMainThreadWithResult` function easier to use.

Finally, the `_eval` and `_exec` functions are called through `maya.utils.executeInMainThreadWithResult` instead of being invoked directly.

Running automated tests in Maya

Running automated tests in Maya is notoriously difficult. While you can use the mayapy interpreter for small, isolated unit tests like we did in *Chapter 1, Introspecting Maya, Python, and PyMEL*, higher-level tests are more difficult. Many people desire automated tests for critical components of a pipeline, such as the startup routine, menu and shelf creation, important plugins, and exporters. However, Maya's complexity makes these a frightening prospect. What happens if the startup code is broken or Maya crashes?

We can use this chapter's automation system to better run high-level tests. A standard Python or mayapy client can start up a Maya process and query information from it. It can run the exporter and compare the result to a known good version, or use PyMEL to check whether the right menu items are created. If Maya crashes, or some fundamental code in the startup routine is broken, the client can timeout and kill the server.

I've used the automation system presented in this chapter extensively for automated testing of Maya and other applications. It has been a key component of creating robust and stable software.

Adding support for logging

A full overview of Python logging is not in the scope of this book. However, with any system that does **input/output** (IO), a robust logging solution is a necessity. Problems happen, usually due to programmer error but often due to environment problems, network disruptions, or faulty hardware. Errors in the server (or network) may mean the client never gets a reply. Without logging, it is difficult or impossible to know what happened. At the very least, you'll want to log when things start up, log what you are about to send, and log what you receive before processing it too much. Logging allows you to reconstruct what happened when the time comes to reproduce and fix a bug.

The following is an abbreviated server with some basic logging. You would want to put similar logging into client functions as well:

```python
import logging

log = logging.getLogger(__name__)

def runserver(handshake_port):
    sock = zmq.Context().socket(zmq.REP)
    appport = sock.bind_to_random_port('tcp://127.0.0.1')
    log.info('Handshaking on %s, sending %s',
            handshake_port, appport)
    # ... do handshake ...
    log.info('Handshake finished, looping.')
    while True:
        recved = json.loads(sock.recv())
        log.debug('recv: %s', recved)
        # ... request processing ...
        log.debug('send: %s', tosend)
        sock.send(json.dumps(tosend))
```

Supporting multiple languages and applications

Suppose all of your tools and programmers are using a language like C# instead of Python, with the sole exception of Maya and people programming in Maya. You can easily hook Maya into a tool written in any language by porting the client into the language of your choice. Of course, the client still needs to assemble its code strings in Python or whatever the language of the server is.

The design of the server is also not limited to Python and Maya. You can practically use the server code as-is in another Python application. You can also use the same concepts and write the server portion in an entirely different language in order to control something like a game engine.

Supporting control from a remote computer

In this chapter, we dealt exclusively with a server and client on the same computer. While it is feasible to have a remote Maya server process that is not started by the client, I've found very limited value in this. That said, it would be useful in a situation where Maya is not your main application, and you only need it to do something like import files and export them into a different format.

You could run several Maya processes on another machine to support this type of pipeline. This increases the complexity of the automation system, however, since you'll need another solution for process lifetimes, debugging, persisting state between client requests, clients interfering with each other, and more. I wouldn't suggest it, but nor would I rule it out.

As a related concern, once you move from local to remote communication, there's the issue of network security. Any communication should go on behind a network firewall, so you can be blissfully unaware of the nasty world outside.

Designing an object-oriented system

It's possible to get quite far without custom classes. The function-based approach presented in this chapter manages to work for the automation system, but it can be simplified by using a few classes. There is an example of a more object-oriented client in *Chapter 7, Taming the Maya API*. If you end up adopting the system presented here for your own use, I suggest using an object-oriented design.

Evaluating other RPC frameworks

We discussed the concept of Remote Procedure Calls earlier, and several frameworks exist for Python. I am sure between me typing these words and you reading them, several more frameworks will come into existence. You may want to try some of these frameworks first, and see if any of them work for your needs. They can conceivably save a significant amount of effort.

Summary

In this chapter, we learned how to create a request-reply automation system in Python using ZeroMQ. We learned some basics about network programming, operating system processes, and how to control Maya's startup routine. We built a system to start, control, and kill an arbitrary number of Maya processes from a single Python or mayapy process. We finished up by exploring ways we can take advantage of and improve our newfound powers.

In the next chapter, we will dive back into Maya. We will learn more about how types and classes work in Python, how the OpenMaya API is designed, and how to use it to perform complex tasks. We will also explore Maya's plugin system and create a command plugin.

7
Taming the Maya API

Maya's Python command system, MEL, is extremely powerful. You can use it
to automate and customize Maya to an incredible degree. Python and PyMEL
have largely superseded MEL because they are much more powerful and flexible.
We've put this power and flexibility to great use by creating composable libraries,
robust error handling, an automation system, and maintainable GUIs.

What we haven't yet discussed is Python's role in augmenting, and in many cases
replacing, C++ in Maya programming. There are some things that the command
system and MEL are designed to not do. Dealing with the Maya **Application
Programming Interface (API)** is one such thing. Python, however, can utilize most
of the Maya API that C++ has access to. In *Chapter 8, Unleashing the Maya API through
Python*, we will see how Python allows us to do things we cannot even do in C++,
and easily create custom Maya plugins in a very Pythonic way with no boilerplate.

Before we jump into that we will use this chapter to explain and demonstrate a number
of concepts central to the Maya API. We start off with learning about types and classes,
since the Maya API is thoroughly object-oriented and designed around them. We
will explore the design of the Maya Python API, see how Maya exposes its C++ API
through Python bindings, and learn how to read the Maya API Reference. We will go
through several examples using the Maya Python API, including callbacks and mesh
creation. Finally, we'll dip our toes into the wonderful world of Maya Python plugins,
and see how the system works by creating a command plugin to play sounds.

Explaining types

There are many definitions of the computer science term **type**. There are so many, in fact, that choosing one is difficult. The best definition depends on what your perspective is. A compiler writer may see a type as an abstract mathematical entity. A statistics programmer may see it as a name and series of values. We will approach types from the perspective of a Python programmer who needs to get work done.

 I consider the terms **type** and **class** interchangeable in Python (though not in all other languages). It can be perhaps argued that they are not exactly the same, but for our purposes they are.

We'll start with the definition that a type is a name associated with some values. A name and value pair is called an **attribute**. Consider the following statement:

```
widget = PySide.QtCore.QWidget()
```

In that statement, the type of the `widget` variable is `Pyside.QtCore.QWidget`. By virtue of `widget` being an instance of the `QWidget` type, it has certain names and values. For example, `widget` has an attribute named `destroyed`. The value of the `destroyed` attribute is an instance of the `PySide.QtCore.QSignal` type.

Usually a type represents some idea, so the names and values seek to describe and support working with that idea, as we will see in the next section.

Dicts all the way down

In this section, we will create a type that represents a collection of unique items. Think of it as only the keys in a dictionary, just like Python's `set` class. The type needs an attribute to hold the items in the collection, which we'll call its state. It also needs a number of attributes to interact with the state, such as adding, removing, and querying items.

We introduced the phrase "dicts all the way down" in *Chapter 1, Introspecting Maya, Python, and PyMEL*. It is relevant again here (of course it is, since Python iss dicts all the way down!). A class can be thought of as a dictionary with special behavior. For example, consider the following class. You can put it into a `myset.py` file in your development root if you'd like to run the examples in this section.

```
class MySet(object):
    def __init__(self):
        self._state = {}
    def add(self, v):
        self._state[v] = None
```

```
    def remove(self, v):
        del self._state[v]
    def items(self):
        return self._state.keys()
```

In the preceding code, the `class` statement defines a class named `MySet`. It inherits from the `object` type, which is the base class of all classes (we will ignore old-style classes in this book). The `MySet` type has an attribute named `_state` which points to a dictionary used to hold the unique items. It has three more attributes which are methods: `add`, `remove`, and `items`. The first argument to every instance method on a type is `self`, that is, the instance of the type. For example, consider the following code, which creates and manipulates two unique instances of the `MySet` class:

```
>>> import myset
>>> s1 = myset.MySet()
>>> s2 = myset.MySet()
>>> s1.add(1)
>>> s2.add('a')
>>> s1.items()
[1]
>>> s2.items()
['a']
```

In keeping which our theme that types are "dicts all the way down," you can access the members of a type or instance through its __dict__ attribute, as shown in the following example:

```
>>> myset.MySet.__dict__
[...('__init__', <function __init__ at 0x...>),
 ('__module__', 'myset'),
 ('add', <function add at 0x...>),
 ('items', <function items at 0x...>),
 ('remove', <function remove at 0x...>)]
>>> s = myset.MySet()
>>> s.__dict__
{'_state': {}}
```

The `MySet.__dict__` attribute holds references to the methods and information about the type itself. The `s.__dict__` attribute just holds the values of the attributes for that instance, such as the `_state` dictionary.

There is much more to types in Python, but the goal of this section is not an exhaustive explanation. It is hopefully enough to get you up and running for the work we do in the rest of this chapter.

If you are confused by some of the terminology here, review the *Adding support for methods* section in *Chapter 1, Introspecting Maya, Python, and PyMEL*.

Using custom types to simplify code

Now that we've seen how to create custom classes, let's put them to work for us. In this section, we will change the automation system client we built in *Chapter 6, Automating Maya from the Outside*, to use a class instead of functions. Rather than rewriting all of the original code, we will just create an easy-to-use wrapper class around the original functions. Place the following code into a `newmayaclient.py` file in your development root:

```python
import zmq
import mayaserver.client as oldmayaclient

class MayaAutomationClient(object):
    def __init__(self): #(1)
        self.realport = oldmayaclient.start_process()
        self.reqsock = self._create_client()

    def _create_client(self):
        return oldmayaclient._create_client(self.realport)

    def sendrecv(self, *args, **kwargs): #(2)
        try: #(3)
            return oldmayaclient.sendrecv(
                self.reqsock, *args, **kwargs)
        except zmq.Again:
            self.reqsock = self._create_client()
            raise
```

Let's walk through the preceding code and compare it to the function-based version from last chapter:

1. Classes can have an __init__ method which is called just after the object is constructed. The __init__ method initializes the object, usually assigning some initial value to its attributes. When a `MayaAutomationClient` instance is created, the Maya server process will be started, the handshake will be performed, and the client's application socket will be created.

2. The only method callers need to worry about is now the `sendrecv` method. They also only need to pass it the data to evaluate or execute, not the socket to send the data with.

3. The timeout behavior, where a new application socket must be created if the server takes too long to respond to the client, is easily integrated into the class' behavior. Previously, the caller needed to handle creating a new client if the original timed out. This design is much simpler, and makes the socket recreation an implementation detail.

Using a class hides complicated logic behind a simple interface. With the function-based approach, it is incumbent upon the caller to know when and how to use the `start_process`, `create_client`, and `sendrecv` functions, and handle timeouts. This is a lot of information for every caller to manage!

Compare this to the preceding code using a custom type. The caller only needs to create a `MayaAutomationClient` instance and invoke the `sendrecv` method on it. That is significantly simpler!

This new class-based client can be used as follows:

```
>>> import newmayaclient
>>> cl = newmayaclient.MayaAutomationClient()
>>> cl.sendrecv(('eval', '1 + 1'))
2
```

Using types is a great way to associate data with the functions that operate on that data.

Introducing inheritance by drawing shapes

Another strength of classes is that they can be **inherited**. We saw the benefits of inheritance in *Chapter 1, Introspecting Maya, Python, and PyMEL*, when working with joints, transforms, and PyNodes. In this section, we will apply inheritance to our own classes. We will create a base class to draw shapes in the Maya viewport. Subclasses will customize the shapes that are actually drawn.

First, let's create our `Shape` base class. It will deal with the low-level drawing code that Python has access to through the Maya Python API. It's okay if you don't fully understand the API calls here or are unfamiliar with OpenGL. In fact, that's precisely the point of putting this code in a base class. Subclasses can inherit its drawing behavior without having to learn about the Maya API or OpenGL:

```
from maya import OpenMayaRender #(1)
renderer = OpenMayaRender.MHardwareRenderer
glFT = renderer.theRenderer().glFunctionTable()

class Shape(object): #(2)
```

```
def coords(self): #(3)
    """Return a list of groups of points,
    each group defining a line segment."""
    return []

def draw(self, m3dview): #(4)
    m3dview.beginGL() #(5)
    for segmentcoords in self.coords(): #(6)
        glFT.glBegin(OpenMayaRender.MGL_LINE_STRIP) #(7)
        for coords in segmentcoords: #(8)
            glFT.glVertex3f(*coords)
        glFT.glEnd() #(9)
    m3dview.endGL() #(10)
```

Let's walk through the preceding example in detail:

1. Import the `maya.OpenMayaRender` module, which exposes classes useful for rendering and drawing to the Maya Python API. Just after the import, assign the OpenGL function table helper to the `glFT` variable. This provides helpers for drawing, which will be used later.

2. Define the `Shape` base class, which inherits from the `object` type.

3. Define a `coords` method and docstring. The subclasses we create next will override the `coords` method, providing an alternative implementation. In the base class, return an empty list of coordinates so nothing will be drawn.

4. Define a `draw` method that takes an `OpenMayaUI.M3dView` instance, which will be passed in later. This function contains the logic for drawing our shape.

5. Tell the view to set itself up for OpenGL drawing. This pattern of paired begin and end calls is unfortunately common throughout the Maya API. It is similar to the `undoInfo(openChunk=True)` and `undoInfo(closeChunk=True)` pattern we wrapped with the `mayautils.undo_chunk` context manager in *Chapter 4, Leveraging Context Managers and Decorators in Maya*. I would encourage you to build a context manager if you use these functions often.

6. Loop through each segment. Each segment is a list of XYZ coordinate tuples.

7. Tell the OpenGL renderer to begin rendering a line strip. Subsequent calls will add points to this line strip.

8. Go through each segment coordinate tuple, and add a point to the OpenGL line strip that was opened in point 7.

9. Close the line strip.

10. Tell the `M3dView` that the OpenGL drawing is complete.

11. Remember, the internals of the draw method are not for the faint of heart. Putting them in the Shape base class means we only have to write it once but can use it many times.

 If you'd like to find out more about any of the API classes used in the preceding example, you should refer to the *Maya API Reference*. See the *Navigating the Maya API Reference* section later in this chapter.

Now, let's create two subclasses that define concrete shapes: Cross and Square.

```
class Cross(Shape): #(1)
    def coords(self): #(2)
        return [
            ((-10, 0, 0), (10, 0, 0)),
            ((0, -10, 0), (0, 10, 0)),
            ((0, 0, -10), (0, 0, 10)),]


class Square(Shape): #(3)
    def coords(self): #(4)
        return [
            ((20, 20, 0),
            (20, -20, 0),
            (-20, -20, 0),
            (-20, 20, 0),
            (20, 20, 0))]
```

Let's go through the preceding code example:

1. Define the Cross class. It inherits from Shape, so it automatically picks up the draw and coords methods.

2. Override the coords method. Return a list of three pairs of XYZ coordinate tuples. Each pair defines a line segment which is an axis of the cross. The first pair goes across the X axis, the second goes across the Y axis, and the third across the z axis.

3. Define a Square class that also inherits from the Shape class.

4. Override the coords method. Return a list containing a single line segment of five points. Each point is a corner of the square. The first corner is repeated at the end, so the segment is closed.

Now, we can test out the drawing of our shapes by running the following code in the Script Editor:

```
from maya import OpenMayaUI #(1)
m3dview = OpenMayaUI.M3dView.active3dView() #(2)
m3dview.beginOverlayDrawing() #(3)
Square().draw(m3dview) #(4)
Cross().draw(m3dview)
m3dview.endOverlayDrawing() #(5)
```

Let's walk over the code line by line to better understand what's going on:

1. Import the `maya.OpenMayaUI` module, which provides Python exposure to useful classes having to do with the Maya user interface.

2. Get the active viewport's `M3dView` instance so we can draw into it.

3. The call to `m3dview.beginOverlayDrawing()` sets up an OpenGL context so we can draw into the viewport. This is another good place for a context manager.

4. Create a new `Square` instance and call its `draw` method with the active `M3dView` instance. Do the same for `Cross`. This will draw into the viewport.

5. Tell the viewport to close the OpenGL context.

You should see the cross and the square drawn in the Maya viewport:

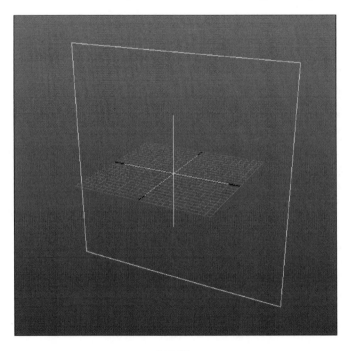

Remember that your types should always adhere to the **Liskov Substitution Principle**, which we learned about in *Chapter 1, Introspecting Maya, Python, and PyMEL*. I consider it among the most important principles in object-oriented programming. It says that if S is a subtype of T, then objects of type T can be used to replace objects of type S without altering a program's correctness. In our case, this means that any subclass of Shape that overrides the coords method should return a list of tuples of XYZ coordinates for drawing.

Inheritance is a key to understanding and using the Maya API. Furthermore, the pattern of having methods such as Shape.coords that are meant to be overridden in subclasses is powerful, especially when we look at Maya plugins later in this chapter.

That said, inheritance can be abused. Designing with inheritance is a skill that will take time to learn. We must use it in many areas of Maya, but think twice when applying it to your own classes or frameworks.

Introducing Maya's API and architecture

Maya, as we know, uses three distinct languages: MEL, Python, and C++. In previous chapters, we've used Python in much the same way as we would have used MEL, by creating high-level functionality and controls for Maya. We have seen, however, that the general purpose design of Python has allowed us to do things that we could not otherwise do in MEL. This includes building pure PySide GUIs in *Chapter 5, Building Graphical User Interfaces for Maya*, and the automation system from *Chapter 6, Automating Maya from the Outside*. These would simply not have been possible in MEL and would have required some Maya-specific C++ coding.

Another unique application of Python in Maya, and the focus of this chapter, is Python's access to the Maya API. In the previous section, we used the Maya Python API to draw into the active viewport. Having Maya's API exposed to Python means that every single artist and Python hacker has the full, raw power of Maya available. No one is any longer bound by its scripting interface. This level of power was once reserved for those with a healthy knowledge of C++, an IDE, compiler, and the dogged determination necessary to create and distribute compiled Maya plugins. Programming in Maya became much more democratic, and the richness of tools exploded.

The explosion started in 2007, when Autodesk added support for Python into Maya 8.5. In this section, we will go over how the Maya Python API bindings work, how Python and C++ work together, and how to navigate the sometimes obtuse Maya API reference.

Understanding the OpenMaya bindings

In *Chapter 5, Building Graphical User Interfaces for Maya*, we used PySide and PyQt, which are Python bindings to the Qt C++ framework. The OpenMaya Python bindings work in the same way and allow us to call C++ code from Python. Autodesk uses the **Simplified Wrapper and Interface Generator (SWIG)** to create bindings between the C++ API and Python. Let's look at how the bindings work in more detail, since the are not as clean as something like PySide.

> In this chapter, I will use the terms *Maya API* or *OpenMaya* when discussing the C++ or general Maya API, and *Maya Python API* when discussing the Python bindings. You can find out more about SWIG at www.swig.org.

There exists an `MPxNode` C++ class in the Maya API. It is exposed to Python via the `maya.OpenMayaMPx.MPxNode` class. All C++ classes, with a few exceptions, are exposed to Python through one of the OpenMaya Python modules. These include the `maya.OpenMaya`, `maya.OpenMayaMPx`, and `maya.OpenMayaUI` modules.

The C++ `MPxNode.name()` method that returns an `MString` object. In Python, the `MPxNode.name()` method returns a Unicode string. Certain types that map directly to Python types are automatically converted by the bindings, and in some cases are not even exposed to Python. For example, the `MString` type maps to the Python `unicode` type, and an `MStringArray` to a list of strings. Neither can be created by Python directly. The `MInt` type maps to the Python `int` type, though `MIntArray` is accessible to Python.

> Not exposing all classes was a mistake by Autodesk. There are special cases in the API where the implicit conversion between Python types and Maya Python API types can cause issues, such as the `MFnMesh.createBlindData` method. Autodesk has recently developed a Maya Python API 2.0, which should eventually fix these issues and replace the original Maya Python API, similar to how PyMEL is superseding `maya.cmds`. I have great hope for it, but as it is still quite new, I've chosen to use the original Maya Python API in this book.

When we program with the Maya Python API, we are almost always calling C++ code under the hood. We are writing Python but using a C++ style. This is why Python code using the API often looks very *non-Pythonic*. The OpenMaya idioms are very different than what we're used to:

- Iteration and dealing with lists is clunky and limited. We must use classes such as `MIntArray`, or populate collections like `MSelectionList` using an `add` method.

- The infamous pass by reference design that leads to methods designed to mutate an object passed in, rather than return something new.

- Function sets, introduced later, are necessary to do nearly anything with a node. Nodes themselves do not have any real functionality.

All of these manifest themselves in the following code block, which converts a node's name into an MObject instance and back into its name. The comments pointing out these three problematic idioms are highlighted.

```
>>> from maya import OpenMaya
>>> sellist = OpenMaya.MSelectionList()
>>> sellist.add(objname) #Can't initialize a list with items.
>>> mobj = OpenMaya.MObject()
>>> sellist.getDependNode(0, mobj) #Pass by reference
>>> jntdepnode = OpenMaya.MFnDependencyNode(mobj) #Function sets
>>> jntdepnode.name()
u'myobj'
```

It is necessary to understand each of these design decisions so that you can use the Maya Python API effectively. They are not intuitive but they are important. We'll learn how to cope with these designs throughout the rest of this chapter.

Navigating the Maya API Reference

Though there are many good examples and tutorials for using the Maya Python API, the Maya API Reference will be your go-to source when you need to look something up. However, it is a reference for C++, so you need to be comfortable translating the documentation into Python in your head. Effective use of the Maya API Reference requires understanding the underlying design and vocabulary.

For example, the MFnMesh.create method has three possible signatures, as shown in the following example. The differences between the three versions are highlighted.

```
MObject create(
    int numVertices,
    int numPolygons,
    const MPointArray &vertexArray,
    const MIntArray &polygonCounts,
    const MintArray &polygonConnects,
    MObjeect parentOrOwner=MObject::kNullObj,
    Mstatus *ReturnStatus=NULL)
MObject create(
    int numVertices,
    int numPolygons,
```

```
    const MFloatPointArray &vertexArray,
    const MIntArray &polygonCounts,
    const MintArray &polygonConnects,
    MObject parentOrOwner=MObject::kNullObj,
    Mstatus *ReturnStatus=NULL)
MObject create(
    int numVertices,
    int numPolygons,
    const MPointArray &vertexArray,
    const MIntArray &polygonCounts,
    const MintArray &polygonConnects,
    const MFloatArray &uArray,
    const MFloatArray &vArray,
    MObject parentOrOwner=MObject::kNullObj,
    Mstatus *ReturnStatus=NULL)
```

This is a very common pattern in the Maya API. Let's go over the important points:

- There are multiple versions of the same method. This is possible due to method overloading, which is a feature of C++ and many other statically-typed languages. Usually, it is enough to understand that any of those methods can be called, and the bindings will choose the right one. In certain cases, Maya may raise an error if the choice between two methods is ambiguous, and you must find some way to disambiguate them. Python normally does not use method overloading. Instead, it relies on optional arguments.

- The signature of each method overload is different, but sometimes in small ways. For example, the type of a certain parameter may be different, such as where the vertexArray parameter changes between MPointArray and MFloatPointArray types. A more significant difference is when the number of parameters change, such as the addition of the uArray and vArray parameters in the third method overload.

- The last argument to each create method is an MStatus instance. This is not used in Python, so ignore it. The Maya C++ API is designed to support programming by status code, so that if a method call fails, it returns or sets a failure status code. In Python, an exception would be raised instead.

- The type of each argument is specified, and many have an inconvenient array type, such as MIntArray. You should use a Python list where possible, but sometimes you must use an OpenMaya collection. If a method does not accept a normal Python list, it will raise an error, and you can try using OpenMaya objects instead.

- The return type of the method is MObject, and is listed before the method name. Methods commonly return an MStatus instance. You can ignore MStatus return values, just like you can ignore it when it is a parameter. Exceptions are automatically used instead.

The Maya API Reference is incredibly detailed and helpful. You should learn to read it fluently to program with the Maya Python API effectively. It can be frustrating at first if you've never used C++. However even if you've never programmed in a language other than Python, you will get the hang of it eventually. I would also suggest learning how to read basic C++ code, so you can better understand the examples included with the reference.

Understanding MObjects and function sets

The Maya API is designed around the concept of using MObjects to represent Maya Dependency Graph nodes, and function sets for operating on those nodes. The Maya API Reference has the following to say about the MObject type:

> *"MObject is the generic class for accessing all Maya internal modeling, animation and rendering Objects, collectively referred to as Model Objects, through the API. This includes all Dependency Graph (DG) Nodes, of which Directed Acyclic Graph (DAG) Nodes are a subset."*

It's important to note that an MObject is not the same as the underlying Maya node. It only provides access to the underlying node. For example, deleting an MObject instance does not delete the Maya node. To work with a Maya node, you must use a function set. A function set is a type prefixed with MFn, and it is usually constructed with an MObject instance. The PyMEL help has this to say about function sets:

> *"Because I am a huge nerd, I like to the think of the function sets as robotic 'mechs' and the fundamental objects as 'spirits' or 'ghosts' that inhabit them, like in Ghost in the Shell."*

I find this description quite illustrative, even though I do not watch any *manga*.

The design of having fundamental objects and function sets works well for the Maya API, which is an interface into an extensible C++ application. It is totally necessary for Python, however. You should not design any Python framework this way.

When you are using PyMEL, you can access a PyNode's underlying API objects through the __api*__ methods, as shown in the following example:

```
>>> p = pmc.PyNode('perspShape')
>>> p.__apimfn__()
```

```
<maya.OpenMaya.MFnCamera; proxy of <Swig Object of type 'MFnCa...
>>> p.__apimdagpath__()
<maya.OpenMaya.MDagPath; proxy of <Swig Object of type 'MDagPa...
>>> a = p.focalLength
>>> a
Attribute(u'perspShape.focalLength')
>>> a.__apimplug__()
<maya.OpenMaya.MPlug; proxy of <Swig Object of type 'MPlug *' ...
```

Truth be told, I've rarely had a need to access these methods, and as the PyMEL help says, they are implementation details and the names could change. They are there if you need them, however, and can be useful when you use the Maya Python API and PyMEL together.

Learning the Maya Python API by example

Something like the Maya API is best explained through demonstration. Once you get the hang of it, the Maya API Reference and its copious examples will be a wonderful source of information. However, it will take some time and effort to become proficient. This section will present several easy-to-tackle problems to help illustrate the Maya Python API.

Converting a name to an MObject node

It's important to remember that when we step into the world of OpenMaya, we leave the Pythonic simplicity of PyMEL behind. The following line of code converts a node name string into a PyMEL PyNode:

```
>>> pmc.PyNode('mynode')
nt.Transform(u'mynode')
```

In the wonderful world of the Maya Python API, though, there is much more code involved to convert a string into the MObject instance that refers to the node:

```
>>> sellist = OpenMaya.MSelectionList() #(1)
>>> sellist.add('mynode') #(2)
>>> node = OpenMaya.MObject() #(3)
>>> sellist.getDependNode(0, node) #(4)
>>> node #(5)
<maya.OpenMaya.MObject; proxy of <Swig Object of type 'MObject...
```

Let's go over the preceding example in more detail:

1. Create an instance of the woefully named `MSelectionList` type. It does not necessarily have anything to do with selections. The `MSelectionList` must be created and populated in separate steps.

2. Use the `MSelectionList.add` method, which can take a MEL-like selection string (the name of the node, in our case) to add the object we are looking for to the list.

3. Create an empty `MObject` instance that will eventually point to the node we are looking for.

4. Pass this empty `MObject` to the `MSelectionList.getDependNode` method, along with the index of the item in the `MSelectionList` instance. Since we added only one item, the index is zero.

5. Finally, we have the `MObject` instance for our node. Note the unsightly string representation of Maya Python API objects.

In most cases, though certainly not all, the API is easier to use than this. Inconvenient patterns can also be hidden behind simpler functions. For example, the preceding code could be wrapped in a `name_to_mobject` function.

Getting the name of an MObject

Finding an `MObject` by name is clunky, but finding the name of an `MObject` isn't so bad. In PyMEL, such a routine is straightforward, involving a single method call:

```
>>> pynode.name()
u'mynode'
```

In the API, the same routine can still be a one-liner. It is also our first use of a function set, which were introduced earlier in the chapter. In the following example, the `MFnDependencyNode` function set it used to find the node's name.

```
>>> OpenMaya.MFnDependencyNode(mobject).name()
u'mynode'
```

Getting the hash of a node

Getting the hash value of a node is similar to getting the name of a node. A hash value is a fixed length value, such as a 32-bit integer, that represents a variable length value, such as a string, which can be of any size. In Maya, because the hash of a node should never change, you can use it for identifying and keeping track of nodes.

Getting the hash of a node in Python is done with the built-in `hash` function. PyMEL is smart enough to return the underlying node's hash value.

```
>>> hash(pynode)
409350872
```

Even if `pynode` is renamed or otherwise changes, it will still have the same hash.

To get the hash of an `MObject`, we use the `maya.OpenMaya.MObjectHandle` class. While not a function set, it works conceptually the same, providing some additional functionality to an `MObject` instance. To get the hash through the Maya Python API, you can use the following:

```
>>> OpenMaya.MObjectHandle(mobject).hashCode()
409350872
```

Given the same underlying node, the hash from PyMEL will be the same as the hash from the Maya API. This allows us to identify Maya nodes between PyMEL and the API, even if names change or all you have is the hash value.

As a final note, the rules around implementing a type that is properly hashable are nuanced, and we will not explore them here. The internet has enough good resources on implementing hashable Python objects properly. How PyMEL handles hashing is explained in its documentation at `http://bit.ly/1v28Gp4`.

Building a mesh

Now we will work on a task well suited for the Maya API: building a mesh from code. You can use this system to write importers for mesh formats that Maya does not support. In our case, we will create a simple cube using the `MFnMesh` function set.

Let's start by looking at what methods we will need to call to fully create a mesh, and what data is used by each method:

- To create the mesh, use the `MFnMesh.create` method. It takes the number of vertices (`numVertices`), number of polygons (`numPolygons`), an `MPointArray` of the positions for each vertex (`vertexArray`), an `MIntArray` for the number of vertices in each polygon (`polygonCounts`), and finally, an `MIntArray` that specifies the indices of vertices in `vertexArray` that are part of each polygon (`polygonConnects`). `polygonConnects` is best thought of as a list of tuples that define the vertex indices for each polygon, except all chained together into one list.

- To set the vertex UVs, use the MFnMesh.setUVs method, which takes an MFloatArray of U coordinates (uArray) and an MFloatArray of V coordinates (vArray) for each vertex. This data could be passed in as part of the call to MFnMesh.create, but we'll call it separately to concentrate on one thing at a time.

- To set the polygon UVs, use the MFnMesh.assignUVs method. It takes in the same polygonCounts and polygonConnects we calculated for the call to the MFnMesh.create method. The assignUVs method maps the actual vertex UVs to the mesh. If you want more information on this admittedly complex topic, see the Maya API Reference. This sort of complexity is not uncommon in the API.

- Call the MFnMesh.updateSurface method when the mesh is built. It will signal to Maya that the mesh has changed and needs to be redrawn.

- We'll deal with mesh normals in the next section.

It's important to remember that all of the arrays and arguments used in the functions in the preceding example match up. The length of numVertices is equal to the length of vertexArray, and the length of uArray is equal to the length of vArray. That said, you may already be aware that the number of vertices in a mesh may not correspond to the number of UVs or normals. A single vertex can have as many distinct normals or UVs as it has faces it is a part of. For example, each vertex in a cube can have zero to four normals and UVs. And of course, any mesh can have multiple UV sets! In this example, each vertex is going to have one UV coordinate and normal because each face in the cube will be a separate polygon.

Now that we have some idea of what we need to call and what we need to pass in, let's define our example data. We will keep it simple and create a cube with non-welded vertices and a UV layout where all faces take the entire UV space.

We are going to use the Python feature of list multiplication to create some data instead of typing duplicate data out. We can see list multiplication at work in the following example:

```
>>> [(0, 1)] * 2
[(0, 1), (0, 1)]
```

The value inside of the list is repeated the specified number of times into a new list. As a note of caution, it is the reference to the value, and not the value itself, that is copied. This can produce some strange results if the value being repeated is mutable, as shown in the following example:

```
>>> value = [1]
>>> newlist = [value] * 2
```

```
>>> newlist
[[1], [1]]
>>> newlist[0].append('a')
>>> newlist
[[1, 'a'], [1, 'a']]
```

Be careful when using list multiplication with mutable values.

Let's go ahead and use list multiplication to set up some data for our mesh. We'll create a list of XYZ position tuples, a list of UV coordinate tuples, a list of polygon counts, and a list defining the vertices for each face.

```
# meshcreate.py
from maya import OpenMaya
import pymel.core as pmc

vert_positions = [
    (1, 1, 1), (1, -1, 1), (-1, -1, 1), (-1, 1, 1), #front
    (1, 1, 1), (1, -1, 1), (1, -1, -1), (1, 1, -1), #right
    (1, 1, -1), (1, -1, -1), (-1, -1, -1), (-1, 1, -1), #back
    (-1, 1, 1), (-1, -1, 1), (-1, -1, -1), (-1, 1, -1), #left
    (1, 1, 1), (1, 1, -1), (-1, 1, -1), (-1, 1, 1), #top
    (1, -1, 1), (1, -1, -1), (-1, -1, -1), (-1, -1, 1), #bottom
]
# all faces have same UVs
vert_uvs = [(0, 0), (0, 1), (1, 1), (1, 0)] * 6
poly_counts = [4] * 6   #Six quad faces
poly_connections = [
    3, 2, 1, 0,
    4, 5, 6, 7,
    8, 9, 10, 11,
    15, 14, 13, 12,
    16, 17, 18, 19,
    23, 22, 21, 20
]
```

The order of the indices in `poly_connections` controls the way the faces of the cube will be created. If you use a different order, you can end up with faces pointing in the wrong direction.

Next, use the Python data to fill up the OpenMaya array objects we will use to create the mesh. Since all we are doing is projecting our Python data structure into an OpenMaya data structure, we can abstract the problem out into a single helper function that turns a Python list into an OpenMaya array:

```python
def py_to_array(values, marray_type, projection=None): #(1)
    result = marray_type() #(2)
    for v in values: #(3)
        newv = v
        if projection is not None:
            newv = projection(v)
        result.append(newv) #(4)
    return result #(5)

def tuple_to_mpoint(p): #(6)
    return OpenMaya.MPoint(p[0], p[1], p[2])

#(7)
vert_pos_array = py_to_array(
    vert_positions,
    OpenMaya.MPointArray,
    tuple_to_mpoint)
poly_counts_array = py_to_array(
    poly_counts, OpenMaya.MIntArray)
poly_conns_array = py_to_array(
    poly_connections, OpenMaya.MIntArray)
```

Let's go through the preceding code in more detail:

1. Create the helper function to convert a Python list (`values`) into an OpenMaya array of a certain type specified by the `marray_type` parameter. We can pass in an optional projection function (`projection`) to apply to each item in the list.

2. Create a new instance of the OpenMaya array.

3. Iterate through each Python item, and apply `projection` to it if supplied.

4. Append the value to the OpenMaya array.

5. Return the OpenMaya array and exit the helper function.

6. Vertex positions need to be converted from tuples into `maya.OpenMaya.MPoint` instances, so create the `tuple_to_mpoint` function to do it.

7. Convert the vertex positions, polygon counts, and polygon connections to OpenMaya arrays. The vertex positions use the `tuple_to_mpoint` function as the projection when converting the Python list into an OpenMaya array.

We also need to convert our pairs of UV coordinates into a list of U and list of V coordinates. Python has the built-in ZIP function which does the opposite of what we want, converting two separate lists into a list of pairs. We can get the desired behavior by passing in our list of pairs with a * symbol, which passes each pair as its own sequence and essentially unzips pairs into individual lists. The following demonstrates the zipping and unzipping behavior.

```
>>> numbers = (1, 2)
>>> letters = ('a', 'b')
>>> zipped = zip(numbers, letters)
>>> print zipped
[(1, 'a'), (2, 'b')]
>>> unzipped = zip(*zipped)
>>> print unzipped
[(1, 2), ('a', 'b')]
>>> unzipped[0] == numbers
True
>>> unzipped[1] == letters
True
```

I love the name "zip" as the function works just like a jacket zipper: it zips n separate strands into one, or unzips a unified strand into n separate ones. Let's use the `zip` function to unzip our UV coordinates into two separate OpenMaya arrays.

```
ulist, vlist = zip(*vert_uvs)
uarray = py_to_array(ulist, OpenMaya.MFloatArray)
varray = py_to_array(vlist, OpenMaya.MFloatArray)
```

The need to zip, unzip, and convert data between Python sequences and OpenMaya arrays is not uncommon. It helps to be comfortable with it and have convenience functions available.

Now that we have all of our data into an OpenMaya compatible form, we can use the `MFnMesh` calls to create our mesh.

```
mesh = OpenMaya.MFnMesh() #(1)
mesh.create( #(2)
    len(vert_positions),
    len(poly_counts ),
    vert_pos_array,
    poly_counts_array,
    poly_conns_array
)
mesh.setUVs(uarray, varray) #(3)
mesh.assignUVs(poly_counts_array, poly_conns_array) #(4)
```

```
mesh.updateSurface() #(5)
pmc.sets(
    'initialShadingGroup',
    edit=True, forceElement=mesh.name()) #(6)
```

Let's walk over the preceding code:

1. Create a new `MFnMesh` instance with no arguments. It does not represent any underlying Maya object.

2. Create an actual mesh object using the `MFnMesh.create` method. Pass in the OpenMaya data we previously created. The `MFnMesh` instance now refers to the newly-created underlying object.

3. Use the `MFnMesh.setUVs` method to set the vertex UVs.

4. Use the `MFnMesh.assignUVs` method to assign UVs to the geometry. One would expect a single call for UV setup, but as we are working at the low level of the Maya API, we have to deal with more complexity.

5. Call `MFnMesh.updateSurface` to tell Maya the mesh has changed and needs to be redrawn.

6. Use PyMEL to assign the default shader to the new mesh. Just because we are creating a mesh with the Maya Python API does not mean we can only use the API. It can save time to use scripting where it is more appropriate.

Running the preceding code will create a cube as shown in the following figure:

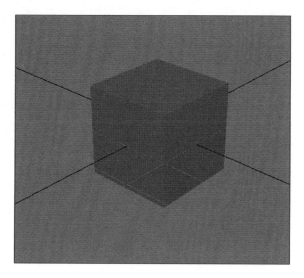

We will continue iterating on this cube in the next section where we deal with mesh normals.

Setting mesh normals

The shading of the cube we created in the previous section looks flat. That is, the lighting between polygons is not interpolated, and the surface receives light from the direction in which it points. The faces of the polygons are all planar, and no vertices are welded, which results in the flat-shaded appearance. If we had created a cube with eight vertices instead of 24, with multiple faces sharing the same vertex, the shading would look smooth. In this section, we will override the normals on the mesh so it looks smooth, even though the geometry will not change otherwise. A similar activity could be done to make the normals of an eight-vertex cube, which looks smooth by default, look flat.

As previously mentioned, a single mesh vertex can have as many normals as it has polygons that include the vertex. The same is true for the vertex's UVs. Long ago, this was a memory concern, so 3D applications devised clever ways of working with normals to save memory. As memory pressures disappeared, less efficient but simpler patterns cam into use. The old mechanisms were left in, so 3D applications often have multiple ways of working with normals.

The preferred way of working with normals is by setting arbitrary vertex normals. Maya calls this feature **per-vertex per-polygon normals**, or in some cases, **per-vertex per-face normals**. In other words, it is identifying the normal of a vertex based on a face. If you are dealing with welded and smooth geometry, where each vertex only has one normal, you can use the **shared normals** Maya uses by default.

We will call the `MFnMesh.setFaceVertexNormal` method for each vertex with the normal, face ID, and vertex ID. The most difficult part of this is writing a function to convert our existing data into an association between face ID, vertex ID, and normal. We can derive the vertex normal from the vertex position by normalizing the position, which will result in smoothly interpolated shading.

We will use the built-in `enumerate` function to help convert our data. The `enumerate` function allows us to iterate over a sequence and get the index of each item in the sequence and the item itself. Without `enumerate` we would need to resort to the following:

```
>>> chars = 'ab'
>>> for i in range(len(chars)):
...     c = chars[i]
...     print 'Item %s is %r' % (i, c)
Item 0 is 'a'
Item 1 is 'b'
```

With enumerate, we can simplify the preceding loop:

```
>>> for i, c in enumerate(chars):
...     print 'Item %s is %r' % (i, c)
Item 0 is 'a'
Item 1 is 'b'
```

Notice we no longer need the c = chars[i] line or the range(len(chars)) call.

We can get the mapping of face ID to vertex ID and normal with the following code:

```
def get_normals_data():
    result = {}
    offset = 0
    for i, pcnt in enumerate(poly_counts):
        vertInds = poly_connections[offset:offset + pcnt]
        positions = [vert_positions[vind] for vind in vertInds]
        normals = [OpenMaya.MVector(p[0], p[1], p[2]).normal()
                   for p in positions]
        result[i] = (vertInds, normals)
        offset += pcnt
    return result
face_to_vert_inds_and_normals = get_normals_data()
```

The face_to_vert_inds_and_normals variable is a complicated data structure. The key is the face index. The value is a two-item tuple. The first item is a list of the indices of each vertex in the polygon. The second item is a corresponding list of the normal of each vertex in the polygon. Or more explicitly, in pseudocode:

```
face_to_vert_inds_and_normals = {
    face0_id: [
        [vert0_index, vert1_index, vert2_index],
        [vert0_norm, vert1_norm, vert2_norm]
    ],
    face1_id: [
        [vert1_index, vert2_index, vert3_index],
        [vert1_norm, vert2_norm, vert3_norm]
    ],
    ...
}
```

Now that we have this data, we can iterate over it, calling the `MFnMesh.`
`setFaceVertexNormal` method which each normal, face index, and vertex index.
I've highlighted the changes in the following code:

```
mesh = OpenMaya.MFnMesh()
mesh.create(
    len(vert_positions),
    len(poly_counts),
    vert_pos_array,
    poly_counts_array,
    poly_conns_array
)
mesh.setUVs(uarray, varray)
mesh.assignUVs(poly_counts_array, poly_conns_array)

items = face_to_vert_inds_and_normals.items()
for faceInd, (vertInds, norms) in items:
    for vind, normal in zip(vertInds, norms):
        mesh.setFaceVertexNormal(normal, faceInd, vind)

mesh.updateSurface()
pmc.sets(
    'initialShadingGroup',
    edit=True, forceElement=mesh.name())
```

After running this code, a new cube should be created with smooth shading. If you
try selecting a face and moving it, you'll see every face is still detached.

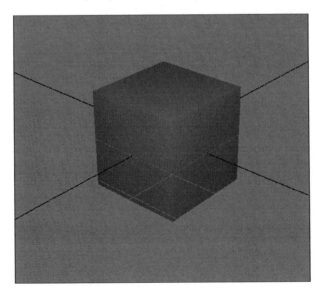

Using MScriptUtil to call a method

In certain cases, the Maya API is fundamentally incompatible with Python. Some API functions take arguments that are passed by reference. The C++ API can do something like the following pseudocode.

```
> value = False;
> Print(value);
False
> MakeTrue(&value);
> Print(value);
True
```

Notice how we never set `value = True` in our code, yet `value` is set to `True` at the end. The `MakeTrue` function is able to change the underlying value of the `value` variable, which is passed by reference.

This is impossible to do in Python. A function cannot change the value of a variable in this manner. However, this pattern is common in the Maya API, and we need to use the `MScriptUtil` class to support it.

I will briefly cover a basic use of the `MScriptUtil` class. It is a real pain to use and is being phased out with the Maya Python API 2.0. However, it is still necessary to use and no coverage of the Maya Python API would be complete without demonstrating this horror.

In the following example, we get the degrees of freedom of a joint. This will involve creating a new joint through the API, and using `MScriptUtil` to get the degrees of freedom:

```
>>> from maya import OpenMaya, OpenMayaAnim
>>> joint = OpenMayaAnim.MFnIkJoint() #(1)
>>> joint.create()
>>> joint.setDegreesOfFreedom(True, False, True) #(2)
>>> utils = [OpenMaya.MScriptUtil() for su in range(3)] #(3)
>>> ptrs = [su.asBoolPtr() for su in utils] #(4)
>>> joint.getDegreesOfFreedom(*ptrs) #(5)
>>> [OpenMaya.MScriptUtil.getBool(ptr) for ptr in ptrs] #(6)
[1, 0, 1]
```

Let's walk over the preceding code line by line:

1. In order to create a joint through the Maya Python API, instantiate a new, empty `MFnIkJoint` instance and call its `create` method to create an underlying Maya node.

2. Call the `MFnIkJoint.setDegreesOfFreedom` method to change the degrees of freedom from the default values. This allows us to verify we are getting the correct values at the end of the example script.

3. Create a list of three `MScriptUtil` instances. They correspond to the *x*, *y*, and *z* axes of freedom. We use them on the next line.

4. Create a list of three pointers by calling the `MScriptUtil,asBoolPtr()` method on each `MScriptUtil` instance. The pointers are not Boolean values themselves, but point to an underlying Boolean value Maya will mutate. Each pointer will be filled with whether the joint is free to move in a particular axis.

5. Pass the pointers to the `MFnIkJoint.getDegreesOfFreedom` method. The arguments of this method are passed by reference, as indicated by the `"&"` character next to each argument name in the method's documentation. The method does not return anything. It mutates the underlying Boolean values of the pointers passed into it.

6. Get the underlying pointer values by calling the `MScriptUtil.getBool` method. Unfortunately `getBool` returns an integer and not an actual Boolean. Verify that the result is `[1, 0, 1]`. This result corresponds to the `[True, False, True]` that the degrees of freedom were set to in point 2.

Astute readers may notice that creating the `MScriptUtil` instances and `asBoolPtr` calls can be combined into a single list comprehension. This can result in bugs due to Maya's memory management. I would suggest you always keep an explicit reference to the original `MScriptUtil` instance as long as you have any references to a pointer created by it. Combining the lines where we set the `utils` and `ptrs` variables may result in a crash, a result of `[1, 1, 1]`, or the correct behavior.

At this point, we're almost done with our tour of what the Maya Python API has to offer. Throughout these examples, you may have said to yourself many times, "I can do this through MEL / Maya commands / PyMEL". We will learn how to set up callbacks using the Maya Python API before exploring this question.

Using OpenMaya for callbacks

There are some areas where it is infeasible to use Maya commands. Callbacks are one such area. We can use script jobs, but for reasons laid out in *Chapter 5, Building Graphical User Interfaces for Maya*, we are not going to. Script jobs are unreliable, brittle, difficult to use, and above all, very limited. Maya API callbacks are much more straightforward and predictable in their design and use.

In this example, we are going to register a callback to be invoked when the name of a node changes. In order to make life easier, we're going to allow the callback to work with PyNodes, rather than instances of MObject or types from the Maya API. The fact that the callbacks use the Maya Python API under the hood will be totally hidden to the caller.

The web of Maya API callbacks can be a bit difficult to navigate. Start with the OpenMaya.MMessage type and look for the callback you need on the appropriate subclass. In our case, we need the OpenMaya.MNodeMessage subclass with its addNameChangedCallback method.

Two things to know about *all* callbacks in OpenMaya are:

- Adding a callback returns an ID which should be passed to the MMessage. removeCallback method to remove the callback.

- Nearly all callbacks take an optional clientData parameter you should just ignore. There is no use for it in Python. We represent it by the underscore (_) parameter in the callbacks, and do not pass it in when we call the "add callback" methods.

We can start by stubbing out the functions to add and remove the callback. Writing good docstrings will help us figure out exactly what we need to do:

```
#callbacks.py
from maya import OpenMaya
import pymel.core as pmc

def addNameChangedCallback(callback, pynode=None):
    """Registers a callback so that
    `callback(pynode, oldname, newname)` is called when
    `pynode`'s name changes.
    If `pynode` is None, invoke the callback for every
    name change.
```

```
Return the callback ID. Hold onto this if you will need to
remove the callback.
"""

def removeNameChangedCallback(callbackId):
    """Removes a callback based on its ID."""
```

The `removeNameChangedCallback` function is straightforward enough to implement, so let's go ahead and do so. It simply calls the `MNodeMessage.removeCallback` function with a given callback ID:

```
def removeNameChangedCallback(callbackId):
    OpenMaya.MNodeMessage.removeCallback(callbackId)
```

Adding support for registering the callback is more complex. We will use what we learned earlier in this chapter to convert `PyNode`s and `MObject`s back and forth. We also use a closure for our callback, so we can easily map between the actual callback (using OpenMaya objects) and the user-supplied PyMEL callback (using PyNodes):

```
def addNameChangedCallback(callback, pynode=None):
    def omcallback(mobject, oldname, _): #(1)
        newname = OpenMaya.MFnDependencyNode(mobject).name()
        changedPynode = pmc.PyNode(newname) #(2)
        # Ignore name changes for manipulators and stuff
        # that have no scene objects
        if not _isvalidnode(changedPynode): #(3)
            return
        callback(changedPynode, oldname, newname) #(4)

    if pynode is None: #(5)
        listenTo = OpenMaya.MObject()
    else:
        listenTo = pynode.__apimobject__()
    return OpenMaya.MNodeMessage.addNameChangedCallback( #(6)
        listenTo, omcallback)

def _isvalidnode(pynode):
    try:
        bool(pynode)
        return True
    except KeyError:
        return False
```

There are a lot of new concepts in the preceding code, so let's go over it in more detail:

1. Inside the `addNameChangedCallback` function, define a closure which will be the actual function invoked by Maya when a node's name changes. It takes the `MObject` that has changed, its old name, and the `clientData` parameter that can be ignored.

2. Inside the closure, convert the node that has changed into a `PyNode`.

3. Check if the changed node is a valid node with the `_isvalidnode` function. If it is not valid, return early and do not call the supplied callback.

4. If the node is valid, invoke the supplied callback with the `PyNode`, old name, and new name. Exit the closure.

5. If the caller of `addNameChangedCallback` does not supply a PyNode to listen to, use an empty `MObject` instance to listen to all name changes. Otherwise, get the `MObject` that underlies the PyNode by calling its `__apimobject__()` method.

6. Install the callback into Maya by calling the `MNodeMessage.addNameChangedCallback` method with the `MObject` to listen to and the closure.

Let's see the callback behavior in action:

```
>>> def cb(n, old, new): #(1)
...     print 'CB: %r, %r, %r' % (n, old, new)
>>> watched = pmc.joint() #(2)
>>> unwatched = pmc.joint()
>>> cbid1 = addNameChangedCallback(cb, watched) #(3)
>>> watched.rename('spam') #(4)
CB: nt.Joint(u'spam'), u'joint1', u'spam'
>>> unwatched.rename('eggs') #(5)
>>> cbid2 = addNameChangedCallback(cb) #(6)
>>> unwatched.rename('eggs2') #(7)
CB: nt.Joint(u'eggs2'), u'eggs', u'eggs2'
>>> watched.rename('spam2') #(8)
CB: nt.Joint(u'spam2'), u'spam', u'spam2'
CB: nt.Joint(u'spam2'), u'spam', u'spam2'
>>> removeNameChangedCallback(cbid2) #(9)
>>> unwatched.rename('eggs3') #(10)
```

Let's walk through the preceding demonstration line by line to see how callbacks work:

1. Define the callback function, which just prints its arguments.

2. Create the two joints. The names of these joints will be changed to demonstrate the callback behavior.

3. Register a callback to fire when the name of the `watched` joint changes.

4. Rename the `watched` joint. The callback fired.

5. Rename the `unwatched` joint. The callback is not fired.

6. Register the callback function to listen for name changes to all nodes.

7. Rename the `unwatched` joint again. The callback function is invoked once due to it being registered for all node name changes.

8. Rename the `watched` joint again. The callback fires twice: once for the callback registered specifically for the `watched` joint, and once for the callback registered for all nodes.

9. Remove the callback registered for all nodes.

10. Rename the `unwatched` joint yet again. No callback is fired because the callback watching all nodes was just removed.

A final thing to keep in mind when using callbacks is that they may be fired at seemingly bizarre times. Don't be shocked the first time an unrelated callback is invoked when you switch active views, render the scene, or delete a node. You must design your code to protect against being called at the wrong time.

Comparing Maya Python API and PyMEL

The main benefit of using the Maya API is clearly the greater power it gives you. Many things are not possible through scripting, and being able to access the API from Python gives you the best of both worlds. We saw this demonstrated several times, such as where we used the API to build a mesh and PyMEL to assign a shader, and where we hid usage of API callbacks behind a function that works with PyMEL arguments.

There is another benefit of the Maya API, however. It allows you to approach Maya programming from the bottom up, rather than the top down. For example, to build a mesh with the Maya API requires a relatively small amount of Maya knowledge (start with the `MFnMesh` reference page and learn from there), but a significant amount of programming skill, such as the code to derive vertex normals. OpenMaya is great for addressing foundational problems.

Building a mesh is certainly possible through script. In fact there are probably dozens of ways you can do it! But instead of working around a unified concept- the `MFnMesh`- you are working from many different angles: commands for creating the mesh, UVs, and normals are not unified except by a user's familiarity with them. It's quite possible for programmers who have little knowledge of Maya to write passable libraries, such as exporters or importers, remarkably quickly with the API. This is because the OpenMaya concepts are so universal and similar to the 3D concepts they may be used to. The scripting and command concepts, in contrast, are very specific to Maya and require some amount of context and familiarity with the program. We saw in *Chapter 2, Writing Composable Code*, how convoluted some of the commands have become!

Oftentimes the reason I recommend the Maya Python API is similar to why I recommend PyMEL over `maya.cmds` and PySide over the Maya UI commands: to improve the quality of the rest of the Python code. Python code that uses OpenMaya can often be more straightforward and readable, especially if the alternative is many script command calls with obscure flags and values. However, code using the API is usually more verbose, in the end requiring more lines of code, though many of those lines can be put in clear, well documented, and tested libraries. Experiment and become skilled with the two, and choose the approach that allows you to write the most appropriate code.

Oh, and it's worth pointing out that the Maya Python API is usually faster than either PyMEL or `maya.cmds`. That isn't always the case, though. Sometimes PyMEL wraps the API so nicely that it can save you a bunch of work, or you can make a single script call instead of thousands of API calls. But if you find that commands become a performance bottleneck, you can try porting your code to use the Maya Python API as a last resort.

Creating a Maya Python plugin

Our tour of the Maya Python API continues with probably its most common use in the wild: creating a Maya plugin with Python. In fact, the entirety of the next chapter is spent working with Maya Python plugins in novel ways. We should have a good understanding of how plugins work before ending our API tour, so the remainder of this chapter will be focused on creating a Maya command plugin with Python. When called, the command will play a sound.

There are several plugin types supported by Maya. Plugin types are denoted by the `MPx` prefix and are inside the `maya.OpenMayaMPx` namespace. You can look at the Maya API Reference to get an idea of what's available. All plugins work with basically the same concepts, which we will cover in this chapter. Custom plugins are handled by subclassing the appropriate Maya plugin type, and registration is handled by the `OpenMayaMPx.MFnPlugin` class.

In this section, we will create a command plugin by subclassing the `maya.OpenMayaMPx.MPxCommand` base class. Command plugins are designed to expose functionality that can be called from script just like native MEL commands. They are becoming less popular because they don't offer much over a regular Python script, as we'll see. Python allows us to access both script commands and the Maya Python API at the same time, so it's much easier to write everything in Python than it is to write C++ or Python commands that are then called from a separate script.

Even though command plugins are not very popular anymore, they provide a straightforward way of becoming familiar with Maya's plugin system. This knowledge will be essential when we tackle Dependency Graph plugins based on `MPxNode` in the next chapter, *Chapter 8, Unleashing the Maya API through Python.*

The life of a Python plugin

All Maya Python plugins behave in roughly the same way. In fact, this sort of unified interface is a fundamental feature of any plugin system. In this section, we will start by defining what a plugin is. Then we will learn how to find, load, initialize, and register it. Finally, we will see how to unload, uninitialize, and deregister it.

A single **plugin** consists of a **plugin module** and any number of **plugin types**. For example, you may have a plugin module named `exporterplugin.py` which contains the commands (plugin types) `exportSelected` and `exportAll`. All of these together can be collectively referred to as the `exporterplugin` plugin.

A Python plugin is defined by a `.py` file placed in one of the directories in the `MAYA_PLUG_IN_PATH` environment variable. All Python files placed there will show up in the **Plugin Manager** window.

Plugins can be **loaded** through the `pymel.core.loadPlugin` function, from the **Plugin Manager** window, or automatically loaded when Maya starts up if the plugin is set to automatically load. The `.py` suffix must be specified when loading or unloading Python plugins through script. C++ (`.mll`) plugins can be loaded and unloaded with or without the `.mll` suffix.

When the plugin is loaded by Maya, whether through the GUI, script, or automatic loading on startup, it is initialized. Maya automatically calls the module-level `initializePlugin` function. The `initializePlugin` function takes in an `MObject` instance which is used to construct an `MFnPlugin` instance.

Methods on the MFnPlugin instance with the register prefix are called perform plugin type registration. Registration of types that store some data in the scene, such as MPxNode plugins, usually require a unique identifier called a type ID. We'll learn more about type IDs in *Chapter 8, Unleashing the Maya API through Python*. Plugins types that do not store data, such as MPxCommand plugins, are usually just identified by a name. Nearly all plugin registration includes a creator function that is used to create an instance of the actual plugin type.

A plugin can be unloaded through the pymel.core.unloadPlugin function. Again, the .py suffix must be specified when loading or unloading Python plugins through script.

When a plugin is unloaded, it is uninitialized and its plugin types are deregistered. This works the same as plugin initialization and registration; the uninitializePlugin module-level function and deregister-prefixed MFnPlugin methods are used.

Be aware that the deregistration method is not always named the same as the registration method. For example, plugins registered through the MFnPlugin. register**Transform** method are deregistered through the MFnPlugin. deregister**Node** method.

I should also warn you that that the uninitializePlugin function is not called when Maya exits. See the MFnPlugin API reference page for instructions on how to handle plugins that must run some sort of cleanup before Maya exits.

Once a plugin is initialized and registered, it can actually be used. Used can mean many different things and depends wholly on the type of plugin.

In this section, we went over the life cycle of a Maya plugin in the abstract. In the next four sections, we will build a command plugin to provide a concrete example.

Creating the sound player library

We will create a command plugin to play a sound in Maya. Before creating the plugin, however, we will write a simple Python library that plays a sound using the QtGui.QSound class. Place the following code into a C:\mayapybook\pylib\ playsound.py file:

```
import os
from qtshim import QtGui

GOBBLE = os.path.join(os.path.dirname(__file__), 'gobble.wav')
GORILLA = os.path.join(os.path.dirname(__file__), 'gorilla.wav')
```

```
def play_sound(wav=GOBBLE):
    QtGui.QSound.play(wav)
```

The preceding code defines the paths to a couple audio files, as well as a `play_sound` function which takes in the path to a file and plays it uses PySide.

You can find `gobble.wav` and `gorilla.wav` alongside the code samples for this chapter. You can also use your own `.wav` files. Place them next to the `playsound.py` file in the `C:\mayapybook\pylib` development root. The `qtshim` library was created in *Chapter 5, Building Graphical User Interfaces for Maya*.

The `playsound` library will do the actual sound playing. Breaking apart generic Python code, like we have here, from Maya-specific plugin code, as we'll write next, is a good practice.

Creating the plugin file

We will need to create the Python plugin file in a location Maya recognizes as a plugin directory. All of the directories on the `MAYA_PLUG_IN_PATH` environment variable are searched for plugins. You can see your available options by running the following code from a mayapy interpreter:

```
>>> import pymel.core, os
>>> for p in os.getenv('MAYA_PLUG_IN_PATH').split(os.pathsep):
...     print p
```

On my OS X machine, this prints out a number of suitable directories, including:

```
/Users/rgalanakis/Library/Preferences/Autodesk/maya/plug-ins
/Users/Shared/Autodesk/maya/plug-ins
```

Choose a location and create a file named `playsoundplugin.py`. Open it up and write the following code:

```
from maya import OpenMayaMPx #(1)
import playsound

class SoundPlayer(OpenMayaMPx.MPxCommand): #(2)
    def doIt(self, args): #(3)
        playsound.play_sound(playsound.GOBBLE)

def create_plugin(): #(4)
    return OpenMayaMPx.asMPxPtr(SoundPlayer())

plugin_name = 'playSound' #(5)
```

```
def _toplugin(mobject): #(6)
    return OpenMayaMPx.MFnPlugin(
        mobject, 'Marcus Reynir', '0.01')

def initializePlugin(mobject): #(7)
    plugin = _toplugin(mobject)
    plugin.registerCommand(plugin_name, create_plugin)

def uninitializePlugin(mobject): #(8)
    plugin = _toplugin(mobject)
    plugin.deregisterCommand(plugin_name)
```

This is all the code we need for a simple version of our sound player plugin. It is very dense, though, so let's go through it in detail.

1. Import `maya.OpenMayaMPx` module and the `playsound` library we just built.

2. Define the `SoundPlayer` class which inherits from the `OpenMayaMPx.MPxCommand` class. Maya plugins are subclasses of plugin base classes. A command plugin is a subclass of the `MPxCommand` class.

3. Command plugins must override the `MPxCommand.doIt` method. The `SoundPlayer.doIt` just calls the `playsound.play_sound` function. Ignore the `args` parameter to the `doIt` method for now.

4. The `create_plugin` function is known as a creator function and it is used during node initialization. A creator function creates a new instance of the plugin type (`SoundHorn`) and passes it to the `OpenMayaMPx.asMPxPtr` function. The call to `OpenMayaMPx.asMPxPtr` is very important. It instructs Maya to manage the memory of the newly created instance, rather than Python. Python would immediately garbage collect the newly instantiated plugin and havoc would ensue. Every plugin registration requires a creator function, and every creator function looks exactly the same: a call to `asMPxPtr` with a newly created instance of the plugin type.

5. Define the plugin name. For a command plugin, the name is what the command is called in Maya. For example, `pmc.playSound` will invoke our command plugin once it is registered.

6. Define a helper to convert an `MObject` to an `MFnPlugin` instance.

7. Define a function to initialize the plugin. It converts the passed `MObject` into an `MFnPlugin` instance, and then calls its `registerCommand` method. The method makes the command available to Maya.

8. Define a function to uninitialize the plugin. It converts the passed `MObject` into an `MFnPlugin` instance, and then calls the `MFnPlugin.deregisterCommand` method. The method means the command can no longer be used by Maya.

We can try out our plugin in mayapy or the **Script Editor**:

```
import time
import pymel.core as pmc
pmc.loadPlugin('playsoundplugin.py')
pmc.playSound()
time.sleep(2)
pmc.unloadPlugin('playsoundplugin.py')
```

You should hear a turkey gobble sound play. If you do not, Qt may not have found the `.wav` file, so make sure it is next to the `playsound.py` file, and not the `playsoundplugin.py` file.

Reloading plugins

Plugins are not normal Python modules. They aren't imported, so they cannot be reloaded through the `reload` function. If there are changes we want to pick up, the plugin needs to be unloaded and loaded again. This can be done by calling the `pymel.core.loadPlugin` and `pymel.core.unloadPlugin` functions or using the **Plugin Manager** window.

Like any other Maya plugin, there cannot be any references to the plugin when it is unloaded. This is usually only a problem for plugins that store data in the scene (such as node plugins), though you may need to clear your Undo Queue and/or Construction History to allow Maya to unload certain types of plugins.

Adding a command flag

Finally, we will add a flag to the `playSound` command so a caller can choose a sound to play. The new contents of `playsoundplugin.py` follow, with the changes highlighted:

```
from maya import OpenMayaMPx, OpenMaya
import playsound

wav_flag_short = '-w' #(1)
wav_flag_long = '-wavname'
```

```
WAVS = {  #(2)
    'gobble': playsound.GOBBLE,
    'roar': playsound.GORILLA,
}

class SoundPlayer(OpenMayaMPx.MPxCommand):
    def doIt(self, args):
        parser = OpenMaya.MArgParser(self.syntax(), args) #(3)
        filename = WAVS['gobble'] #(4)
        if parser.isFlagSet(wav_flag_short):
            key = parser.flagArgumentString(wav_flag_short, 0)
            filename = WAVS[key]
        playsound.play_sound(filename) #(5)

def create_syntax(): #(6)
    syn = OpenMaya.MSyntax()
    syn.addFlag(
        wav_flag_short, wav_flag_long, OpenMaya.MSyntax.kString)
    return syn

def create_plugin():
    return OpenMayaMPx.asMPxPtr(SoundPlayer())

plugin_name = 'playSound'

def _toplugin(mobject):
    return OpenMayaMPx.MFnPlugin(
        mobject, 'Marcus Reynir', '0.01')

def initializePlugin(mobject):
    plugin = _toplugin(mobject)
    plugin.registerCommand(
        plugin_name, create_plugin, create_syntax) #(7)

def uninitializePlugin(mobject):
    plugin = _toplugin(mobject)
    plugin.deregisterCommand(plugin_name)
```

Let's go through the differences between the previous version and this new version with flag support. Adding flag support is not trivial and requires learning a number of new, confusing API concepts:

1. Define the flags. The flag -w is the short name and -wavname is the long name. Short names must be less than four characters and long names must be greater than three. If your names do not conform, you will get a mysterious `RuntimeError: You are not licensed to use the "<command name>" command` error when using the plugin.

2. Create a dictionary that will map flag arguments to .wav files. This is just a convenient mapping for callers. You may also want to provide -f and -file flags if you want the caller to be able to supply a full path to a .wav file.

3. Inside of the `doIt` method, create an `OpenMaya.MSyntax` instance by calling the `self.syntax()` method. Create a new `OpenMaya.MArgParser` instance using the `MSyntax` instance. Refer to point 6 for more information about the `self.syntax()` method.

4. Set the default key to `'gobble'`, and if the user supplies a flag value, parse that.

5. At the end of the `doIt` method, play the .wav file specified by the key.

6. The `create_syntax` function returns an `MSyntax` instance that is used to parse arguments from the `args` parameter passed into the command's `doIt` method. The syntax instance is retrieved through the `MPxCommand.syntax()` method, which was used in point 3. The `create_syntax` function is associated with the plugin type when calling the `MFnPlugin.registerCommand` method, as shown in point 7.

7. Pass the `create_syntax` method into the `MFnPlugin.registerCommand` method when registering the plugin type.

Let's try out the plugin again using mayapy or the **Script Editor**. Make sure the changes have been picked up by unloading and loading the plugin, or restarting Maya. In the following example, we call the `playSound` command with no argument to play the turkey sound, and then with an argument to play the gorilla sound.

```
import time
pmc.loadPlugin('playsoundplugin.py')
pmc.playSound()
time.sleep(2)
pmc.playSound(wavname='gorilla')
time.sleep(2)
pmc.unloadPlugin('playsoundplugin.py')
```

You should hear a turkey gobbling, and then a gorilla roaring. That completes the `playSound` command plugin. Before we wrap things up, however, we will see why plugins like this are largely unnecessary.

Comparing the OpenMaya and scripting solutions

I mentioned earlier there is a reduced need for command plugins. The example of adding a flag should demonstrate why. The design makes sense in a C++ world, but is totally unnecessary in Python. We could keep all the same functionality but get rid of the plugin by using the `playsound` library directly as shown in the following example:

```
import playsound, time
playsound.play_sound(playsound.GOBBLE)
time.sleep(2)
playsound.play_sound(playsound.GORILLA)
time.sleep(2)
```

What are the main benefits of using the Python library approach over command plugins?

- There is no plugin creation dance. Instead, just call functions directly.

- Keyword arguments are part of the language. There's no need to deal with `MArgParser` or `MSyntax`. Supporting a single flag using the API is complex enough. Can you imagine how the argument parsing code for something like the `ls` command looks?

- Code is not registered ahead of time. Functions can be imported when they are needed. This makes code more understandable. For example, if you run across a call to `pymel.core.explode` somewhere, you cannot immediately know whether it is a built-in Maya command you didn't know about, or a command from a random plugin. If you run across a call to `somelib.explode`, you know the `explode` function lives in the `somelib` module.

- Undo and redo are easier to handle. Command plugins that manipulate the scene must be careful to support undo and redo. It is much easier to create undo and redo blocks from script, as we did in *Chapter 4, Leveraging Context Managers and Decorators in Maya*.

Clearly there's less of a need for command plugins because it's easier to accomplish the same as a script. I chose not to demonstrate a command that requires undo and redo support or other advanced topics because the complexity can quickly become overwhelming. Be aware, though, that any command plugin that manipulates the Maya scene should provide undo and redo support. Such a plugin is included with this book's sample code in the `zerooutplugin.py` file.

Using PyMEL in a plugin that loads during startup

Maya will import plugin files that are set to auto-load very early in its startup routine, much earlier than any user-specified startup scripts. Earlier, even, than PyMEL. This means that the initialization of your plugin must not use (or even import) PyMEL if it is set to auto-load.

For example, I've included part of the `deferpymel.py` plugin in the following code. The rest of the code can be found with the book's examples. Notice the `import pymel.core` line at the top of the file.

```
from maya import OpenMayaMPx
import pymel.core

# ... Other code here ...

def initializePlugin(mobject):
    plugin = _toplugin(mobject)
    plugin.registerCommand(plugin_name, create_plugin)
```

If we start Maya, set this plugin to auto-load, and restart Maya, we should see the following in the **Script Editor** after Maya starts up:

```
# // pymel.core : Updating pymel with pre-loaded plugins: deferpymel
```

PyMEL was loaded but it is in an incomplete state. On import, PyMEL dynamically analyzes Maya and makes all of its commands available. This analysis happened too early and some plugins are missing.

Instead, we need to defer the importing of PyMEL until Maya is finished initializing. We can change the imports and the `initializePlugin` method as follows:

```
from maya import cmds, OpenMayaMPx

# ... Other code here ...

def initializePlugin(mobject):
    plugin = _toplugin(mobject)
    def register():
        import pymel.core as pmc
        plugin.registerCommand(plugin_name, create_plugin)
    cmds.evalDeferred(register)
```

First, remove the import of `pymel.core` from the top of the file. Instead, import the `maya.cmds` module.

Inside `initializePlugin`, create the `MFnPlugin` instance as normal. Also create a closure that does the PyMEL import and calls the `plugin.registerCommand` method. Then pass the closure to the `maya.cmds.evalDeferred` function. This function will invoke what is passed to it when Maya becomes idle. Fortunately, Maya will not be idle until its startup routine has finished, at which point the plugin can be safely registered.

If you start Maya, you should see the following output to the top panel of the **Script Editor**. The output will be different depending on what other plugins you have set to auto-load.

```
# # pymel.core : Updating pymel with pre-loaded plugins: deferpymel,
fbxmaya, objExport
```

This should fix our problem, though it is sometimes an inconvenient way of getting around the restriction of not being able to import PyMEL during plugin initialization.

Summary

In this chapter, we learned about object-oriented programming and how to use the Maya Python API. We saw the power of inheritance and how to draw shapes into the Maya viewport using OpenGL. Then we learned about the inner workings of the Maya Python API bindings, how to navigate the Maya API Reference, and how `MObjects` and function sets work.

We accomplished a number of tasks with the API which demonstrated common patterns. We used the powerful `MFnMesh` class to build a mesh from scratch, wrestled with the `MScriptUtil` class and pass by reference pattern, and saw how OpenMaya callbacks are used. We ended the chapter by implementing a command plugin for playing sound.

Throughout this chapter we also saw various problems with the Maya Python API. More and more code is being written as Python scripts instead of plugins, though some plugin types, especially for rendering, often still belong in C++. Next, in *Chapter 8, Unleashing the Maya API through Python*, we will look at `OpenMayaMPx.MPxNode`, a very common type of plugin to write that cannot be replaced with a simple Python script and PyMEL. We will build a system that provides a Pythonic wrapper around building `MPxNode`s so we can write elegant, Pythonic code, and we do not need to go through the pain and boilerplate we were forced to endure in this chapter.

8
Unleashing the Maya
API through Python

In this chapter, we will synthesize everything we've learned so far into a module that may change the way you think about Python and Maya programming. We will develop a library that will allow you to create Maya plugins with minimal code in a very Pythonic style, hiding away the complexities of working with the Maya Python API. It will show you how well designed and powerful both Maya and Python are, and the beautiful things they can create together.

We'll start by building a Maya dependency graph plugin using standard API techniques. This will demonstrate Maya's Dependency Graph concepts of input attributes, output attributes, and the `compute` method. We'll look at the gotchas, boilerplate, and complexities involved in creating a dependency graph plugin.

After that, we will learn about Python metaprogramming. We will put this knowledge to use building the node factory module, which will eliminate the difficulties encountered while building the first version of our plugin. We'll end with some ways you can expand and extend the node factory.

Understanding Dependency Graph plugins

The Maya API Guide's *Python Learning Path* help document covers the basics of creating **dependency graph plugins**, which are also called **node plugins** for short. You can get quite far by **cargo culting** (copy, pasting, and adjusting) examples without knowing why something is done. Even if most of the explanations are in the Maya help documents somewhere, it can be difficult to find and put it all together. So in this section, we'll create a dependency graph plugin and explain each new topic along the way, making sure some old ones are understood as well.

 The term cargo cult programming refers to when a programmer uses some code without understand why or how it does what it does. It originates from the practice some Pacific tribes adopted after World War II, where they would make mock-ups of airplanes and landing strips with the hope of bringing back the cargo planes that visited them during the war.

A node plugin is a plugin type that inherits from the `maya.OpenMayaMPx.MPxNode` Maya API class. Plugin nodes can be hooked into the Maya dependency graph, which means their inputs and outputs can connect to the inputs and outputs of other nodes. All of the nodes you interact with in Maya, from the transform and shape of a `polySphere`, to the viewport camera, to the node representing the scene time, are all part of Maya's dependency graph. Compare this to the command plugin we created in *Chapter 7, Taming the Maya API*, which can affect the scene directly but cannot be connected to anything.

Nodes are the molecules that make up a Maya scene. By creating our own dependency graph plugins, we can synthesize new chemicals that mesh into the rest of Maya.

Building a simple node plugin

For our example node plugin, we'll port the Maya API Reference's C++ example circle node to Python. The original source code for the circle node is in the `circleNode.cpp` file in Maya's development kit.

The circle node is pretty simple. It outputs a sine and cosine computed from its inputs. When connected to the X and Z translation of a transform node, the outputs will move the transform in circle through the XZ plane, hence the name "circle node."

The circle node also has three inputs which control the phase, amplitude, and frequency of the outputs:

- The scale attribute is a multiplier against the sine and cosine and controls amplitude, or height. Without scaling, the outputs would only be between -1 and 1.

- The frames attribute controls the sine and cosine's period, or length of a cycle. A higher frames value means a slower rate of change.

- The input attribute controls the phase of the outputs. It is normally the current frame number. For example, at frame 0, the sin is at 0. If the value of input is 10 and frames is 20, the sine is halfway through its cycle. If the value of input is 40 and frames is 20, the sine is back at 0.

With that description out of the way, it's time to stub out the plugin's initialization and registration. Add a circlernode.py file somewhere in your MAYA_PLUG_IN_PATH. Refer to *Chapter 7, Taming the Maya API*, if you need help finding where to place the plugin. Inside of circlernode.py, type the following code:

```python
import math
from maya import OpenMaya, OpenMayaMPx

class Circler(OpenMayaMPx.MPxNode): #(1)
    def compute(self, *args):
        pass

def create(): #(2)
    return OpenMayaMPx.asMPxPtr(Circler())

def init(): #(3)
    return

nodeName = 'circler' #(4)
nodeTypeID = OpenMaya.MTypeId(0x60005) #(5)

def _toplugin(mobject): #(6)
    return OpenMayaMPx.MFnPlugin(
        mobject, 'Marcus Reynir', '0.01')

def initializePlugin(mobject): #(7)
    plugin = _toplugin(mobject)
    plugin.registerNode(nodeName, nodeTypeID, create, init)

def uninitializePlugin(mobject): #(8)
    plugin = _toplugin(mobject)
    plugin.deregisterNode(nodeTypeID)
```

Most of this should be familiar from the command plugin we built in *Chapter 7, Taming the Maya API*, but let's go over each distinct concept in the preceding example:

1. After importing the necessary modules, define the `Circler` class, which inherits from the `OpenMayaMPx.MPxNode` class. The `MPxNode` class or one of its subclasses must be the base class of any node plugin. Other types of plugins inherit from different MPx-prefixed OpenMaya types. Stub out the `Circler.compute` method for now. We will write the code for it in a coming section.

2. Define the `create` function, known as the node creator. It looks and works the same way as it does for the command plugin we built in *Chapter 7, Taming the Maya API*.

3. Define the `init` function, known as the node initializer. We will look at the node initializer in more detail in a coming section.

4. Define the node's name. You can create the node using this name by calling something like `pymel.core.createNode('circler')`.

5. Define the node's type ID. We look at type IDs in detail in the next section.

6. The `initializePlugin` and `uninitializePlugin` functions look like they do for command plugins. The only difference is that they use the `MFnPlugin.registerNode` and `MFnPlugin.deregisterNode` methods, which take different arguments than the `MFnPlugin.registerCommand` and `MFnPlugin.deregisterCommand` methods we used in *Chapter 7, Taming the Maya API*.

In the next three sections, we will go over the new concepts introduced in the preceding breakdown: type IDs, the node initializer, and the `MPxNode.compute` method.

Understanding plugin type IDs

Node plugins, along with a few other plugin types, store data in the Maya scene that is persisted across sessions. Maya identifies the node by storing its type ID. Identifying a node by ID is very different from simply using a name. Names can change, but even more importantly, names can easily conflict. Imagine saving a scene that uses a custom node, and someone else with a different node plugin with the same name loads your scene. Because the behavior of the nodes is different, even though the name is the same, the scene may be entirely broken, or worse, it may technically work but look different! All because two people thought "circler" is a great name for a node.

To avoid this fate, Maya has the concept of the type ID, implemented through the MTypeID class. This class just wraps an unsigned integer, commonly referred to as a uint. By convention, type IDs are represented in hexadecimal form, such as 0x60005 in the circle node example.

A normal (signed) 32-bit integer can be between approximately -2 billion and 2 billion. An unsigned integer, lacking a positive or negative sign, can be between 0 and approximately 4 billion. We just use normal integers in Python since it does not natively support unsigned integers.

I have absolutely no idea why it's common to use hexadecimal notation for the unsigned integer represented by an MTypeID instance.

Autodesk has established a set of rules that should govern the choice of ID number. A quite thorough tutorial, including most of the following information, is included on the *MTypeID* page in the Maya API Reference.

- Type IDs for plugins that are and will forever be internal use only can be between 0 and 0x7ffff. We will use this range for this chapter.

- The plugins Autodesk ships with the Maya plugin development kit use IDs between 0x80000 and 0xfffff.

- Any plugins that ever have the potential to be used outside of your tight control should use a unique ID from Autodesk. You can reserve a block of 256 IDs through the Autodesk Developer's Network. See the MTypeID reference page for more details. I strongly suggest that you get a block of type IDs reserved. You never know when your plugin will need to be used in a new environment!

Defining inputs, outputs, and the initializer

Now that we know about type IDs, we can start building the node itself. Let's define the inputs and outputs on the class definition as is normally done in Maya Python API plugin examples.

```
class Circler(OpenMayaMPx.MPxNode):
    inputFrame = OpenMaya.MObject() # input
    frequency = OpenMaya.MObject() # input
    scale = OpenMaya.MObject() # input
    outSine = OpenMaya.MObject() # output
    outCosine = OpenMaya.MObject() # output
```

This code, though common in examples, does nothing. It is one of many C++ *isms* that have infected Python plugin code. The actual code that sets up our inputs and outputs goes into the node initializer, which we are about to build. However, for this first example, we will not stray far from the rest of Maya's Python plugin examples, and simply port the C++ code into Python.

Generally porting C++ code into Python generates huge **code smells** and this is no different. The ported code will look alien to the Python we've been writing in the rest of the book. By the end of this chapter, we will have a way to use Python to create Maya node plugins in a much more pleasing fashion.

The node initializer is what sets up the node's real input and output attributes. Again, this is a straight port from the C++ code, so it looks distinctly non-Pythonic.

```python
def init():
    nAttr = OpenMaya.MFnNumericAttribute() #(1)
    kFloat = OpenMaya.MFnNumericData.kFloat

    #(2) Setup the input attributes
    Circler.input = nAttr.create('input', 'in', kFloat, 0.0)
    nAttr.setStorable(True)
    Circler.scale = nAttr.create('scale', 'sc', kFloat, 10.0)
    nAttr.setStorable(True)
    Circler.frames = nAttr.create('frames', 'fr', kFloat, 48.0)
    nAttr.setStorable(True)

    #(3) Setup the output attributes
    Circler.outSine = nAttr.create('outSine', 'so', kFloat, 0.0)
    nAttr.setWritable(False)
    nAttr.setStorable(False)
    Circler.outCosine = nAttr.create(
        'outCosine', 'co', kFloat, 0.0)
    nAttr.setWritable(False)
    nAttr.setStorable(False)

    #(4) Add the attributes to the node
    Circler.addAttribute(Circler.input)
    Circler.addAttribute(Circler.scale)
    Circler.addAttribute(Circler.frames)
    Circler.addAttribute(Circler.outSine)
```

```
Circler.addAttribute(Circler.outCosine)

#(5) Set the attribute dependencies
Circler.attributeAffects(Circler.input, Circler.outSine)
Circler.attributeAffects(Circler.input, Circler.outCosine)
Circler.attributeAffects(Circler.scale, Circler.outSine)
Circler.attributeAffects(Circler.scale, Circler.outCosine)
Circler.attributeAffects(Circler.frames, Circler.outSine)
Circler.attributeAffects(Circler.frames, Circler.outCosine)
```

Let's go over what the preceding code is doing:

1. The `nAttr` variable behaves like an attribute factory. A factory is an object that returns new instances of some other type of object. In this case, the factory creates attributes and returns `MObject` instances representing those attributes.

2. Create the input attributes. Call the `nAttr.create` method to create the `MObject` representing an attribute, and assign it to the `Circler` class so it can be used in the `Circler.compute` method we create in the next section. Every attribute requires a long name (such as "scale"), short name (such as "sc"), and type (such as `OpenMaya.MFnNumericData.kFloat`). Each input is also given an explicit default value. Set each input as storable so Maya will save its value into the scene. Methods like `nAttr.setStorable` work on the last attribute created by the `nAttr.create` method.

3. Create the output attributes. Output attributes are prefixed with "out" by convention, but it is not necessary. They are also set as not storable and not writable. Outputs are not storable because they should be calculated only from inputs. They are not writable because they cannot be written to in the dependency graph. When we connect the inputs and outputs of different nodes, outputs are the source and inputs are the destination. Only destination attributes (inputs) should be writable. Attributes are writable by default so we did not have to call `nAttr.setWritable` for the input attributes.

4. Add every attribute to the `Circler` class by calling the `Circler.addAttribute` method.

5. Set up which inputs affect which outputs. When an input attribute changes, Maya will look up what output attributes need to be recalculated. Usually, each input should affect every output.

Conceptually, node initialization is elegant: describe the input attributes, output attributes, and how they affect each other. In practice, however, the code becomes unwieldy, and is always filled with copy and paste. This elegant concept with clumsy implementation is even more apparent when we look at a node's `compute` method.

Creating the compute method

The `compute` method is the heart of a Maya plugin node and is called to recalculate an output attribute. An output needs to be recalculated when an input that affects it changes. Recall that we set up the attribute affection relationships by calling the `Circler.attributeAffects` method. The purpose of `compute` is to set the values of the node's output plugs, which repeats the process for all downstream nodes in the graph. For example, given the following node hierarchy:

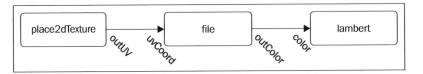

some value on the `file` node changes, the `file.compute` method will be called. This method will recalculate the `outColor` attribute, which will change the `lambert.color` input attribute, causing `lambert.compute` to be called. However, the `place2dTexture.outUV` attribute, which is upstream from the `file` node, will not affected, so `place2dTexture.compute` will not be called. It is helpful to think about these relationships by laying out all nodes with children on the left and parents on the right. Then you can think of changes happening at one point in the graph causing `compute` to be called for nodes to the right of it (*downstream*) but not to the left of it (*upstream*).

The concept of `compute` is simple, flexible, and brilliant. The way it is traditionally implemented, however, is not. Our `compute` method looks like the following:

```
class Circler(OpenMayaMPx.MPxNode):
    ...
    def compute(self, plug, data): #(1)
        if plug not in (Circler.outSine, Circler.outCosine): #(2)
            return OpenMaya.MStatus.kUnknownParameter
        inputData = data.inputValue(Circler.input) #(3)
        scaleData = data.inputValue(Circler.scale)
        framesData = data.inputValue(Circler.frames)

        inputVal = inputData.asFloat() #(4)
        scaleFactor  = scaleData.asFloat()
        framesPerCircle = framesData.asFloat()

        angle = 6.2831853 * (inputVal/framesPerCircle) #(5)
        sinResult = math.sin(angle) * scaleFactor
```

```
cosResult = math.cos(angle) * scaleFactor

sinHandle = data.outputValue(Circler.outSine) #(6)
cosHandle = data.outputValue(Circler.outCosine)
sinHandle.setFloat(sinResult) #(7)
cosHandle.setFloat(cosResult)
data.setClean(plug) #(8)
return OpenMaya.MStatus.kSuccess #(9)
```

This implementation of the `compute` method has the same trademark duplication and verbosity as the node initializer function. Let's better understand what's going on:

1. Define the `compute` method. It takes the instance of the `Circler` class (`self`), an `OpenMaya.MPlug` instance (`plug`), and an `OpenMaya.MDataBlock` instance (`data`).

2. Check if the plug instance is one of the node's outputs. If it is, we will compute the output. If it is not, we return `OpenMaya.MStatus.kUnknownParameter`. The `kUnknownParameter` constant tells Maya we did not know how to handle the `plug`. For Python plugins, these status codes are unnecessary. We should use exceptions instead if an error is encountered during evaluation of the `compute` method. I include them here to achieve parity with most Maya Python API examples.

3. Call the `MDataBlock.inputValue` method for each input attribute. The `inputValue` method returns an `OpenMaya.MDataHandle` instance which we can fetch values from and store values into.

4. Call the `MDataHandle.asFloat` method for each attribute. This gives us the actual value of the attribute we can use in Python. All of this boilerplate is necessary to extract useful data from OpenMaya objects.

5. The next three lines of code use the attribute values to calculate the sine and cosine value that will go into our outputs. These are the only three lines that are truly unique for our node. The rest of the lines in the `compute` method are just for converting the values from and to OpenMaya objects.

6. Get an `MDataHandle` instance from each output attribute.

7. Call the `MDataHandle.setFloat` method to set the sine and cosine output values.

8. Call `MDataBlock.setClean` with the `MPlug` instance to tell the Maya Dependency Graph that the given plug has been recalculated.

9. Finally, return `MStatus.kSuccess` status code, which is superfluous as discussed previously.

Taming the non-Pythonic Maya API

After we've spent so much of this book writing clean, Pythonic code, I hope the plugin presented here leaves you either furious or dejected at the idea of writing node plugins this way. It is depressing to think that after all the work of integrating Python into Maya, and learning how to program in a Pythonic way, we would need to throw it all out the window when using Maya plugins.

I wouldn't have been so hard on creating Maya plugins through the Maya Python API if I didn't have an alternative. What if the entire node, including the creator, initializer, compute, and everything else about it, could be written as follows:

```python
inputnames = ['input', 'scale', 'frames']
create_node(
    NT_DEPENDSNODE, 'circler', 0x60005,
    [
            floatattr('input', 'in'),
            floatattr('scale', 'sc', default=10.0),
            floatattr('frames', 'fr', default=48.0),
            floatattr('outSine', 'so',
                    affectors=inputnames,
                    transformer=sin),
            floatattr('outCosine', 'co',
                    affectors=inputnames,
                    transformer=cosine),
    ])
```

There are no special Maya types you need to remember or error-prone patterns you can hurt yourself with. There is no mangling of beautiful Python into an ugly and verbose design. There is no boilerplate! Instead, you can write elegant, descriptive, declarative code that does exactly what it says; nothing more and nothing less.

What's the secret? It lies with a moderately advanced Python technique called metaprogramming.

Demystifying Python metaprogramming

To metaprogram is to write a program that writes or manipulates itself or another program. It sounds much more intimidating than it is. In fact, metaprogramming has been a large part of two chapters in this book.

We were metaprogramming in *Chapter 6, Automating Maya from the Outside*, with our use of eval and exec to run arbitrary code. The following is an example of metaprogramming using the eval function. We evaluate a string to sum the numbers from 1 to 5.

```
>>> s = '+'.join([str(i) for i in range(1, 6)])
>>> s
'1+2+3+4+5'
>>> eval(s)
15
```

We were also metaprogramming when creating closures and decorators in *Chapter 4, Leveraging Context Managers and Decorators in Maya*. The following is an example of metaprogramming using a function to return a different function.

```
>>> def _make_sort(reverse):
...     def dosort(items):
...         return sorted(items, reverse=reverse)
...     return dosort
>>> sort_ascending = _make_sort(False)
>>> sort_descending = _make_sort(True)
>>> sort_ascending([1, 3, 2])
[1, 2, 3]
>>> sort_descending([1, 3, 2])
[3, 2, 1]
```

These examples should be encouraging. Metaprogramming can be simple and natural and affords a tremendous amount of power. We will use this power to turn the Maya Python API into something much more beautiful. The next three sections will focus on a specific area of metaprogramming: creating types dynamically.

Rethinking type creation

In *Chapter 7, Taming the Maya API*, we defined a type in Python as, more or less, a dictionary with some particular semantics. We can construct two similar classes like the following:

```
>>> class Dog(object):
...     def make_sound(self):
...         print 'Woof!'
>>> class Cat(object):
...     def make_sound(self):
...         print 'Meow!'
>>> Dog().make_sound()
Woof!
>>> Cat().make_sound()
Meow!
```

The preceding code creates a `Dog` type and `Cat` type, each with a `make_sound` method that prints a string. But what if we wanted to make hundreds of different animals, or read and construct types at runtime from a database?

We could try creating a string that contains our class definition, use string formatting to insert our class name and animal sound, and call `exec` to create the actual class definition.

```
>>> template = """class %s(object):
...     def make_sound(self):
...         print '%s'"""
>>> exec template % ('Bird', 'Tweet')
>>> Bird().make_sound()
Tweet
>>> exec template % ('Mouse', 'Squeek')
>>> Mouse().make_sound()
Squeek
```

Such a technique would cut down our repetitive three lines of code into a single line that, while slightly less repetitive, is quite ugly. We can metaprogram types in Python by creating and evaluating strings, but the code becomes nightmarishly difficult to read and debug. Fortunately, there's a simpler way: the `type` function.

Exploring the type function

In several places in this book, we used the `type` function to return the underlying *type* or class of an instance, as in the following example:

```
>>> c = Cow()
>>> c
<__main__.Cow object at 0x0...>
>>> type(c)
<class '__main__.Cow'>
```

What's much less known is that the `type` function has an overloaded form that can be used to construct a new type. This form takes three arguments: the name of the type, its base classes, and an attribute dictionary. It returns the new type. This type can then be instantiated.

Let's rewrite our previous attempt at metaprogramming with the `exec` statement to use the `type` function instead:

```
>>> def make_animal(name, sound): #(1)
...     def mksound(self): #(2)
...         print sound
...     return type(name, (object,), {'make_sound': mksound}) #(3)
>>> Fish = make_animal('Fish', 'Blub') #(4)
```

```
>>> Fish
<class '__main__.Fish'>
>>> make_animal('Seal', 'Ow ow ow')() #(5)
<__main__.Seal object at 0x0...>
>>> make_animal('Fox', '?')().make_sound() #(6)
?
```

There is no more string magic going on in the preceding code. Let's walk through it:

1. Define the `make_animal` function which takes the name of the animal and the sound it makes. The name of the animal will become the new type's name, and the sound it makes will be printed in the `make_sound` method.

2. Define the `mksound` closure, which has a `self` argument just like a normal instance method would have. In this case, we do not use the `self` argument with the function, but it still needs to be there.

3. Call the `type` function. It takes the name of the class, a tuple of the base classes, and a dictionary where the keys are the method names and the values are the method implementations. The `type` function returns a new class, just as if we had used the `class` keyword.

4. Call the `make_animal` function and get back a new class. Assign this class to a variable in order to use it later.

5. Invoke the new `Seal` class without arguments to create an instance of it. Then call that instance to see what a seal says.

6. The class creation, instance creation, and call to the `make_sound` method can now happen in a single line of clear, readable Python code.

Metaprogramming was needed to remove the duplicated code, and I hope it demonstrates that a metaprogram does not need to be impossible to decipher. Using the `type` function kept our code straightforward and readable.

The importance of being declarative

In normal Python, using the `type` function to create new types is very rare. Metaprogramming in general is rare, and you should keep it that way! However, one place it often comes up is when mapping non-Pythonic systems into Pythonic interfaces. Many web frameworks and database relationship mapping systems are often implemented with some amount of metaprogramming. This allows users of these frameworks to write elegant Python code, and have the framework code do the heavy lifting.

For example, using the popular third-party **SQL Alchemy** object-relational mapper framework (see http://www.sqlalchemy.org for more information), we can create a database table that contains animal class information using the following code:

```
from sqlalchemy import Column, Integer, String
# ... code to create the Base subclass
class Animal(Base):
    __tablename__ = 'animals'
    id = Column(Integer, primary_key=True)
    name = Column(String)
    sound = Column(String)
```

In olden times, the preceding code would have been written in a way that was all about how to do something. There would be a SQL statement to create a database table, create each column and constraint, and more. It would describe how to represent the Animal class in the database. This is known as programming in an **imperative style**: defining a sequence of commands that change the program's state.

Instead, you should prefer to program in a declarative style. To be declarative we write code that describes what something is. The conversion from a declarative description to code that actually does something, which may be imperative, is hidden. Furthermore, the conversion from declaration into imperative database access code only needs to be written once.

Declarative code is simple to read, often documenting itself. In the preceding example, we can know at a glance that instances of the Animal class are stored in a table named animals, which has an id primary key column, and name and sound string columns. If this information were written out as SQL statements, it would be much more difficult to read.

The node plugin code we wrote earlier in this chapter is very imperative. In the node initializer, we used a series of statements to establish which inputs affect which outputs. It would be more declarative to state what inputs affect an output when we describe the output. In the compute method, the bulk of our code involved getting data from and to OpenMaya objects. It would be more declarative to only state what the transformations from input to output values are, and allow some other code to convert between OpenMaya and Python types.

Keep this pattern in mind as we go forward. We will create a declarative, Pythonic interface for the imperative Maya Python API. It will allow us to succinctly describe Maya nodes, instead of writing out the long series of commands involved in creating them.

Designing the node factory

For the rest of this chapter, we will be creating a node factory library which will help create dependency graph plugins. It will provide the following benefits:

- **Less code and duplication**. Creating nodes through the node factory requires 75-90% less code than an equivalent node created with the raw Maya Python API. The node declarations should also involve little to no duplication, as they only need to describe data and behavior unique to the node. The repetitiveness of working with the Maya Python API is hidden.

- **Intuitive and consistent**. Using the node factory should be conceptually close to designing a Maya node and not require learning many new concepts. For example, we uphold the concepts of name, type ID, inputs, outputs, and compute, but provide a way of working with them that does not require knowledge of the Maya API. The node factory should also provide a consistent and complete abstraction, not requiring the user to jump between PyMEL and the API except for advanced usage.

- **Lightweight**. In the worst case, a user should be able to port her code back to the original Maya Python API style. Furthermore the library should be flexible and easy to understand by reading the source code, and for users to maintain and extend. These things make the library easy to use.

- **Extensible**. New functionality should be easy to add. For example, we do not cover array attributes in this chapter, but adding support is straightforward. Advanced use cases requiring access to the API should be possible as well.

Clearly these goals together justify the relatively small amount of work involved in getting the node factory up and running. It can be written once and reused endlessly for many different applications.

Designing plugin nodes

The node factory will map how we think about Maya nodes into how we code Maya nodes. For example, we normally think of the following when designing a Maya node:

- The name of the node.
- The type ID of the node.
- The input attributes of the node.
- For each input attribute: the type of the input, the default value of the input, the minimum and maximum values, and some other optional information.

- The output attributes of the node.

- For each output: the type of the output, the minimum and maximum values, the inputs that affect the output, the transformation of those input values into the output value, and some other optional information.

- More advanced nodes may need to override methods such as `MPxNode.connectionMade` or `MPxNode.connectionBroken`.

As we experienced when we built the circle node, the code that creates a node does not reflect this simple design. It is filled with boilerplate calls to the Maya Python API, and its structure does not reflect the elegance of the underlying Maya architecture. The node factory we are developing will reflect the design of Maya nodes onto the code used to construct them.

Designing the attribute specification

One of the key concepts of the node factory is that we can provide a homogeneous interface for attributes of all types. Using traditional techniques, if you have a float attribute, you need to use methods like `asFloat` and `setFloat` to get and set values. For different types of attributes, we need to use different methods, such as `asString` and `setString`. This problem gets progressively worse the deeper you dig. Float2 attributes can be created by calling the `MFnNumericAttribute.create` method, but color attributes must call the `MFnNumericAttribute.createColor` method. And string attributes use `MFnTypedAttribute`, a different attribute type entirely.

To provide a homogenous interface, we must come up with a specification that describes any attribute, and implement the specification for each concrete attribute type. We will use a base class to define the specification, and subclasses to implement it for each attribute type. Alternatively, you could use a dictionary with a common set of keys. The following is the specification for a float attribute. We will cover this design in more detail later.

```
class _FloatAttr(AttrSpec):
    def createfnattr(self):
        return OpenMaya.MFnNumericAttribute()
    def getvalue(self, datahandle):
        return datahandle.asFloat()
    def setvalue(self, datahandle, value):
        datahandle.setFloat(value)
    def create(self, fnattr, longname, shortname):
        return fnattr.create(
            longname, shortname, OpenMaya.MFnNumericData.kFloat)
    def setdefault(self, fnattr, value):
        fnattr.setDefault(value)
A_FLOAT = _FloatAttr()
```

Because the specifications are immutable and unchanging, we hide the class definition (`_FloatAttr`) and expose a single instance of it (`A_FLOAT`). We use an *ALL_CAPS* naming convention to denote that the variable is a constant. The caller does not really need to know anything about the implementation; they just need to pass the specification around.

Similar specifications will be built for other attribute types. When we need to support other attribute types, such as `color` or `enum`, we only need to figure out how to implement the specification in terms of that type. We will not need to change the node factory code itself.

See *Supporting string and color attributes* and *Supporting enum attributes* later in this chapter for examples of other attribute types.

Designing the node type specification

In the same way we can provide a homogenous interface for an attribute through a specification, we can do the same for a node. Let's look at the specification of a dependency graph node. We will go over this code in more detail later.

```
class _DependsNode(NodeSpec):
    def nodebase(self):
        return (OpenMayaMPx.MPxNode,)
    def _nodetype(self):
        return OpenMayaMPx.MPxNode.kDependNode
    def register(self, fnplugin, typename, typeid, create, init):
        fnplugin.registerNode(
            typename, typeid, create, init,
            self._nodetype())
    def deregister(self, fnplugin, typeid):
        fnplugin.deregisterNode(typeid)
NT_DEPENDSNODE = _DependsNode()
```

Our node type specification defines the common information we need to create a node, including the base class and methods for registering and deregistering it. That's all there is to a node-type specification. The rest of the information about a node, such as its attributes, is specific to the custom nodes we will create.

See *Supporting transform nodes* later in this chapter for a transform node specification.

Building the node factory

In the following sections, we will implement the concepts explained in *Designing the node factory*. This will involve moving incrementally from the traditional circle node plugin we built in *Understanding Dependency Graph plugins*, first extracting out some of the duplication to use attribute specifications, then tying in the node specification, and finally overriding the `compute` method.

Specifying attributes

The first step in building the node factory is to create the attribute specification base class and the concrete subclass we will need for float attributes. Create a file at `C:\mayapybook\pylib\nodefactory.py` and type into it the following code:

```python
from maya import OpenMaya, OpenMayaMPx


class AttrSpec(object): #(1)
    def createfnattr(self):
        raise NotImplementedError()
    def getvalue(self, datahandle):
        raise NotImplementedError()
    def setvalue(self, datahandle, value):
        raise NotImplementedError()
    def create(self, fnattr, longname, shortname):
        raise NotImplementedError()
    def setdefault(self, fnattr, value):
        raise NotImplementedError()


class _FloatAttr(AttrSpec): #(2)
    def createfnattr(self):
        return OpenMaya.MFnNumericAttribute()
    def getvalue(self, datahandle):
        return datahandle.asFloat()
    def setvalue(self, datahandle, value):
        datahandle.setFloat(value)
    def create(self, fnattr, longname, shortname):
        return fnattr.create(
            longname, shortname, OpenMaya.MFnNumericData.kFloat)
    def setdefault(self, fnattr, value):
        fnattr.setDefault(value)
A_FLOAT = _FloatAttr() #(3)
```

Let's walk through the preceding code:

1. Define the attribute specification base class. Concrete attribute specifications will override the methods on this class. This class is the homogenous interface for attributes; any attribute can be implemented by these methods. A `NotImplementedError` is raised inside each method because the `AttrSpec` class should not be instantiated and used directly.

2. Define the float attribute specification class `_FloatAttr`. We make the class definition protected by preceding it with an underscore; callers should use the `A_FLOAT` variable (see next point). The methods use the appropriate mechanisms for manipulating float data, such as `asFloat` and `setFloat`.

3. Define a single instance of the float specification class: the global `A_FLOAT` variable. We will use the `A_` prefix on our specification instances to group them as concrete attribute specifications.

Remember, these are all implementation details for the node factory. Callers do not need to know how specifications work at all. They only need to pass around the concrete specifications.

Creating attributes

Next, we will create a function that uses attribute specifications to simplify the attribute creation process. You may recall from *Defining inputs, outputs, and the initializer* that creating an attribute requires a subclass of `MPxNode`, a long name, short name, and attribute type. Attributes can also have a default value. Outputs require a collection of inputs that affect them.

Place the following code into the `nodefactory.py` file. It will handle all the attribute creation.

```
def create_attr(
        nodeclass, attrspec, ln, sn,
        affectors=(), default=None):
    attr = attrspec.createfnattr() #(1)
    plug = attrspec.create(attr, ln, sn) #(2)
    if default is not None:
        attrspec.setdefault(attr, default) #(3)

    isinput = not bool(affectors) #(4)
    attr.setWritable(isinput)
    attr.setStorable(isinput)

    nodeclass.addAttribute(plug) #(5)
```

```
    setattr(nodeclass, ln, plug) #(6)

    for affectedby in affectors: #(7)
        inattrobj = getattr(nodeclass, affectedby)
        nodeclass.attributeAffects(inattrobj, attrobj)
```

The entire thirty-three line `init` function inside `circlernode.py` can be simplified into six lines:

```
from nodefactory import create_attr, A_FLOAT
def init():
    create_attr(Circler, A_FLOAT, 'input', 'in')
    create_attr(Circler, A_FLOAT, 'scale', 'sc', default=10.0)
    create_attr(Circler, A_FLOAT, 'frames', 'fr', default=48.0)
    inputnames = ['input', 'scale', 'frames']
    create_attr(Circler, A_FLOAT, 'outSine', 'so', inputnames)
    create_attr(Circler, A_FLOAT, 'outCosine', 'co', inputnames)
```

Now that we've seen how the `create_attr` function is called, let's go through its code in more detail. The function is designed to work with any plugin class and attribute specification, but I will use concrete specifications and types here to make the explanation more clear.

1. Calling the `A_FLOAT.createfnattr` method returns a new `OpenMaya.MFnNumericAttribute` instance.

2. Calling the `A_FLOAT.create` method calls the `MFnNumericAttribute.create` method and returns the result, an instance of `MObject` that represents the new attribute.

3. If a default value is provided, call the `A_FLOAT.setdefault` method, which calls the `MFnNumericAttribute.setDefault` method to set the attribute's default value.

4. Determine whether something is an input or output based on whether it is affected by other attributes. No affectors means it is an input. Inputs should be writable and storable, outputs should not be.

5. Call `Circler.addAttribute` to add the attribute to the class, just like the old code. This adds the attribute to the Maya representation of the node.

6. Call `setattr(Circler, ln, attrobj)` to set the `MObject` representing the attribute on the `Circler` class, so it is accessible in the `Circler.compute` method. This adds the attribute to the Python representation of the node.

7. If the attribute is an output, loop over the affectors. For each affector, get the `MObject` for the input attribute from the Python type (see point 6), and call `Circler.attributeAffects(<input attr>, <output attr>)`.

If you're having trouble following, try going through the `create_attr` method for any of the `Circler` attributes. Thinking through a concrete use case can often bring clarity to code.

This is a huge improvement. The node has the same behavior and less code. However, we can simplify much more. The `circlernode.py` file still contains a lot of boilerplate. Next, we will remove the `Circler` class definition, node creator function, and node initializer function.

Specifying a node

We can create nodes using a design similar to what we used for attributes. We should continue to identify boilerplate and figure out how to remove it. A node specification is quite simple:

- The tuple of the node's base classes. The tuple `(OpenMayaMPx.MPxNode,)` would be used for dependency graph nodes.

- A function to register the node. Registration requires an `MFnPlugin` instance, the type name, the type ID, the creator function, and an initializer function.

- A function to deregister the node. Deregistration requires an `MFnPlugin` instance and the type ID.

We can specify every type of Maya node with that specification. Concrete nodes such as `Circler` also consist of:

- The name of the node.
- The type ID of the node.
- The input and output attributes of the node.
- A way to convert input values into output values, such as the three lines of math in the `Circler.compute` method which calculate the sine and cosine.
- Optional overrides for methods other than `compute`, such as the `MPxNode.connectionMade` method.

Other information, such as the node creator function, is the same for every node. The node factory can take care of it.

We can take the requirements for our specification to build a base class and concrete subclass for dependency nodes inside `nodefactory.py`:

```python
class NodeSpec(object): #(1)
    def nodebase(self):
        raise NotImplementedError()
    def register(self, fnplugin, typename, typeid, create, init):
        raise NotImplementedError()
    def deregister(self, fnplugin, typeid):
        raise NotImplementedError()


class _DependsNode(NodeSpec): #(2)
    def nodebase(self):
        return (OpenMayaMPx.MPxNode,) #(3)
    def register(self, fnplugin, typename, typeid, create, init):
        fnplugin.registerNode( #(4)
            typename, typeid, create, init,
            OpenMayaMPx.MPxNode.kDependNode)
    def deregister(self, fnplugin, typeid): #(5)
        fnplugin.deregisterNode(typeid)
NT_DEPENDSNODE = _DependsNode() #(6)
```

Let's walk through the preceding code. The ideas are the same as for attribute specifications.

1. Define the `NodeSpec` base class. This class contains the three methods that define the specification. Subclasses must override these methods, so the default implementations raise multiple `NotImplementedError`.

2. Define the `_DependsNode` subclass, which inherits from the `NodeSpec` base class. The implementation should be familiar from the original circle node. See the *Supporting transform nodes* section for an example of a different subclass.

3. The `nodebase` method returns a tuple containing `MPxNode`.

4. The `register` method calls `MFnPlugin.registerNode` with the given arguments. It passes in `MPxNode.kDependNode`, which Maya confusingly calls the node type, to indicate to Maya this is a basic dependency node. There are other node types available, such as `kDeformerNode`. You can create other types of nodes by using a different node type flag. We won't deal with other values of this flag for the sake of simplicity.

5. The `deregister` method calls the `MFnPlugin.deregisterNode` with the given arguments.

6. Define a single instance of the dependency node specification class named `NT_DEPENDSNODE`. Use the `NT_` prefix to identify objects as concrete node specifications.

By using the node specifications from this section, and the `type` function which was explained in the *Demystifying Python metaprogramming* section, we can simplify the remaining boilerplate and duplication away into a node creator function. However, we'd like to declare an entire node and all attributes in a single expression and not across multiple statements. This presents a problem, because attributes need to know about the node type, but the node type is declared with its attributes. To solve this problem, we can use a technique called partial application.

Using partial application to create attributes

Partial application (often called **partial function application**) means processing a function with *n* arguments into a function with less than *n* arguments. We've actually used this technique throughout this book without knowing it, usually by creating closures as in the following example:

```
>>> def add(a, b): # Our 'full' function
...     return a + b
>>> def partial_add(a):
...     def add2(b): # Create a closure
...         return add(a, b)
...     return add2
>>> adder = partial_add(1) # Create the partial function.
>>> adder(2) # Call the partial function
3
```

We can use partial application to turn the `nodefactory.create_attr` function, which takes an `MPxNode` subclass and returns a concrete attribute, into a function that takes everything except the subclass and returns a closure that takes only the subclass. The closure then returns the concrete attribute.

Inside the `nodefactory.py` file, replace the `create_attr` function with a `create_attrmaker` function as in the proceeding code:

```
def create_attrmaker(
        attrspec, ln, sn,
        affectors=(), default=None):
    def createattr(nodeclass):
        fnattr = attrspec.createfnattr()
        attrobj = attrspec.create(fnattr, ln, sn)
        if default is not None:
            attrspec.setdefault(fnattr, default)
        isinput = not bool(affectors)
        fnattr.setWritable(isinput)
        fnattr.setStorable(isinput)
        nodeclass.addAttribute(attrobj)
        setattr(nodeclass, ln, attrobj)
        for affectedby in affectors:
            inattrobj = getattr(nodeclass, affectedby)
            nodeclass.attributeAffects(inattrobj, attrobj)
    return createattr
```

The code has changed slightly. The `create_attr` function becomes the `create_attrmaker` function, which takes the same arguments as the original minus the node type. The nested `createattr` function closes over all of those arguments and is returned by `create_attrmaker`. The `createattr` function is called with only the node type. This way, we can declare the attributes along with the node, but create them after the node type is synthesized.

Creating a node

In this section, we will create the first version of our node builder function, which will support a node name, type ID, and attributes. In the next section we will add support for the `compute` method, and later on in the *Overriding MPxNode methods* section we will add support for methods such as `connectionMade`.

The code for `create_node` follows. It should go into `nodefactory.py`.

```
def create_node(nodespec, nodename, typeid, attrmakers):  #(1)
    def compute(*_):  #(2)
        print 'Compute not yet implemented.'
    methods = {'compute': compute}
    nodetype = type(nodename, nodespec.nodebase(), methods)  #(3)
```

```
tid = OpenMaya.MTypeId(typeid) #(4)
def creator(): #(5)
    return OpenMayaMPx.asMPxPtr(nodetype())
def init(): #(6)
    for makeattr in attrmakers:
        makeattr(nodetype)
def register(plugin): #(7)
    nodespec.register(plugin, nodename, tid, creator, init)
def deregister(plugin):
    nodespec.deregister(plugin, tid)
return register, deregister #(8)
```

Let's walk through the preceding code for creating a node:

1. Define the `create_node` function. It takes in a node specification, node name, type ID, and attribute maker functions. An attribute maker function is returned from the `create_attrmaker` function we built in the previous section. Each attribute maker is called with the node type constructed inside the `create_node` function that we are building.

2. Define a nested `compute` function, which is just a stub for now.

3. Create a new type using the `type` function. Pass in the node name as the type name, the node specification's tuple of base classes, and the method dictionary which for now only contains the stub `compute` function.

4. Convert the `typeid` argument, which is an integer, into an `MTypeId` instance. This way, the caller does not need to worry about the `MTypeId` class and only needs to pass an integer as the type ID.

5. Define the node creator function, which tells Maya to manage the Python object's memory. Notice that we use the newly constructed `nodetype` as the class.

6. Define the node initializer function. The node initializer just sets up the node's attributes. For now, this only entails calling each attribute maker closure with the newly constructed node type.

7. Define nested `register` and `deregister` functions. These functions have a simple interface that only needs an `MFnPlugin` instance passed in. They capture other arguments, such as the node's type ID, from local variables.

8. Return the `register` and `deregister` functions. The caller is responsible for invoking them with an `MFnPlugin` instance.

Next we will hook up the new `create_node` method to the `circlernode.py` plugin file. The following is the entire contents of the file. Notice how small it is.

```python
from nodefactory_final import (
    NT_DEPENDSNODE, A_FLOAT, create_attrmaker, create_node)
_deregister_funcs = [] #(1)
def floatattr(*args, **kwargs): #(2)
    return create_attrmaker(A_FLOAT, *args, **kwargs)
def register_circler(fnplugin): #(3)
    inputnames = ['input', 'scale', 'frames']
    reg, dereg = create_node(
        NT_DEPENDSNODE, 'circler', 0x60005, [
            floatattr('input', 'in'),
            floatattr('scale', 'sc', default=10.0),
            floatattr('frames', 'fr', default=48.0),
            floatattr('outSine', 'os', inputnames),
            floatattr('outCosine', 'oc', inputnames),
    ])
    reg(fnplugin)
    _deregister_funcs.append(dereg)

def _toplugin(mobject):
    return OpenMayaMPx.MFnPlugin(mobject, 'Marcus Reynir', '0.01')
def initializePlugin(mobject):
    register_circler(_toplugin(mobject)) #(4)
def uninitializePlugin(mobject):
    plugin = _toplugin(mobject) #(5)
    for func in _deregister_funcs:
        func(plugin)
```

Let's go through the preceding code to see how the original `circlenode.py` file with over eighty lines has shrunk in half.

1. Create the `_deregister_funcs` list at the module level. It contains all the functions to deregister the plugin's nodes during uninitialization. This makes it much easier to define several nodes in the same file. Even if more nodes are defined, the code in `uninitializePlugin` will not need to change.

2. Define the `floatattr` helper function to simplify the float attribute creation code; this is optional and I only use it so attribute declarations fit on a single line.

3. Define the `register_circler` function. It registers the `circler` node type, which calls the `nodefactory.create_node` function. It invokes the registration function returned from `create_node` with the passed `MFnPlugin` instance. It also adds the deregistration function to the `_deregister_funcs` list for later usage.

4. When the plugin is initialized, call the `register_circler` function with an `MFnPlugin` instance.

5. When the plugin is uninitialized, call every function in `_deregister_funcs` with the `MFnPlugin` instance.

To complete the node factory version of the `circler` node, all that remains is implementing the `compute` method.

Slaying the compute method

In this section, we will create an abstraction for the `compute` method so that callers do not need to worry about using the Maya Python API. They can instead focus on the actual transformation of inputs into outputs.

To implement the `compute` method, the node factory will grab OpenMaya values from input attributes, convert them to regular Python values, and pass them to a user-supplied transformer function which returns a Python value. The node factory will convert that into an OpenMaya type and set the output attribute. This process is illustrated in the following figure:

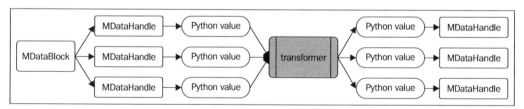

The transformer function will take the number of arguments equal to, and in the same order as, the inputs that affect the output. For example, the following would be the transformer to calculate the `outSine` output attribute on the `circler` node.

```
def sin_xformer(input, scale, frames):
    angle = 6.2831853 * (input / frames)
    return math.sin(angle) * scale
```

The `sin_xformer` function takes the float values of the three input attributes, and calculates what the value of the output should be. There is not a Maya Python API type in sight!

 This technique of converting values into a different form, processing them, and converting them back is conceptually similar to the *decorate-sort-unsort* pattern. You may want to research it if you find the idea of the transformer laid out here unfamiliar or confusing.

It is important to note that a transformer is not associated with the node as a `compute` method would be. A transformer is associated with each output attribute. This allows us to think of outputs individually and build separate transformers for each. I find this much simpler than a `compute` method with a number of `if/else` conditions determining which output is being computed.

The node creator function needs more information about a created attribute so it can work with the transformer. Let's make the following small change to the `createattr` closure inside the `create_attrmaker` function in `nodefactory.py`. The previous version of the closure did not return anything. It should now return the attribute's long name, specification, transformer, and affectors. The changes are highlighted.

```
def create_attrmaker(
    ...
    def createattr (nodetype):
        ...
        for affectedby in affectors:
            inputplug = getattr(nodetype, affectedby)
            nodetype.attributeAffects(inputplug, plug)
        return ln, attrspec, transformer, affectors
    return createattr
```

Finally, we must add a significant amount of code to the `nodefactory.create_node` function. In the following listing, the nested `compute` function is fleshed out, and the node initializer sets up some associations between output and input attributes.

```
def create_node(nodespec, name, typeid, attrmakers):
    attr_to_spec = {} #(1)
    outattr_to_xformdata = {}
    def compute(mnode, plug, datablock):
        attrname = plug.name().split('.')[-1]
        xformdata = outattr_to_xformdata.get(attrname) #(2)
        if xformdata is None:
            return OpenMaya.MStatus.kUnknownParameter
```

```
        xformer, affectors = xformdata
        invals = []
        for inname in affectors: #(3)
            inplug = getattr(nodetype, inname)
            indata = datablock.inputValue(inplug)
            inval = attr_to_spec[inname].getvalue(indata)
            invals.append(inval)
        outval = xformer(*invals) #(4)
        outhandle = datablock.outputValue(plug) #(5)
        attr_to_spec[attrname].setvalue(outhandle, outval)
        datablock.setClean(plug)
    methods = {'compute': compute}
    nodetype = type(name, nodespec.nodebase(), methods)

    mtypeid = OpenMaya.MTypeId(typeid)
    def creator():
        return OpenMayaMPx.asMPxPtr(nodetype())
    def init():
        for makeattr in attrmakers: #(6)
            ln, attrspec, xformer, affectors = makeattr(nodetype)
            attr_to_spec[plug] = attrspec
            if xformer is not None:
                outattr_to_xformdata[plug] = xformer, affectors
    # ... Unchanged code elided ...
```

This is by far the most advanced code in the chapter, and possibly the book. Let's go over it in detail.

1. The attr_to_spec dictionary holds the long name of each attribute as the key and the attribute's specification as the value. The outattr_to_xformdata dictionary holds the long name of each output attribute as the key and a tuple of the transformer function and affectors (list of names of input attributes that affect the output attribute) as the value. These dictionaries will be filled with the values returned from the attribute creator during node initialization (see point 9). I've chosen to use attribute names as keys out of convenience, but you can also try using the MObject representing the attribute.

2. Inside the nested compute function, find the transform and affectors for the attribute. If there is no entry, it means the plug can't be handled so return the MStatus.kUnknownParameter value.

3. For each affector, get the value of the attribute. To do this, get the MObject that represents the input attribute, get the MDataHandle for it, and then use the attribute specification to retrieve the actual Python value, which is a float in our case.

4. Invoke the transformer function with these values.

5. Get the `MDataHandle` for the output attribute, and use the output attribute specification to set the output's value. Finally, set the plug clean.

6. When the node is initialized and attributes created (which happens before `compute` is called, remember), fill out the `attr_to_spec` and `outattr_to_xformdata` dictionaries. The remaining code in the `create_node` function is the same.

The preceding code follows the transformer function concept quite closely. It converts input attributes from OpenMaya to Python types using their specifications, calls the transformer with Python types, and sets the output attribute's value using the transformer's return value and the output's specification.

Notice how similar this `compute` function is to the old `compute` method. Lots of API access and boilerplate. The important thing is we only need to write this code once and can reuse it many times.

Let's see how the transformer is hooked up in `circlernode.py`. The new code is highlighted.

```python
def make_transformer(mathfunc):
    def inner(input, scale, frames):
        angle = 6.2831853 * (input / frames)
        return mathfunc(angle) * scale
    return inner
sin = make_transformer(math.sin)
cosine = make_transformer(math.cos)


def register_circler(plugin):
    inputnames = ['input', 'scale', 'frames']
    reg, dereg = create_node(
        NT_DEPENDSNODE, 'circler', 0x60005,
        [
            floatattr('input', 'in'),
            floatattr('scale', 'sc', default=10.0),
            floatattr('frames', 'fr', default=48.0),
            floatattr('outSine', 'so',
                affectors=inputnames,
                transformer=sin),
            floatattr('outCosine', 'co',
                affectors=inputnames,
                transformer=cosine),
        ])
```

It is exciting to see how our sine and cosine calculation went from 20 lines to 4, and how we've really pulled the essence of the math into a function that has nothing to do with Maya.

With that, we can verify the node factory design works. It can handle float attributes with ease. The rest of the chapter will expand on the design laid out so far, adding support for other attribute and node types, and more advanced use cases.

Extending the node factory

The following sections cover extending the node factory's functionality. We will add support for string, color, and enum attributes, transform nodes, and overriding `MPxNode` methods other than `compute`.

There are many more features to support than what's covered here, such as string and array attributes. When it comes time to add a new feature to the node factory, I suggest you start by getting comfortable with its implementation using the Maya Python API directly. Only then should you support it in the node factory. This is due, first and foremost, to the fact that many examples and tutorials exist for the API. Second, it is due to the fact that diagnosing issues in the node factory can be difficult due to its dynamism.

Supporting string and color attributes

Adding support for string and color attributes demonstrates the power of the attribute specification design. For string attributes, add the following code to `nodefactory.py`:

```python
class _StringAttr(AttrSpec):
    def createfnattr(self):
        return OpenMaya.MFnTypedAttribute()
    def getvalue(self, datahandle):
        return datahandle.asString()
    def setvalue(self, datahandle, value):
        datahandle.setString(value)
    def create(self, fnattr, longname, shortname):
        return fnattr.create(longname, shortname,
                             OpenMaya.MFnData.kString)
    def setdefault(self, fnattr, value):
        fnattr.setDefault(OpenMaya.MFnStringData().create(value))
A_STRING = _StringAttr()
```

Now you can just use A_STRING to declare string attributes in the same way you use A_FLOAT to declare float attributes. Supporting color attributes is equally straightforward, as the following specification demonstrates:

```
class _ColorAttr(AttrSpec):
    def createfnattr(self):
        return OpenMaya.MFnNumericAttribute()
    def getvalue(self, datahandle):
        return datahandle.asFloatVector()
    def setvalue(self, datahandle, value):
        datahandle.setMFloatVector(OpenMaya.MFloatVector(*value))
    def create(self, fnattr, longname, shortname):
        return fnattr.createColor(longname, shortname)
    def setdefault(self, fnattr, value):
        fnattr.setDefault(*value)
A_COLOR = _ColorAttr()
```

See the next section for an example plugin that uses string and color attributes.

Notice that we did not need to change anything else in the node factory to support new attribute types. This is a good thing as it makes the code easy to extend and understand.

Supporting enum attributes

Enum attributes can be set to any member of an enumeration of values. For example, the OpenMaya.MStatus type defines the MStatusCode enumeration. Each MStatusCode enum has a name, such as kSuccess and kFailure, and a value. The value itself is usually not important, since enums are meant to be used by name and not by value.

Enum attributes are very similar to integer attributes. However when we create the attribute, we need to define the possible name and value pairs, called fields.

> There's more to enumerations as a general concept than we are going to cover here. For example, they are commonly used with bitwise operations so they can act as masks. However, it is much more common for enum attributes to be used for explicitly defined and mutually exclusive values, like the rotation order of an Euler angle solver.

Even though only enum attributes support fields, you should always avoid special case code such as:

```
if attrspec is A_ENUM:
    # ... do special code ...
```

Avoiding special cases will keep your code clean. However, we will need to change code in a couple places, since fields are a new concept for the node factory. Add an `allow_fields` method to the `AttrSpec` base class. It will return `False` by default.

```
class AttrSpec(object):
    # ... Other methods elided ...
    def allow_fields(self):
        return False
```

Now create a new attribute specification for enum attributes. Override the `allow_fields` method to return `True`.

```
class _EnumAttr(AttrSpec):
    def createfnattr(self):
        return OpenMaya.MFnEnumAttribute()
    def getvalue(self, datahandle):
        return datahandle.asInt()
    def setvalue(self, datahandle, value):
        datahandle.setInt(value)
    def create(self, fnattr, longname, shortname):
        return fnattr.create(longname, shortname)
    def setdefault(self, fnattr, value):
        fnattr.setDefault(value)
    def allow_fields(self):
        return True
A_ENUM = _EnumAttr()
```

The `create_attrmaker` function must also change to support fields. I've highlighted the changes and marked where the unchanged code has been elided:

```
def create_attrmaker(
    attrspec, ln, sn, affectors=(), default=None,
    transformer=None, fields=()): #(1)

    if not attrspec.allow_fields() and fields: #(2)
        raise RuntimeError(
            'Fields not allowed for %s.' % attrspec)

    def createattr(nodeclass):
        fnattr = attrspec.createfnattr()
        attrobj = attrspec.create(fnattr, ln, sn)
        for name, value in fields: #(3)
            fnattr.addField(name, value)
        # ... unchanged code elided ...
```

Let's go over the changes in the preceding code:

1. Add a `fields` parameter which defaults to an empty tuple.

2. If the attribute specification does not support fields, but the caller has supplied fields, raise an error. This sort of aggressive checking, especially around trickier areas, is a good idea. A better idea still would be to redesign our code to not need incompatible parameters at all!

3. Iterate over the name and value for each field and pass them into the `MFnEnumAttribute.addField` method.

The following demonstrates the use of string, color, and enum attributes:

```
nodefactory.create_node(
    nodefactory.NT_DEPENDSNODE, 'otherdemo', 0x60006,
    [
        nodefactory.create_attrmaker(
            nodefactory.A_COLOR, 'col', 'c'),
        nodefactory.create_attrmaker(
            nodefactory.A_ENUM, 'enum', 'e', default=1,
            fields=[
                ['field1', 1],
                ['field2', 2]]),
        nodefactory.create_attrmaker(
            nodefactory.A_STRING, 'string', 's', default='hi')])
```

Supporting transform nodes

The node factory at this point supports a variety of attribute types, but only a single node type: `MPxNode`, for basic dependency nodes. In this section, we will add support for the transform node type, which inherits from `OpenMayaMPx.MPxTransform` and has a representation in the Maya viewport. The creation of transform nodes is considerably more complex than dependency nodes, requiring a special `OpenMayaMPx.MPxTransformationMatrix` subclass as well. However, all of this complexity can be hidden behind the node specification. The `_TransformNode` class in the following code has some helpers on it, including the transformation matrix subclass and the function to create the transformation matrix. We put the helpers here to avoid dirtying the module, and keep our code self-contained.

```
class _TransformNode(NodeSpec):
    xform_typeid = OpenMaya.MTypeId(0x60080)
    class TransformMatrix(OpenMayaMPx.MPxTransformationMatrix):
        pass
```

```
    def nodebase(self):
        return (OpenMayaMPx.MPxTransform,)
    def _make_node_matrix(self):
        return OpenMayaMPx.asMPxPtr(TransformMatrix())
    def register(self, fnplugin, typename, typeid, create, init):
        fnplugin.registerTransform(
            typename, typeid, create, init,
            self._make_node_matrix, self.xform_typeid)
    def deregister(self, fnplugin, typeid):
        fnplugin.deregisterNode(typeid)
NT_TRANSFORMNODE = _TransformNode()
```

Those are the only changes required to support transform nodes. The core of the node factory was not modified and no special cases were made. We also kept things simple for the caller, by hiding the MPxTransformationMatrix class and other boilerplate behind the NT_TRANSFORMNODE specification. The calling code is as simple as it was for dependency nodes, as in the following example:

```
nodefactory.create_node(
    nodefactory.NT_TRANSFORMNODE, 'transformdemo', 0x60007, [])
```

Overriding MPxNode methods

Up until now, the compute node is the only MPxNode method we've needed to override. In many cases, this is sufficient and even recommended. Nodes should be self-contained and not depend on outside state, and connection compatibility is ideally based on attribute type alone. There will inevitably be cases, however, where certain rules may need to be broken. We can handle this in two ways.

We can add first-class support for other MPxNode methods like connectionMade and connectionBroken. This has lots of benefits, but considerable costs to cover a limited number of use cases. It would take similar effort to what was required for the compute function. It is worth the effort if you have methods that are commonly overridden.

The second option, which I find preferable and which we will pursue in the following example, is to allow the caller to pass in the method dictionary themselves. This exposes the Maya Python API to advanced users of the node factory, but is fully extensible and requires almost no extra work.

It only takes one extra line to support `MPxNode` method overrides, highlighted in the following code (unchanged code is elided):

```
def create_node(nodespec, name, typeid, attrmakers,
                override_methods=None):
    # ... unchanged code elided ...
    methods = {'compute': compute}
    methods.update(override_methods)
    nodetype = type(name, nodespec.nodebase(), methods)
    # ... unchanged code elided ...
```

With those very small changes, a caller can now pass in their own override methods. The signature of the override method must be the same as the normal `MPxNode` method. In the following example, we override `MPxNode.connectionMade`:

```
def connection_made(nodeself, plug, other_plug, as_src):
    print 'Connection made!'

nodefactory.create_node(
    nodefactory.NT_DEPENDSNODE, 'overridesdemo', 0x60010, [
        nodefactory.create_attrmaker(
            nodefactory.A_COLOR, 'color', 'c')],
    {'connectionMade': connection_made})
```

Whenever a connection is made to an `overridesdemo` node, the string `"Connection made!"` will print to the **Script Editor**. We can use this same technique to override any method on `MPxNode`, or whatever your node's base class may be.

Summary

In this chapter, we used the power and flexibility of Python and the Maya Python API to develop a node factory that allows us to create Maya dependency graph plugins in a declarative and Pythonic style. We started this process by going through the frustrating experience of building a plugin node using C++-based Maya API patterns. We then saw how Python metaprogramming allows us to simplify the boilerplate and duplication required by imperative frameworks. Finally, we put this knowledge to use by building the node factory and seeing how it simplified the original plugin code. We also saw how easy it is to add more features to the node factory.

I hope that this chapter, as well as all preceding chapters, demonstrated how using and thinking with Python can transform the way you program with Autodesk Maya. In the next and final chapter, we will learn how to both leverage and contribute to the Python community. Integrating effectively with the larger Python ecosystem will allow you to exploit the language's full potential.

9

Becoming a Part of the Python Community

Over the previous eight chapters, I hope you have learned a lot of useful programming skills. Knowing how to handle errors, create context managers and decorators, leverage PySide, and get around the Maya Python API are concrete topics you now have experience in. Recognizing Pythonic code and understanding how to abstract poor designs into elegant ones are ongoing journeys you have a head start on.

To unlock Python's full potential, this book is not enough. No amount of training alone will turn you into a Python expert. Python is so powerful, and so exciting, because it is the unifying force behind an incredible community. It is in this community where Python's true strength lies and where you can unleash your creativity as a developer. All great Python programmers are also a part of its community.

In this chapter, we will look at the Python community in more depth and go over how to integrate with it and take advantage of what it has to offer. We'll start by understanding what Open Source Software is. Next we will learn how to create a site directory, and fill it with third-party modules others have developed. After that, we will find out how to contribute back to a project. For the truly adventurous, I will explain how to get your own open source project up and running. Finally, we will list some hubs of activity in the Maya Python community.

Understanding Open Source Software

There is no single and universal definition for **Open Source Software (OSS)**. The simplest definition would be software for which the source is freely available, meaning you do not need to license or buy it to use it legally (thus leaked source code does not make a program open source). This lack of clarity is reflected in the number of open source licenses available. There are nearly seventy open source licenses as classified by the **Open Source Initiative (OSI)**, which has a relatively strict definition. There are countless more *sort of* open source licenses which may not meet a fully open source criteria for any number of reasons (and thus should not really be considered open source licenses). The Open Source Initiative is, according to its website, "a non-profit corporation with global scope formed to educate about and advocate for the benefits of open source, and to build bridges among different constituencies in the open source community."

Entire books have been written about open source licensing, and I am not naive enough to try and cover the topic in depth. That said, the most popular licenses are probably the MIT License, Apache License, the GPL, and the BSD licenses. The `http://www.choosealicense.com` website provides an excellent overview of different open source licenses. To learn more about open source licensing in general, visit the Open Source Initiative at `http://www.opensource.org`.

Differentiating OSS from script download sites

In addition to the licensing situation, there's also the issue of development model. A good open source project can easily integrate changes submitted by its community into its main version. For example, you can clone the Python source code repository, find or create an issue for a bug, fix it, create and submit a patch for the change, and one of Python's core developers will review and commit your patch. The change would then be released along with the next version of Python. Obviously this is a simplistic description, but the key is that users can get changes back into the software, and that all of this is open.

 You can find the CPython source code repository at `http://hg.python.org/cpython/`. The repository allows you to see all the work that goes into the much simpler distribution you use on your computer. If you are interested in contributing to Python, from CPython interpreter fixes to correcting typos in standard library documentation, you can find the *Python Developer's Guide* at `http://docs.python.org/devguide/`.

That said, nothing stops you from posting a bunch of code on the Internet without a license. And in fact, the 3D community has a long history of doing precisely this!

If you browse one of the popular script download sites like `http://creativecrash.com`, you can find thousands of potentially useful scripts. Some you must buy, but most are free. Of the free scripts, many do not have any license information, making them technically not open source. Of those with license information, some have Open Source Initiative-approved licenses and are technically Open Source Software.

However, this download and extract a zip file distribution model which has been so prevalent in the 3D community is not a model for sustainable open source software. Even though some scripts may technically be open source, the ecosystem they are developed and released in lacks vital features.

The key feature of mature open source software is that the entire source tree is freely available, listing all changes to the source code. It is not enough to release only an executable or zip file containing code. Though you can have a healthy project with only one person submitting changes, it is unusual. Users are often willing and able to contribute back changes, and authors are excited to get contributions! Contributions by users is the sign of a healthy open source project, and without a freely available source tree, it is impossible.

While script download sites can and will continue to serve an important role in the community for getting scripts and tools to end users, they are not meant to, and have never effectively been, a way to share code. This is a shame, as there is a great deal of commonly useful code written by the 3D community that has been developed and redeveloped many times.

With a good grasp of Python, and the rest of the information in this chapter, I propose that Maya Python programmers can now do better. The remainder of this chapter will show you how to use available open source projects, and contribute or start your own.

Defining what a third-party module is

The most common way to use open source software in Python is simply finding and installing third-party modules. A third-party module is a module not included with Python, and not developed by you or your team/project/company. In other words, a third party that you do not control developed the module.

For example, PyMEL is a third-party module in Maya 2010 because it is not included with Maya 2010. Maya 2011 and newer versions include PyMEL so to users of those versions, it is not a third-party module. To Luma Pictures, the creators and core developers of PyMEL, PyMEL is a first-party module, developed in house. To Autodesk, who create Maya and bundle PyMEL with Maya, PyMEL is still a third-party module.

The bundling of PyMEL with Maya 2011 and newer has generally been a good thing by making PyMEL available by default. However, it can cause problems if you want to use a newer version of PyMEL. To get around this, check out PyMEL's installation guide. Since it is hosted in several locations (a side effect of OSS), there's no authoritative location so I will not provide a link here. But, again, you don't need to do this unless you want to upgrade the PyMEL bundled with Maya.

With these definitions out of the way, let's learn how to use third-party modules in Python.

Creating a site directory for third-party modules

In the next three sections, we will learn how to prepare Maya to use third-party modules. We will learn how Python's site directories work, create a site directory for Maya, and hook up the new site directory so third-party modules are available in Maya.

Before starting, I must make a disclaimer: there are no established conventions for setting up Maya to use third-party modules. In this book I present what I think is a middle ground between correctness and complexity. If you are comfortable with Python package management systems and virtual environments, you can take a more complex but also more correct approach. If you are just starting out and don't even feel comfortable with what's presented here, you can also place third-party modules into your development root and sidestep the entire issue of segregating third-party and first-party code.

The most important thing, in my opinion, is that you are reusing code from others, and not wasting effort reinventing the wheel.

Explaining the site directory

The third-party modules for a Python installation are in its `site-packages` directory. Its location is dependent on the operating system but is usually something like `<PythonRoot>/Lib/site-packages`. If you look at your `sys.path` in Python, as we did in *Chapter 1, Introspecting Maya, Python, and PyMEL*, you will see the `site-packages` directory is present.

If there is a `spam.py` file inside of `site-packages`, it will be importable in Python through `import spam`. Of course, you can also use a Python package instead of a module. Recall that a Python package is a folder with an `__init__.py` file (and usually other files) inside.

In the case of a clean Python install, the `site-packages` directory is empty. For Maya's Python, the `site-packages` directory contains `maya` and `pymel` folders. This is where the code comes from when you call `import maya.cmds` or `import pymel.core`. We will define a new site directory in the next section to control where Maya loads third-party modules from.

Creating a new site directory for Maya

As previously mentioned, Maya already has a `site-packages` directory. However, it is generally a very bad practice to modify program installation directories for various reasons. It is such a bad idea that most modern operating systems restrict non-administrator access to installation directories. So instead, we will create a `thirdparty` folder which will contain third-party modules. We will add to this directory later in the *Working with Python distributions in Maya* section.

The `thirdparty` folder will be next to our development root, which for this book has been the `C:\mayapybook\pylib` directory. So our third-party modules will go in the `C:\mayapybook\thirdparty` directory. Go ahead and create that directory now.

Establishing the site directory at startup

After creating our folder, we need to tell Maya that the `thirdparty` directory is a site directory so it will load modules from there. There are a number of ways to do this. My suggested way is to use a `sitecustomize.py` module, as explained in the `site` module's documentation at `https://docs.python.org/2/library/site.html`. Unlike using the `-command` flag or a `userSetup.py` file, this will also ensure the necessary code is run when using the mayapy interpreter.

In your development root, which we put in our `sys.path` in *Chapter 1, Introspecting Maya, Python, and PyMEL*, create a `sitecustomize.py` file. We will use relative paths to find the `thirdparty` directory. Type the following code into the `C:\mayapybook\pylib\sitecustomize.py` file. Obviously you will need to adjust for the location of your `thirdparty` directory and operating system:

```
import os
import site
site.addsitedir(
    os.path.join(os.path.dirname(__file__), '..', 'thirdparty'))
```

When Maya or mayapy start up, they will import this file and turn the `thirdparty` directory into a site directory. Python modules and packages in there are now importable.

Note that `sitecustomize` and `usercustomize` are imported during the startup of the Python interpreter. You should avoid doing any work that isn't about setting up the Python environment. For example, the `sitecustomize.py` file would not be an acceptable place to create custom Maya menus! Use a `userSetup.py` file or some other mechanism for this.

Working with Python distributions in Maya

Now that our `thirdparty` folder is available to Maya, let's add some modules to it. First we'll see how to find packages on the Python Package Index. Then we will add source distributions and binary distributions to the directory. We will also go over some caveats using third-party modules in Maya on Windows systems. Finally, we will briefly look at pip, Python's package management tool.

Using the Python Package Index

The **Python Package Index (PyPI)** at `http://pypi.python.org` contains a nearly comprehensive list of community-developed Python modules that you can browse, install, and use however you need. PyPI is not just important for hosting files but for providing a common interface for users and tools to pull down information and packages, as we'll see later.

Using PyPI's website should be self-explanatory. You can search for packages and download distributions. We will install a distribution in the next section.

Adding a source distribution to Maya

A project that consists of only Python code is usually distributed as a source distribution, which is an archive such as `.tar`, `.gz`, or `.zip`. An example of a project that uses a source distribution is the mock library at `https://pypi.python.org/pypi/mock/`. Download the latest version from its PyPI page. Open the archive and copy `mock.py` into `C:\mayapybook\thirdparty`. Assuming that the `thirdparty` directory is set up as a site directory in Maya, you can now use mock from within Maya and mayapy.

Putting third-party modules into the `thirdparty` folder allows us to keep them segregated from our own code, which we have in C:\mayapybook\pylib. It has a few drawbacks, however.

- It can be difficult to know what version of a module is in use. The source files do not always contain version information. When you run into a bug or need to upgrade, you usually want to know what version you are using, so you can see any backwards-incompatible changes introduced, bugs that have been fixed, and features added. To mitigate this, you can include the `egg-info` or similar folder from the distribution, which usually contains this information.

- Dependencies of the module need to be installed manually. For example, if `mock` depended on some other third-party module, we'd need to install both of them by hand. To get around this, you can use pip, which is covered in the upcoming *Using pip to install third-party modules* section.

- For packages with compiled C extensions, you cannot just copy code out of the source archive like we did for `mock`. You will need to properly install the third-party module and copy the files into the `thirdparty` directory. Refer to the next section for more information.

Even with these drawbacks, I've successfully used this strategy with few regrets. There are certainly improvements that can be made, but for most setups this technique should be enough.

Adding an egg or wheel to Maya

Some projects have code written in C that must be compiled before the module can be used. Many projects provide precompiled binary distributions for various Windows and OS X platforms.

A binary distribution is packaged as a wheel (`.whl`) or egg (`.egg`) file. These formats are actually just `.zip` files with a different extension. You can support binary distributions in Maya using the same techniques we used for source distributions in the previous section. Extract the code from within the archive into the `thirdparty` directory and it should be usable in Maya and mayapy. Just make sure you get the right binaries for your operating system and Maya's version of Python!

On Linux, it is assumed that the code will be locally compiled, so binary distributions are usually not available. To acquire compiled files, you have three choices:

- Compile the files yourself from the package's source distribution.
- Use a Python package manager, as we will do in *Using pip to install third-party modules*.

- Use your system's package manager. For example, on an Ubuntu/Debian Linux 64-bit machine with a default Python 2.6, you could do `sudo apt-get install python-zmq`, and then copy the installed `zmq` files from `/usr/lib/python2.6/dist-packages` into `~/mayapybook/thirdparty`.

If a binary distribution is not available for OS X, you should follow the preceding instructions for Linux.

Using binary distributions on Windows

On Windows, there are two significant complications.

The biggest issue is with Maya 2013 and newer. PyPI's binary distributions will not work. They are compiled with Visual Studio 2008, which is the compiler normally used for Python 2.6 and 2.7. However, Maya 2013 and newer are compiled with more recent Visual Studio compilers. Maya 2013 and 2014 use Visual Studio 2010, and Maya 2015 uses Visual Studio 2012. This means the normal Python Windows binaries will not work. You need to compile from source using the appropriate Visual Studio compiler. I do not provide instructions for doing so in this book. You can also check out `http://www.robg3d.com/maya-windows-binaries/`, which hosts precompiled binaries for various versions of Python and Maya.

The second problem is that many packages on PyPI do not provide binary distributions at all, and Windows does not have a C compiler by default. Fortunately, you can find many precompiled Python libraries for Windows at `http://www.lfd.uci.edu/~gohlke/pythonlibs`. Unfortunately, they are usually `.exe` files, not wheels or eggs. To work with these binaries, you should:

1. Install a standard Python interpreter that matches the Python version of the Maya you are using.

2. Download and install the required `.exe` packages to that interpreter.

3. Copy the files from the interpreter's `site-packages` directory into the `C:\mayapybook\thirdparty` directory.

Installing binary packages is not always painless, especially on Windows. If you run into problems, seek help from one of the sources listed in the *Engaging with the wider community* section.

Using pip to install third-party modules

You can use Python's package management tool, pip, to install third-party modules. You can install pip by following the instructions at `http://pip.readthedocs.org/installing.html`. It involves downloading and running the `get-pip.py` file. I would install it for a standard Python interpreter, and not for mayapy.

On Linux, OS X, and properly configured Windows systems, pip will compile C extensions as well. For the binaries to be usable in Maya, however, the interpreter needs to be compatible with Maya's. This is not a big deal on OS X and Linux but is a problem on Windows, as detailed earlier.

You can use pip to install modules into arbitrary directories such as the `thirdparty` directory using the `--target` option (there are many other ways to do this). For example, to install the PyZMQ package there, you can run:

```
pip install --target=C:\mayapybook\thirdparty pyzmq
```

Note that pip will also install dependencies by default, so it can be much easier to use pip to install modules than doing it by hand.

Contributing to the open source community

At this point, you should be able to use open source code from other people in a way more maintainable than copying and pasting the bits you need into your own scripts. Inevitably, at some point while using third-party code you will find a bug or some vital missing feature. You will be at a crossroads and must decide between the following:

- Throw away the existing code and build your own. In the open source world, this is almost never preferable. If you are tempted down this path, think twice. The less experience you have with a problem, the more likely you are to underestimate how much work went into solving it. Since you are using someone else's library to solve a problem, the existing code is likely better than the first thing you'd come up with. Throwing away code is throwing away knowledge!

- Edit your local copy of the code. While less tragic than abandoning the open source version entirely, this is still a bad decision. When you upgrade to a newer version of the code, you will lose your work. Also, no one benefits from your changes.

- File a bug or issue with the project's issue tracker, edit your local copy, create a patch, and submit the patch as a fix. From there, you may need to iterate on the patch and watch for when it gets into a release so you can upgrade and overwrite your local version. This is how many open source projects are run, and contributing this way is relatively lightweight and flexible.

- Finally, with some version control systems (such as Git), you can fork a source repository, make your changes, and use that. Then you can create a pull request to the original source repository to look over and potentially bring in your changes. This is, in the eyes of many (including myself), a superior model.

The last two points would require several pages to cover and the exact steps are often specific to where the open source project is hosted. Check out the README or developer's guide for the project you are using, or see how a similar project is doing it.

The key thing to keep in mind here is that you should almost never edit open source code locally without trying to get those changes back. Not only is it short sighted by creating a maintenance burden, but it is bad for your personal development: you can learn a lot by contributing even a trivial fix to an open source project. It's also bad for the health of the project you are benefiting from. The more active a project is, the healthier it is, and authors usually love when users want to help out.

Designing Maya Python code for open source

In *Chapter 2*, *Writing Composable Code*, we discussed the concept of reusable code and libraries in some detail. Designing an open source project is an extension of this, and requires a somewhat different way of thinking about how code is structured.

A good open source library is focused around a single domain, and depends on other libraries for when it needs to work in other domains. An example project would be boto (https://github.com/boto/boto), a Python interface for **Amazon Web Services (AWS)**. As an example of the first principle (focusing on a single domain), boto is not some sort of generic Amazon Python API. It is for AWS and AWS alone. As an example of the second principle (reusing other libraries), boto uses libraries including requests (https://github.com/kennethreitz/requests) and rsa (https://bitbucket.org/sybren/python-rsa) for making HTTP requests and working with cryptography, respectively.

If we were to graph out how a project can be designed, with dependencies on one axis and how many different things it does on the other, we'd want to target few enough dependencies to manage effectively and enough unique functionality to make it useful. This sweet spot is marked on the following image:

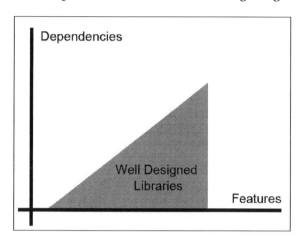

The unfortunate truth is that the vast majority of scripts available in the 3D community do not fall into this sweet spot. Authors reinvent basic functionality, or sometimes copy in other libraries wholesale.

The difficulty here is that the technology and culture of the 3D space has colluded to limit our exposure to OSS and best practices. There's been no good way to reuse third-party code so the community hasn't learned the skills or habits required to write, use, and trust code written by other people. A monolithic project was not only the best choice in many cases, it was the only choice. Programs such as Maya did not have any sort of package or dependency-management system. Maya still does not have one, so if our code relies on `boto`, we would require that the user manually install at least three packages for `boto` and its dependencies.

In order to break out of this unfortunate situation, we need to start by at least getting away from monolithic package design. If your animation tools have a very nifty set of utilities for working with skin weights, you should create the skinning utilities as its own project, and layer on the user-facing features such as menus, toolbars, and icons, in a separate project. This way, other developers can reuse your utilities without the overhead of user-facing features they don't want.

As a final note about design, it should go without saying that configuration needs to be extensible. For example, in *Chapter 3, Dealing with Errors*, we wrote some code that sent an email if an error was raised. If we want to generalize and release that code as open source, we would need to allow the email server and recipient to be configured. We can do this by using any of the following options. We will use the third-party nose library (`http://nose.readthedocs.org`) to illustrate each option:

- Pass the email server and address in as function arguments. This is preferable if the design supports it. For example, you can pass a configuration object into the `nose.run` function to control its behavior.

- Set the email server and address through environment variables. For example, you can use the `NOSE_VERBOSE` environment variable to make nose run in verbose mode and print diagnostic information.

- Set the email server and address through command line flags. You can pass `--verbose` to the nose executable so it runs in verbose mode. Though command line interfaces are an important topic in general, they can be advanced and are not relevant to Maya so we will not cover them.

- Set the email server and address in a configuration file. This is often done using a well-known filename in the current working directory or home directory. For example, nose will load its configuration from a `nose.cfg` or `.noserc` file if found. These configuration files use the `.ini` file format. Another option is to use a Python file for configuration that is executed or imported at runtime. The Sphinx project (`http://sphinx.readthedocs.org`), used for building documentation, uses a `conf.py` file that is imported at runtime. Sphinx provides a template `conf.py` for users to customize and check into source control.

Making your project general enough to be reused is an investment, but it pays off not only for future users (since they could not reuse your code without editing the source in a custom way), but for you as well (your code becomes less coupled and more data-driven).

Starting an open source project

Once you're comfortable with using and contributing back to open source projects, you may want to start your own. This is a very noble thing. Before you start, however, you should ask if someone else doing the same thing already. If the answer is even marginally yes, you should contribute to the existing project instead of starting your own, especially early on. Once you have used and contributed to it and you are still unsatisfied, you'll be in a much better place to start a new project. You can also make a competing fork of the existing one. To fork is to take a copy of a project's code, and do things with it that aren't meant to integrate back into the original version. It splits the community and isn't something to be done lightly.

Assuming you want to go ahead with a new project, you need to pick a way to host it, which also may decide your **source code management (SCM)**. The de facto way to host an open source project right now is to use GitHub (http://github.com), which uses Git source control (http://gitscm.com/), or Bitbucket (https://bitbucket.org/), which supports Git and Mercurial (http://mercurial.selenic.com/).

> The acronym "SCM" can expand out to many different phrases that all mean the same thing: a way to version files. Perforce, Subversion, Git, Mercurial, and CVS are all types of SCM or version control systems.

Once you decide on SCM and hosting, you should follow the tutorials on your site of choice for creating a new repository.

When creating a new Python project, there are established conventions for how to lay out your files. I should note that many older projects do not conform to this, even popular ones like the *Python Imaging Library* and *PyWin32*, so you should make sure you base your project off of libraries that follow good practices. The best source for learning how to set up your Python code is *Hitchhiker's Guide to Packaging*, located at http://guide.python-distribute.org/index.html.

> Some old or abandoned projects that do not conform to modern practices have been forked into new versions. The Python Imaging Library has a modern fork named *Pillow*, available at https://pypi.python.org/pypi/Pillow/.

Once your repository and files are created, you can begin programming away and building awesome stuff!

Distributing your project

The way you choose to distribute your project depends on who the users are. If your project is a library, providing a set of functionality to be called through code, your users are other developers. PyMEL, which we've used extensively in this book, is an example of a library (or framework). As discussed earlier in this chapter, Python has good ways of distributing and using libraries through PyPI, but they are unavailable in Maya. But as long as your project is set up properly, it should be easy enough for other developers to figure out how to reuse your code. You should also upload a version to PyPI to make it easier to find.

If your project is more of an application, which in the Maya context means it presents tools to the other, you need to figure out how you want to install your code onto a user's machine. The easiest way to distribute an application is to upload it to a script-hosting site like `http://creativecrash.com` with installation instructions. Installation usually consists of the user extracting files into a directory and editing a file so your code will be run when Maya starts up. You can also get more creative, with the installer being a Python script that downloads the full code. At the top end would be an auto-updating project.

Remember, even if your end goal is to distribute your tools to users in the form of shelves and menus, you should develop most of the functionality as libraries that can be distributed and consumed independent of the tools.

Neither of these last two options is particularly difficult to implement, but neither are they particularly robust either. Maya is not set up for this sort of thing, and trying to shoehorn a sensible package manager done in an ad hoc way can be error prone and more trouble than it's worth. My hope is that at some point in the next few years, Autodesk adds a sensible package manager to Maya that will begin to solve these problems.

Engaging with the wider community

In this chapter, we have focused mostly on how to use and contribute to open source software. While the coding part of open source is certainly vital, focusing only on code misses the larger point of open source. Open source, by its very nature, encourages a robust and active community. Knowing how to engage with the community will make you a more effective developer because you will have more resources available to you. Beyond that, it's worth thinking about the sense of fulfillment you get from helping people, and the good *karma* others can earn by helping you.

Most discussion about Python, and for many open source projects in general, happens on mailing lists. The official `python.org` mailing lists can be found at `https://mail.python.org/mailman/listinfo`. Also of interest is the `comp.lang.python` Usenet group. Quite a community has sprung up around Python, centered on its mailing lists and other groups.

There are other more general resources, such as the question and answer website `http://stackoverflow.com`, though they lack some of the tight-knit Python community flavor.

Popular individual projects usually also have their own discussion forums, mailing lists, Usenet/Google groups, and IRC channels. All of these resources are incredibly valuable and we are lucky to have them. Make sure to use them!

For Maya Python issues, the situation is a bit different since it doesn't have the same type of open source community. Two Maya programming forums are those at Autodesk's Area (`http://autode.sk/1qLutSc`), and CG Society (`http://bit.ly/1jpMrpm`). I usually choose the latter over the former since it's more active and the community seems to be more cohesive. If you prefer newsgroups over forums, there is the *Python Inside Maya* Google Group located at `https://groups.google.com/forum/#!forum/python_inside_maya`.

For Maya Python issues and 3D application scripting in general, there's `http://tech-artists.org`, which is a forum for technical artists and those that do the technical and programming side of 3D work. I am one of the founders of `tech-artists.org`.

Finally, blogs are an excellent way to learn and spread knowledge. There are two especially relevant feed aggregators. The first is `http://planet.python.org`, an aggregator for most of the popular Python blogs. The second is `http://planet.tech-artists.org`, a feed aggregator for many popular technical artist blogs. Of course, both sites run aggregation software written in Python. I also have a blog at `http://www.robg3d.com`.

Summary

In this chapter, we took a tour around the Python community. We learned what Open Source Software is and how it underpins Python the language and its ecosystem. We saw how to find third-party Python modules and what a Python site directory is. We set up Maya with its own site directory and learned how to add modules to it. We learned about source and binary distributions, and some issues specific to Windows. We then went over what's involved in creating a new open source project, including its design, hosting, and distribution. Finally, we took a quick tour around the wider community.

Python Best Practices

In this book, we used many Python features without diving into the details about how they work. There were also various other issues that were mentioned which could use more explanation. In this appendix, we will cover those topics in more detail. This chapter does not need to be read sequentially; if you are familiar with a topic, feel free to skip its section.

The args and kwargs parameters

We frequently use functions and methods with **asterisk** or **star** characters (*) in their definitions, as shown in the following code snippet:

```
def spam(*args, **kwargs):
    ...
```

Programmers unfamiliar with Python are often puzzled when they encounter this for the first time. What does the single and double asterisk/star character do?

We'll start with *args. The single * character tells Python that the function takes a variable number (zero or more) of positional parameters.

```
>>> def countargs(*args):
...     print 'Passed in', len(args), 'args.'
>>> countargs('a', 'b', 'c')
Passed in 3 args.
>>> countargs()
Passed in 0 args.
```

You can combine normal positional parameters and `*args` to require some arguments. The `os.path.join` method, for example, requires at least one positional argument. Its signature is `os.path.join(a, *p)`.

```
>>> import os
>>> os.path.join('a', 'b', 'c')
'a\\b\\c'
>>> os.path.join('a')
'a'
>>> os.path.join()
Traceback (most recent call last):
TypeError: join() takes at least 1 argument (0 given)
```

In the last call to `os.path.join`, we did not supply any arguments, so a `TypeError` was raised.

You can also use the `*` character when calling a function to expand a sequence (such as a list or tuple) into positional arguments. This does not require the function being called has a `*args` parameter. It can be used to expand to any positional arguments. For example, if we use the `countargs` function defined previously with a list of values, we will get two very different results depending on whether we use a `*` to expand the list when `countargs` is called.

```
>>> items = ['a', 'b', 'c']
>>> countargs(items)
Passed in 1 args.
>>> countargs(*items)
Passed in 3 args.
```

The first call to `countargs` would be equivalent to `countargs(['a', 'b', 'c'])`. It passes the list as the only argument. The second call would be equivalent to `countargs('a', 'b', 'c')`. It passes each item in the list as a separate positional argument.

The `**kwargs` parameter is basically the same as `*args`, but for keyword instead of positional parameters. The `**` characters tell Python a function takes a variable number of keyword parameters.

```
>>> def countkwargs(**kwargs):
...     print 'Passed in', len(kwargs), 'kwargs.'
>>> countkwargs(a=1, b=2)
Passed in 2 kwargs.
>>> countkwargs()
Passed in 0 kwargs.
```

Just like you can specify both required and variable positional parameters (as we saw in `os.path.join`), you can specify regular keyword parameters along with using `**kwargs`.

```
>>> def countkwargs2(strfunc=None, **kwargs):
...     msg = 'Passed in %s kwargs.' % len(kwargs)
...     if strfunc:
...         msg = strfunc(msg)
...     print msg
>>> countkwargs2(strfunc=str.upper, a=1)
PASSED IN 1 KWARGS.
>>> countkwargs2(str.lower, a=1, b=2)
passed in 2 kwargs.
```

As the second call to `countkwargs2` shows, you can still use normal keyword arguments by either position or name.

And finally, you can use `**` to expand a mapping, such as a dictionary, into keyword arguments that are passed into a function:

```
>>> mapping = dict(a=1, b=2, strfunc=str.upper)
>>> countkwargs2(arg=mapping)
Passed in 1 kwargs.
>>> countkwargs2(**mapping)
PASSED IN 2 KWARGS.
```

The `*args` and `**kwargs` parameters are important features of Python with many useful applications, just a fraction of which are presented in this book. They allow a level of dynamic programming that would otherwise be extremely difficult.

As a final note, the names `args` and `kwargs` are convention only. You can just as well name them `*spam` and `**eggs`.

String formatting

You will need to know a few things about string formatting to follow along with this book's examples. The topic itself can get very deep, but we will just stick to some basics.

There are two types of string formatting in Python. The older and still popular version uses the percent character (`%`), while the newer and more flexible version uses the `format` method on strings. Here is a very basic example of each.

```
>>> name = 'Jon'
>>> 'Hi, %s!' % name
```

```
'Hi, Jon!'
>>> 'Hi, {0}!'.format(name)
'Hi, Jon!'
```

We use the % version exclusively in this book because it is more concise. I would encourage you to use the format method for new code. Translating this book's examples should be straightforward.

Inside the string being formatted, the % character indicates something that will be replaced, and the characters following the % specify how it will be replaced. For example, consider the difference between %s and %r.

```
>>> '%s' % 'hi'
'hi'
>>> '%r' % 'hi'
"'hi'"
>>> str('hi')
'hi'
>>> repr('hi')
"'hi'"
```

The %s sequence converts the argument being formatted using the str function, whereas the %r sequence uses the repr function. We will use %s and %r almost exclusively, but two other common format characters that are good to know about are d and f for integer and floating point representations.

```
>>> '%d' % 100.0
'100'
>>> '%03d' % 10
'010'
>>> '%f' % 1
'1.000000'
>>> '%.3f' % 1
'1.000'
```

If the format string has only one positional replacement, the argument can be a tuple with a single value, or a value that is not a tuple. If the format string needs multiple positional replacements, the value should be a tuple with a number of items equal to the number of replacements needed. If the two do not match (there are too few or too many arguments to format), a TypeError will be raised.

```
>>> 'Hi, %s!' % ('Jon',)
'Hi, Jon!'
>>> '%s, %s!' % ('Hi', 'Jon')
'Hi, Jon!'
>>> '%s, %s!' % 'Hi'
```

```
Traceback (most recent call last):
TypeError: not enough arguments for format string
>>> '%s' % ('Hi', 'Jon')
Traceback (most recent call last):
TypeError: not all arguments converted during string formatting
```

Finally, you can also use keywords for formatting strings. The keyword name goes between the % and format characters, like %(keyword)s. Instead of a tuple you provide a mapping, such as a dictionary, after the % operator. The mapping's keys and values become the format string's keywords and the values being formatted. Extra keys are ignored.

```
>>> mapping = {'value': 1.2345, 'units': 'km', 'ignore': 1}
>>> '%(value).3f%(units)s' % mapping
'1.234km'
```

An interesting Pythonic idiom is to use the locals() function as the mapping. The locals() function returns a dictionary where each key and value is a variable and its value.

```
>>> value = 1.2345
>>> units = 'km'
>>> '%(value).3f%(units)s' % locals()
'1.234km'
```

There is a lot more to string formatting but this section covers the basics. If you need more in-depth instruction, resources abound on the Internet.

String concatenation

In a few places in this book, we built short strings into longer strings. This process is called string concatenation. We often did this through the str.join method:

```
>>> planets = 'Venus', 'Earth', 'Mars'
>>> ', '.join(planets)
'Venus, Earth, Mars'
```

We also used string formatting:

```
>>> '%s, %s, %s' % planets
'Venus, Earth, Mars'
```

Why didn't we use string addition, such as:

```
>>> planets[0] + ', ' + planets[1] + ', ' + planets[2]
'Venus, Earth, Mars'
```

When adding more than two strings, Python ends up creating temporary strings. When the strings are large, this can cause unnecessary memory pressure. Consider all the work Python has to do when adding more than two strings:

```
>>> a = planets[0] + ', '
>>> b = a + planets[1]
>>> c = b + ', '
>>> d = c + planets[2]
>>> d
'Venus, Earth, Mars'
```

Of the four strings created to get our result, three of them were immediately unnecessary!

String addition should be avoided when concatenating more than two strings. As a bonus, using addition requires the most code and it is extremely unreadable.

Raw strings and string literals

In order to represent something like a new line in a string, you usually use a special series of characters: \n. "\n" is an escape sequence that indicates to whatever is using the string (writing to a file, printing to the console) that there is a newline present. For example, we can see "\n" in action quite easily:

```
>>> print 'hello\nworld'
hello
world
```

There are many escape sequences of which "\n" is just one. A problem can occur when you want an actual backslash in the string, such as for file paths on Windows operating systems. We need to escape the actual backslash with another backslash so the path will be interpreted properly. The first example in the following code is not escaped, so the results are printed on two lines. The second example is properly escaped, so the path prints properly, on a single line.

```
>>> print 'C:\newfolder'
C:
ewfolder
>>> print 'C:\\newfolder'
C:\newfolder
```

Because of this double-backslash inconvenience, we will sometimes use raw strings. A raw string is prefixed with the `r` character and it tells Python that the string should not be interpreted with escape sequences. In the following example, notice how the leading `r` causes the string to print properly, on a single line.

```
>>> print r'C:\newfolder'
C:\newfolder
```

I most commonly use raw strings to get around the double-backslash path issue on Windows, as I find the double-backslashes make the code significantly more cluttered.

Path building and manipulation

You will often have to construct file system paths using Python. For example, given the variable `mydir` which points to some path, you may want to get the path two folders up:

```
otherdir = mydir + '\\..\\..'
```

Do not build or manipulate paths this way. There are a number of things wrong with this code. The obvious problem is that it is platform-dependent. Windows and Linux-based systems use different path separators.

Even more importantly, this code (and code that uses the value of `otherdir`) can break depending on the value of `mydir` and which operating system is being used. In Windows, drive roots like `C:\` are usually returned with a trailing slash, while other folders, like `C:\Windows`, are not. There are all sorts of other edge cases that can cause bugs if you do not handle paths properly.

As another strike against it, adding paths has the same downsides as adding strings, including poor performance and readability. Refer to the *String concatenation* section from earlier.

These problems are totally unnecessary. Python includes a robust set of path manipulation functionality in the `os.path` module. Use it. The correct version of the preceding code would be:

```
otherdir = os.path.join(mydir, '..', '..')
```

The `os.path` module also includes a number of OS-dependent variables, such as `os.path.sep` (the folder separator character) and `os.path.pathsep` (the separator between paths in an environment variable). There are also higher-level path manipulation libraries available, such as the `pymel.util.common.path` module.

Finally, you will find that doing path manipulation properly creates code that is easier to read, and you will be unable to tolerate building paths with inferior techniques.

Unicode strings

I can think of nothing else that has caused programmers more confusion than
Unicode strings. I will not even attempt to explain the issues surrounding Unicode,
but I feel it's important to bring up so when you see something like the following,
you will be prepared.

```
>>> import pymel.core as pmc
>>> xform = pmc.polyCube()[0]
>>> myname = 'cubexform'
>>> xform.rename(myname)
>>> xform.name()
u'cubexform'
```

Unicode strings in Python 2 are prefixed with a u character. So how come even
though we named our node using a "regular" (byte) string with no prefix, we got
back a Unicode string from the xform.name() method?

Well, "regular" strings in Python 2 (the str type) support ASCII characters only.
ASCII is able to represent a very limited number of characters, but all the characters
of the world can be represented by the Unicode system. So if you are creating a
program that needs to be localized or support more than basic English, your strings
need to be Unicode. Autodesk Maya needs to be localized, of course, so all the user-
facing strings are Unicode.

Fortunately the two types share the same base class (basestring) and compare
equal, so cause minimal inconvenience for us most of the time.

```
>>> myname == xform.name()
True
>>> type(myname), type(xform.name())
(<type 'str'>, <type 'unicode'>)
>>> str.__mro__
(<type 'str'>, <type 'basestring'>, <type 'object'>)
>>> unicode.__mro__
(<type 'unicode'>, <type 'basestring'>, <type 'object'>)
```

Most people programming in Maya can get by without understanding Unicode
or localization. If your needs get more complex and you need to build localizable
tools or applications (for example, to supply translated tools to another studio), be
prepared to do a significant amount more work and testing. These topics are well
outside of the scope of this book, though, so we will just leave our discussion of
Unicode here.

Using the doctest module

All of the example code in this book that is executed at the interactive interpreter (like the *String formatting* example code in this appendix) was created using Python's doctest module. The doctest module allows the writing of executable test code within the docstrings of modules, classes, functions, and methods. It is a great way to not just test your code, but provide executable documentation. For example, we could create a file C:\mayapybook\pylib\doctestexample.py with the following:

```
def adder(a, b):
    """
    Return a added to b.

    >>> adder(1, 2)
    3
    >>> adder('a', 'b')
    'ab'
    >>> adder(1, 'b')
    Traceback (most recent call last):
    TypeError: unsupported operand type(s) for +: 'int' and 'str'
    """
    return a + b
```

Now if you run this file through the doctest module, it will run all the prompt-like lines and ensure they produce the correct result. If the module is successful, you will get no feedback.

```
> mayapy -m doctest doctestexample.py
```

If we change one of the tests to force a failure (for example, change adder(1, 2) to adder(1, 3)) and run the command line again, we should get the following feedback:

```
> mayapy -m doctest doctestexample.py
**********************************************************************
File " C:\mayapybook\pylib\doctestexample.py", line 6, in doctestexample.
adder
Failed example:
    adder(1, 3)
Expected:
    3
Got:
    4
**********************************************************************
1 items had failures:
   1 of 3 in doctestexample.adder
***Test Failed*** 1 failures.
```

There is a lot more to `doctest` that isn't covered in this section, including how to customize the way it runs. I mention `doctest` here for two reasons. The first is that it was used extensively behind the scenes to develop the code for this book. If you look at the source code repository (see the *Using the GitHub repository for this book* section later in this appendix), you will see it used in every chapter. It was an essential tool for writing correct examples.

The second reason I mention `doctest`, which is personal for me, is that `doctest` was my first introduction to unit testing. I consider unit testing an essential Python practice (see the *Starting Test-Driven Development* section next). It is much easier to get into `doctest` than any unit testing framework, and even when you start to use a different test framework heavily, using `doctest` to achieve correct, executable examples in your docstrings is a great practice.

If you have never done automated testing in Python, I highly recommend taking a look at `doctest`.

Adopting Test-Driven Development

I've mentioned several times in this book that I am an advocate of **Test-Driven Development**, or **TDD**. TDD means writing tests before writing feature code, and sticking to TDD is a proven way to generate high-quality and maintainable software.

But what is a section about TDD doing in an appendix of a book about using Python inside Autodesk Maya?

An instructional book is about growth. Both mine and yours. I hope that learning about the OpenMaya API will encourage your creativity. I hope that building a request-reply framework will increase your productivity. I hope that the several chapters we spent learning techniques towards building better code will grow you into a better programmer.

But all the growth and improvement the chapter topics can possibly inspire pales in comparison to what you can do if you adopt Test-Driven Development. It is the single most important technique you can use to make your programming life better (and an improved programming life often leads to an improved personal life!).

If you are looking to get started with TDD, I'd suggest starting in standard Python, leaving Maya alone for the time being. Find some good tutorials or examples, and just dive in. It takes rigor and practice, but keep at it and your programming will be transformed.

Using the GitHub repository for this book

All the code samples in this book are hosted in a GitHub repository at `https://github.com/rgalanakis/practicalmayapython`. There are folders for the code in each chapter and appendix. In many cases, there is some divergence between code in the book and the source code, usually done to avoid duplication or to remove clutter, but it should be easy to find the source code for the chapter samples.

In general, running a file through the mayapy interpreter should execute the code and/or tests in the file. Code entered at the interactive prompt is usually in the `interactive.py` file in the chapter's directory. Most functions that can be tested automatically have unit tests written. Code for GUIs, which cannot be automatically tested so easily, should be simple enough to run by copying and pasting the code into the **Script Editor** and then executing it. To make examples more clear and concrete, many paths are hard-coded. You will need to change those paths to whatever is appropriate for your environment.

Few things annoy me more than code in technical books that does not work. If you find broken examples, they are probably due to an unfortunate copy and paste error from IDE to word processor, or some written instructions I did not test thoroughly enough. Also watch out for mixing tabs and spaces; Python code should be using four spaces for indentation, and never tabs. I sincerely apologize for any mistakes, and ask that you follow the instructions in the *Preface* for reporting problems, or create an issue in the GitHub repository.

Index

Symbols

__init__ method 220
_normalize function 99
.py suffix 248
_py_to_helpstr function 28
%r sequence 314
%s sequence 314

A

accidental complexity 61
add_influences function 74
addNameChangedCallback function 245
advanced decorator concepts
  about 138
  decorators, defining with
      arguments 138, 139
  decorators, stacking 139, 140
  PyMEL attributes, decorating 139
  PyMEL methods, decorating 139
  Python's decorator library, using 140
alternatives, hierarchy converter GUI
  complete test setup 162
  functions versus classes 161
  specific versus general controller 161
Amazon Web Services (AWS) 304
application
  hooking up, to be effected by hierarchy
      converter GUI 156-158
application events
  simulating 160, 161
application level
  exceptions, handling at 83, 84
Application Programming
      Interface (API) 217

args parameter 311-313
arguments
  decorators, defining with 138
assignUVs method 233
asterisk character 311
at_time context manager
  building 126
attribute 218
Autodesk 263
Autodesk 3ds Max 118
automated tests
  running, in Maya 214
automation 179
automation system
  batch processing, with Maya 211, 212
  control, supporting from remote
      computer 215
  improvements 211
  multiple applications, supporting 215
  multiple languages, supporting 215
  object-oriented system, designing 216
  practical uses 211
  RPC frameworks, evaluating 216
  support, adding for logging 214, 215
automation system, designing
  about 184
  client and server, pairing 184
  client-server handshake 185-187
  exceptions, handling between client
      and server 189-191
  requests, serializing 188
  responses, serializing 188
  server, bootstrapping from client 185
  server loop, defining 188
  working of server, selecting 189

B

background thread
used, for sending email 107
batch mode 192
batch processing, Maya 211, 212
benefits, node factory
extensible 273
intuitive and consistent 273
less code and duplication 273
lightweight 273
best practices, Python
args parameter 311-313
doctest module, using 319, 320
GitHub repository, using 321
kwargs parameter 311-313
path, building 317
path, manipulating 317
raw strings 316
string concatenation 315, 316
string formatting 313-315
string literals 316
TDD, adopting 320
Unicode strings 318
binary distribution
about 301
using, on Windows 302
binding 144, 183
Bitbucket
URL 307
boilerplate 47
Boolean flags
usage, avoiding 44, 45
bootstrapping 185
bound methods 32
built-in exceptions
URL 79

C

callable method 113
callbacks
about 146
OpenMaya, used for 243-246
caller 123
cargo cult programming 260
catch keyword 92
character creator

convert_hierarchies function,
implementing 66
convert_hierarchies_main function,
implementing 65
convert_hierarchy function,
implementing 68
decomposing, into composable
functions 66-68
inevitable modification, supporting 69-72
stubbing out 64
writing 63
child class 18
child process 196
circle node
about 260
frames attribute 261
input attribute 261
scale attribute 261
class methods 31
client-server handshake 185-187
closures
about 60, 114
using 60
code
simplifying, custom types used 220, 221
code objects
inspecting 97, 98
code smell 44, 264
command flag
adding 252-254
command line options 192
community
engaging with 308, 309
composable code
about 41
anti-patterns, identifying 42, 43
Boolean flags, avoiding 44, 45
defining 41, 42
first item, obtaining in sequence 46, 47
head function, writing 48
legacy code, evolving into 45
rewriting 46
tail function, writing 48
compute method
abstraction, creating for 285
creating 266, 267

connection strings 183, 184
container widget
    defining 153, 154
contextlib module 121
context managers
    about 111, 118
    creating 119, 120
    undo_chunk context manager, writing 121
    undo_on_error context manager,
        writing 122
    versus decorators 123
context managers, for scene state
    about 124
    at_time context manager, building 126
    set_file_prompt context manager,
        building 125
    set_namespace_active context manager,
        building 127, 128
    set_renderlayer_active context manager,
        building 127
    with_unit context manager,
        building 126, 127
contribution, to open source community
    about 303, 304
    Maya Python code, designing for
        open source 304-306
    open source project, starting 306, 307
    project, distributing 307, 308
contract 55
control widget
    defining 153, 154
convert_hierarchies function
    implementing 66
convert_hierarchies_main function
    implementing 65
convert_hierarchy function
    implementing 68
CPython 118
CPython source code repository
    URL 296
create_plugin function 251
create_syntax function 254
critical path 85
custom types
    used, for simplifying code 220, 221

D

data types, PyMEL 21-23
debugging 84
declarative code 272
decorator library
    using 140
decorators
    about 111-113
    creating, for recording metrics 133
    defining, with arguments 138
    doing 140
    explaining 113-116
    exporter, wrapping with 117
    stacking 139, 140
    URL, for blog posts 113, 140
    URL, for information 140
    versus context managers 123
decorators, for metrics recording
    duration, recording 134, 135
    duration, reporting 135
    errors, handling 136, 137
    unique key, obtaining 134
denormalized_skin context manager
    creating 129
    performance concerns, addressing 131, 132
    vertex influences, swapping 129, 130
dependency graph plugins. *See* **also**
        node plugins
development root
    selecting, for library 11, 12
docstring
    about 25, 53
    writing, for skeleton converter library 52
doctest module
    using 319, 320
draw method 222
dunder methods 28

E

Easier to Ask for Forgiveness than
        Permission (EAFP) 37
ehook function 93
email
    sending, background thread used 107
emit_selchanged function 167

enumerate function 238
environment variables 192
error e-mail
  sending 103, 104
error e-mail contents
  assembling 100, 101
error handler
  background thread used, for sending
      mail 107
  creating 95
  improving 96, 97, 106
  installing 104
  locals, capturing 107
  log files, attaching 108
  other mechanisms 107
  user interface, adding 106
  What If Two Programs Did This
      rule 105, 106
error handling, Maya
  about 88
  exception design, dealing with 91
  expensive state, dealing with 88, 89
  Maya application, dealing with 92
  Maya application, leveraging 92
  mutable state, dealing with 88, 89
  Python, leveraging 92
  undo blocks, leveraging 90
essential complexity 61
eval
  Python, controlling through 180
event loop 151, 152, 213
exception design
  dealing with 91
exception hook. *See* sys.excepthook
    function
exception info. *See* exc_info tuple
exceptions
  about 77, 78
  exc_info tuple 82
  handling, at application level 83, 84
  traceback objects 81
  try/catch/finally flow control 79-81
exception types 78, 79
except keyword 79
exc_info tuple 82
exec
  Python, controlling through 180

exec_ method 151
execution scope 200
exit handler 196
expensive state
  dealing with 88, 89
exporter
  wrapping, with decorators 117
expression 199

F

failing fast 83
filtering behavior 43
filters
  adding, based on filename 98-100
finally keyword 81
function
  creating, in IDE 12, 13
  postcondition 55
  precondition 55
function sets, Maya API 229

G

garbage collected 118
generational garbage collector 118
get_next_message function 152
get_type_hierarchy function 74
GitHub repository
  URL 321
  using 321
graphical user interface (GUI)
  about 143
  crafting, rules 146
GUI, crafting rules
  .ui files usage, avoiding 147
  command-style UI, using 146
  pure PySide GUIs preference 146
GUI mode 192

H

handshake 186
handshake port 187
hash value
  obtaining, of node 231, 232
head function
  writing, for composable code 48

hierarchy converter GUI
  alternatives 161, 162
  application events, simulating 160, 161
  application, hooking up 156-158
  building 153
  container widget, defining 153, 154
  control widget, defining 153, 154
  creating 149
  designing 153
  event loop 151, 152
  executing 152
  hooking up, to be effected by
      application 158, 159
  integrating, with Maya 162
  main Maya window, getting as
      QMainWindow 163, 164
  Maya, connecting to signal 167, 168
  opening, from Maya 162, 163
  Python file, running as script 150
  Python reload function, using 165, 166
  QApplication class 151
  signal, emitting from Maya 166, 167
  verifying 169
  widgets, adding 155
  window, creating 149, 150
  window widget, defining 154
high-level error handler
  building 92
  code objects, inspecting 97, 98
  error e-mail contents, assembling 100, 101
  error e-mail, sending 103, 104
  error handler, creating 95
  error handler, improving 96, 97
  filter based, adding on filename 98-100
  sys.excepthook 93
  sys.excepthook, used in Maya 94
Hitchhiker's Guide to Packaging
  URL 307

I

IDE
  about 9
  function, creating in 12, 13
imperative style programming 272
implementation detail, of function 117
info function 23

inheritance
  creating, by drawing shapes 221-225
inherited 221
initializePlugin function 248
inner function. *See* **closures**
input/output (IO) 214
installation, PySide 147
installation, ZeroMQ 181
Integrated Development
      Environment. *See* **IDE**
interactive mode 10
introspection function
  creating 15, 16
IPC
  problems, handling with 181
IronPython 118
is_exact_type function
  implementing 50

J

JavaScript Object Notation file format 175
JIRA
  URL 107

K

kwargs parameter 311-313

L

LBYL 37
library
  code changes, reloading 13
  creating 9
  creating, mayapy interpreter used 10
  development root, selecting 11, 12
  function, creating in IDE 12, 13
  path, finding for 10, 11
Liskov Substitution Principle 21, 225
list comprehensions
  about 15
  is_exact_type function, implementing 50
  URL 48
  using 48, 49
  versus, map and filter 51
locals
  capturing 108

locals() function 315
log files
  attaching 108
Look Before You Leap. *See* **LBYL**

M

magic methods 28
MakeTrue function 241
map and filter
  versus, list comprehensions 51
math types, PyMEL 21-23
Maya
  about 9
  architecture 225
  automated tests, running in 214
  connecting, to signal 167, 168
  controlling, through request-reply 180
  exploring 13-15
  future versions, improving 129
  hierarchy converter GUI,
      integrating with 162
  hierarchy converter GUI, opening
      from 162, 163
  launching, from Python 194, 195
  signal, emitting from 166, 167
  site directory, creating for 299
  source distribution, adding to 300
  sys.excepthook, using 94
  working with Python distributions 300
Maya 2013 English PyMEL
  URL 25
Maya API
  about 225
  function sets 229
  Maya API Reference, navigating 227, 228
  MObjects 229
  OpenMaya bindings 226, 227
Maya API Reference
  navigating 227, 228
Maya application
  dealing with 92
  leveraging 92
maya.cmds.file command 91
Maya, controlling through request-reply
  about 180
  Maya server, using 180

  problems, handling with IPC 181
  Python client, using 180
  Python, controlling through eval 180
  Python, controlling through exec 180
  request-reply, demonstrating with
      ZeroMQ 182, 183
  ZeroMQ, installing 181
Maya GUI session
  server, running in 213
**maya.OpenMayaMPx.MPxNode
      Maya API class 260**
Maya path
  Qt object, getting from 170
mayapy interpreter
  about 9
  used, for creating library 10
Maya Python API
  about 230
  and PyMEL, comparing 246
  hash value, obtaining of node 231, 232
  mesh, building 232-237
  mesh normals, setting 238-240
  MScriptUtil, used to call method 241, 242
  name, obtaining of MObject 231
  node name conversion, to MObject
      node 230, 231
  OpenMaya, used for callbacks 243-246
Maya Python code
  designing, for open source 304-306
Maya Python plugin
  command flag, adding 252-254
  creating 247
  OpenMaya and scripting solutions,
      comparing 255, 256
  plugin file, creating 250-252
  plugins, reloading 252
  sound player library, creating 249
Maya server
  using 180
Maya shelves
  working with 177
Maya's Script Editor
  using 94
Maya startup routine
  about 191
  batch mode, versus GUI mode 192
  command line options, using 192

environment variables, using 193
startup configuration mechanism,
    selecting 192
Maya window
  getting, as QMainWindow 163, 164
MEL
  types 17, 18
menus
  marker, verifying 176
  marking, as new 172
  persistence registry, adding 174-176
  Qt object, getting from Maya path 170
  test case, creating 173
  top level menu, creating 169
  widget font, changing 171
  widgets styling, alternative methods 176
  working with 169
Mercurial
  URL 307
mesh
  building 232-237
mesh normals
  setting 238-240
method
  calling, MScriptUtil used 241, 242
Method Resolution Order. *See* **MRO**
method types, class definition
  bound methods 32
  class methods 31
  static methods 31
  unbound method 32
metrics recording
  decorator, creating for 133
MObject
  about 229
  name, obtaining 231
MObject node
  name node, converting to 230, 231
model-view-controller (MVC) 158
module type 29
MPxNode methods
  overriding 293, 294
MRO
  using 18
MScriptUtil
  used, for calling method 241, 242

MultiplyDivide node 42
mutable state
  dealing with 88, 89
MySet.__dict__ attribute 219
MySet type 219

N

name
  obtaining, of MObject 231
namespaces 61
nested function. *See* **closures**
node
  hash value, obtaining 231, 232
node connections 61
node factory
  benefits 273
  building 276
  designing 273
  extending 289
node factory, designing
  abstraction, creating for compute
      method 285-289
  attributes, creating 277-279
  attribute specification, designing 274, 275
  attributes, specifying 276, 277
  node, creating 282-285
  node, specifying 279, 280
  node type specification, designing 275
  partial application, used for creating
      attributes 281, 282
  plugin nodes, designing 273
node factory, extending
  color attribute, supporting 289, 290
  enum attributes, supporting 290-292
  MPxNode methods, overriding 293, 294
  string attribute, supporting 289, 290
  transform nodes, supporting 292, 293
node name
  converting, to MObject node 230, 231
node plugins
  about 260
  building 260-262
  compute method, creating 266, 267
  initializer, defining 263-265
  inputs, defining 263-265
  non-Pythonic Maya API, taming 268

outputs, defining 263-265
plugin type IDs 262
node to joint conversion
simplifying 58, 59
non-operation program (no-op) 132
non-Pythonic Maya API
taming 268
nose library
URL 306

O

object oriented programming 119
OpenMaya
and scripting solutions, comparing 255, 256
used, for callbacks 243-246
OpenMaya bindings 226, 227
open source
Maya Python code, designing for 304-306
Open Source Initiative. *See* **OSI**
open source licenses
URL 296
open source project
starting 306, 307
Open Source Software. *See* **OSS**
OSI
about 296
URL 296
OSS
about 296
differentiating, from script download
sites 296, 297

P

parent class 18
parent process 196
partial application
used, for creating attributes 281, 282
path
finding, for library 10, 11
PEP8
about 15
URL 15
PEP 343
URL 118
persistence registry
adding, in menus 174-176

per-vertex per-face normals 238
per-vertex per-polygon normals 238
Pillow
URL 307
pip
used, for installing third-party modules 303
plugin
about 248
PyMEL, using 256, 257
reloading 252
plugin file
creating 250-252
plugin module 248
plugin nodes
designing 273
plugin type IDs 263
plugin types 248
pmhelp function, building
about 24
code issues 38
EAFP versus LBYL 37
help, opening in web browser 38-40
query string, creating for PyMEL
object 25-27
support, adding for functions 33, 34
support, adding for methods 30-32
support, adding for modules 29
support, adding for non-PyMEL
objects 34-36
support, adding for types 30
test cases, writing 27, 28
ports 183
postcondition, function 55
precondition, function 55
predicate 46
problems, handling with IPC
availability 181
monogamy 181
pairing 181
process lifetime 181
timeout mechanism 181
process_message function 152
ProxyUnicode class 21
pseudocode
about 25
writing, for skeleton converter library 52

PyMEL
about 297
and Maya Python API, comparing 246
attributes, decorating 139
data types 21-23
exploring 13-15
math types 21-23
methods, decorating 139
used, in plugin 256, 257
pymel.core.unloadPlugin function 249
PyMEL object
query string, creating for 25-27
PyMEL performance
defining 73
improving 72
inner loops, rewriting to use maya.cmds 75
refactoring 73, 74
PyNodes 19, 20
PyQt
about 143, 144
and PySide, supporting 148
PySide
about 143, 144
and PyQt, supporting 148
installing 147
URL 148
Python
about 9, 19
best practices 311-321
leveraging 92
Maya, launching from 194, 195
types 17, 18
URL 308
Python client
using 180
Python Decorator Library
URL 140
Python Developer's Guide
URL 296
Python distributions
binary distributions, using on
Windows 302
egg, adding to Maya 301
pip, used for installing third-party
modules 303

source distribution, adding to Maya 300
wheel, adding to Maya 301
working with 300
Python Enhancement Proposal (PEP) 49
Python file
running, as script 150
Python library
benefits 255
Python metaprogramming
declarative code 271, 272
demystifying 268, 269
type creation 269, 270
type function, exploring 270, 271
Python Package Index (PyPI)
about 140
URL 300
URL, for mock library 300
using 300
Python plugin
defining 248, 249
PyZMQ
about 181
URL 181

Q

QApplication class 151
Qt 143, 144
Qt Designer
using 147
Qt layouts 145
Qt main windows 145
Qt object
getting, from Maya path 170
qtshim.py module
QtCore namespace 148
QtGui namespace 148
Signal class 148
wrapinstance function 148
Qt signals 146
Qt sorting 145
Qt widgets 144, 145
Qt window
making, child of Maya window 164, 165
query string
creating, for PyMEL object 25, 26

R

race condition 185
raise statement 80
Raven client
  URL 108
raw strings 316
read-copy-update 88
Read-Evaluate-Print Loop. *See* REPL
refactor 38
refactoring 57
reference counting 118
reload function
  about 94
  using 165, 166
remote procedure call (RPC) 189
remove_selected function 73
REPL
  about 23
  leveraging 23, 24
request-reply
  demonstrating, with ZeroMQ 182, 183
  Maya, controlling through 180
request-reply automation system, building
  about 193
  basic Maya server, creating 197
  code, running at Maya startup 198, 199
  eval statement 199-201
  exec statement 199-201
  Maya, launching from Python 194, 195
  Python package, creating 194
  server, killing automatically 196, 197
  support, adding for client-server
      handshake 208-210
  support, adding for eval 201, 202
  support, adding for exception
      handling 202-205
  support, adding for exec 201, 202
  support, adding for timeouts 206, 207
request-response 180
reStructured Text 53
rules, error handling
  about 84
  critical path, focusing 85
  errors, catching 86, 87
  partial mutations, avoiding 87
  tool distribution, avoiding 85, 86

S

safe_setparent utility function
  extracting 56, 57
script download sites
  OSS, differentiating from 296, 297
scripting solutions
  and OpenMaya, comparing 255, 256
s.__dict__ attribute 219
selection behavior 43
Sentry server
  URL 108
serializer 188
server
  about 180
  running, in Maya GUI session 213
set_file_prompt context manager
  building 125
set_namespace_active context manager
  building 127, 128
set_renderlayer_active context manager
  building 127
shapes
  drawing, through inheritance
      creation 221-225
shared normals 238
Simplified Wrapper and Interface Generator
    (SWIG)
  about 226
  URL 226
site directory
  creating, for Maya 299
  creating, for third party modules 298
  establishing, at startup 299
  explaining 298
skeleton converter library
  closures, using 60
  coding 51
  contract 55
  docstring, using 53
  docstring, writing 52
  implementation, breaking 54, 55
  implementation, writing 53, 54
  namespaces, dealing with 61
  node connections, dealing with 61
  node to joint conversion, simplifying 58, 59
  pseudocode, writing 52

refactoring 57
reStructured Text, using 53
safe_setparent utility function,
    extracting 56, 57
wrapping up 62, 63
sound player library
creating 249
source code management (SCM) 307
source distribution
adding, to Maya 300
Sphinx project
URL 306
SQL Alchemy
URL 272
stack trace. *See* **traceback**
startup
site directory, establishing at 299
statement 199
static methods 31
status codes 190
string concatenation 315, 316
string formatting 16, 313-315
string literals 316
subroutine
inverting 111, 112
superclass 18
sys.excepthook function
about 93
using, in Maya 94
sys.exc_info() function 82

T

tail function
writing, for composable code 48
Test-Driven Development (TDD)
about 27
adopting 320
third-party modules
about 297, 298
site directory, creating for 298
**third-party modules, putting in thirdparty
    folder**
drawbacks 301
top level menu
creating 169
traceback 81

traceback2 module
URL 108
traceback objects 81
Trello
URL 107
try/catch/finally flow control 79-81
tuple_to_mpoint function 235
type
about 14, 218
creating 218, 219
custom types used, to simplify
    code 220, 221
inheritance creation, by drawing
    shapes 221-225
type function
about 16
exploring 270, 271
type hierarchies 145
type introspection 9
types, MEL 17, 18
types, Python 17, 18

U

unbound method 32
undo blocks
leveraging 90
undo_chunk context manager
writing 121
undoInfo
drawbacks 90
undo_on_error context manager
writing 122
unhandled exceptions 83
Unicode strings 318
unit 41
user-defined scripts 192
user interface
adding 106
utility functions 56

V

vertexArray parameter 228

W

What If Two Programs Did This
 rule 105, 106
What-You-See-Is-What-You-Get
 (WYSIWYG) 147
widget font, menu
 changing 171
widgets
 styling, alternative methods 176
Windows
 binary distributions, using on 302
Windows Presentation Foundation 147
window widget
 defining 153, 154
WinForms 147
with_unit context manager
 building 126, 127

Z

ZeroMQ
 installing 181
 request-reply, demonstrating with 182, 183
ZMQ- The Guide
 URL 182

About Packt Publishing

Packt, pronounced 'packed', published its first book "*Mastering phpMyAdmin for Effective MySQL Management*" in April 2004 and subsequently continued to specialize in publishing highly focused books on specific technologies and solutions.

Our books and publications share the experiences of your fellow IT professionals in adapting and customizing today's systems, applications, and frameworks. Our solution based books give you the knowledge and power to customize the software and technologies you're using to get the job done. Packt books are more specific and less general than the IT books you have seen in the past. Our unique business model allows us to bring you more focused information, giving you more of what you need to know, and less of what you don't.

Packt is a modern, yet unique publishing company, which focuses on producing quality, cutting-edge books for communities of developers, administrators, and newbies alike. For more information, please visit our website: www.packtpub.com.

Writing for Packt

We welcome all inquiries from people who are interested in authoring. Book proposals should be sent to author@packtpub.com. If your book idea is still at an early stage and you would like to discuss it first before writing a formal book proposal, contact us; one of our commissioning editors will get in touch with you.

We're not just looking for published authors; if you have strong technical skills but no writing experience, our experienced editors can help you develop a writing career, or simply get some additional reward for your expertise.

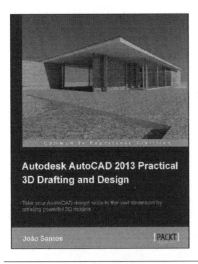

Autodesk AutoCAD 2013 Practical 3D Drafting and Design

ISBN: 978-1-84969-935-8   Paperback: 374 pages

Take your AuotoCAD design skills to the next dimension by creating powerful 3D models

1. Obtain 2D drawings from 3D models.

2. Master AutoCAD's third dimension.

3. Full of practical tips and examples to help take your skills to the next dimension.

Building Machine Learning Systems with Python

ISBN: 978-1-78216-140-0   Paperback: 290 pages

Master the art of machine learning with Python and build effective machine learning systems with this intensive hands-on guide

1. Master Machine Learning using a broad set of Python libraries and start building your own Python-based ML systems.

2. Covers classification, regression, feature engineering, and much more guided by practical examples.

3. A scenario-based tutorial to get into the right mind-set of a machine learner (data exploration) and successfully implement this in your new or existing projects.

Please check **www.PacktPub.com** for information on our titles

Programming ArcGIS 10.1 with Python Cookbook

ISBN: 978-1-84969-444-5   Paperback: 304 pages

Over 75 recipes to help you automate geoprocessing tasks, create solutions, and solve problems for ArcGIS with Python

1. Learn how to create geoprocessing scripts with ArcPy.

2. Customize and modify ArcGIS with Python.

3. Create time-saving tools and scripts for ArcGIS.

Learning IPython for Interactive Computing and Data Visualization

ISBN: 978-1-78216-993-2   Paperback: 138 pages

Learn IPython for interactive Python programming, high-performance numerical computing, and data visualization

1. A practical step-by-step tutorial which will help you to replace the Python console with the powerful IPython command-line interface.

2. Use the IPython notebook to modernize the way you interact with Python.

3. Perform highly efficient computations with NumPy and Pandas.

4. Optimize your code using parallel computing and Cython.

Please check **www.PacktPub.com** for information on our titles

Made in the USA
San Bernardino, CA
30 July 2016